JEAN LACOUTURE was born in Bordeaux in 1921 and attended the Jesuit Collège de Trivoli à Bordeaux, the Faculté des Lettres de Bordeaux, Faculté de Droit de Paris, and Ecole des Sciences Politiques de Paris. During World War II he was attached to the Resident General in French Morocco. A correspondent for *Le Monde*, M. Lacouture has covered politics in Morocco, Egypt, Indochina, and the Middle East. In 1965 he was a Research Fellow at Harvard. He has contributed to such American periodicals as the *New Republic*, *The New York Review of Books*, and *The New York Times Magazine*. M. Lacouture is the author of VIETNAM: BETWEEN TWO TRUCES and the recent, highly acclaimed HO CHI MINH: A POLITICAL BIOGRAPHY.

DE GAULLE

Jean Lacouture

Translated by Francis K. Price

PUBLISHED BY AVON

AVON BOOKS
A division of
The Hearst Corporation
959 Eighth Avenue
New York, New York 10019

First Printing (Discus Edition), December, 1968

Cover photo courtesy of United Press International

DISCUS BOOKS TRADEMARK REG. U.S. PAT. OFF. AND
FOREIGN COUNTRIES, REGISTERED TRADEMARK—
MARCA REGISTRADA, HECHO EN CHICAGO, U.S.A.

Printed in the U.S.A.

Table of Contents

DE GAULLE

1
The Taste
of Madeleines

Things being what they are, men are what they do. De Gaulle believes in free will—in his own, in any case. On this point, we can take his side.

But let us not pretend to believe that he is the product of any ancestry or class, of any region or profession, or of any fiscal policy or recruiting law.

Nothing either explains or conditions this individual to whom flamboyance is both native and studied, this national sleepwalker whose reflexes never sleep, this legitimist of himself, this solitary usurper of collective truths. A man can grow up in an intellectual climate dominated by Taine, and be a Frenchman of the North—intensely so—and owe it less to soil and climate than to his cultural formation and his will.

In 1962, when someone professed astonishment that he should so often have dissociated himself from the obvious interests and aspirations of the French bourgeoisie, though he had himself been born into a typically conservative class, Charles de Gaulle replied: "Bourgeois? I have never been that. The bourgeoisie is wealth: the consciousness of having it, or the desire to acquire it. My family and I have always been poor. I have never felt myself bound to the interests or the aspirations of that class."

What is the baroque style? The rupture of line and pattern by the affluence of invention, the rising of the sap: the base overflows the form. A passionate admirer of classical art, De Gaulle himself is baroque: a landmark example of the baroque in history, a character in search of an author, fortuitous and disjointed, rococo and futurist. The last man of the pre-Marxist age; the first man of the post-Marxist age?

But he is, profoundly, a contemporary of "his" time —of the time when he began to carve out his statue and to contemplate the prospect of "General de Gaulle." He is a man who was ten years old at the end of the nineteenth century—at the time when, as he later wrote, "France cultivated melancholy while savoring her wealth."

He left this period hastily, like a man escaping to sea. But there still remains, as for the young Proust, the childhood taste of madeleines on the tongue, a certain music in the ear.

The year 1890 was made up almost entirely of ordinary days: the Eiffel Tower had been completed in 1889, and it was not until 1891 that negotiations for the Russian alliance were completed.

That year did, however, mark the disappearance of one rather remarkable group—that of the professional camp followers, who had never recovered (or at least so it was said) from the aftereffects of the Crimean War. It was also the year that the Panama Canal Company, due to a national scandal, closed its doors; that Wilhelm II dropped his pilot, Bismarck; and that the ultra-Nationalist General Boulanger, who had just failed to seize power, halted on the far side of the Rubicon to gather forget-me-nots for a charming lady who was soon to die of consumption—Madame de Bonnemain. Ordinary times for average politicians of the Fourth Republic, or for Monsieur Pompidou.

A reading of the newspapers of November 22, 1890, is not, however, altogether lacking in interest. Although *Le Gaulois* was primarily concerned with the return to France of Prince Henri d'Orléans after a trip to China, *Le Temps* called attention to a series of outrages committed in Algeria "against private persons," and reported these remarks of the attorney general of Algiers: "The Moslem fears only one punishment—death. The time for clemency is past; the scaffold must be set up wherever a crime has been committed, and justice must be done on the spot."

Le Figaro, which was publishing a series entitled "The King is not the Master," announced that since the Senate had decided to concern itself with the "reorganization of the colonies," the secretary of state, Eugène Étienne, had obtained a "useful adjournment." And lastly, according to the *Journal des Débats:* "The only topic of conversation in military and diplomatic circles at the moment is the resolution attributed to Monsieur Crispi—he is thought to have definitely refused to adopt smokeless powder, for rifles as well as for cannon. . . ."

This was also the date of birth, at No. 9 rue Princesse, in Lille, of the second son of Henri de Gaulle and Jeanne Maillot. His parents, who had given their older son the snobbish name of Xavier, had the good sense to call this one Charles: excellent for a public and popular destiny.

Charles André Marie Joseph de Gaulle was born in the twilight of a century overflowing with noble ardor and scholarly apathy into a family containing two very different lines—one, that of petty parliamentary aristocracy in which the Norman, the Flemish, and the Burgundian mingled, and the other, that of a half-ruined bourgeoisie in which there had once been talk of tobacco-processing factories and where there was still talk of Irish grandmothers and German cou-

11

sins. He was born, at the very moment when the International Exposition had proclaimed the apparently definitive triumph of the industrial and secular Republic, into a monarchist circle deserted by the Comte de Chambord and not caring much for the Orléans branch of the family.

He was born at a time when French nationalism spoke in the strident voice of Déroulède, the trumpet-poet, and when the French army was about to pass into the hands of the generals of the Dreyfus case. He was born on the wrong slope of history.

On the facade of the house in the rue Princesse, the residence of the Maillot family in which Charles de Gaulle was born, there is a niche—to the left of the tall entrance doors and on a level with the second-floor rooms—which shelters a statuette, almost invisible behind the iron grillwork, of Notre-Dame-de-la-Foy. Aside from this, the facade is rigorously austere, contrasting sharply with the ornamentation—restrained and northern though it is—of the neighboring buildings. The rue Princesse was situated in the heart of the Jansenist quarter. The De Gaulle children were to learn at an early age that life is not just a party.

But we must not dwell too strongly on Lille, or on Flanders. The maternal line was there, but the De Gaulles had been Parisians for four generations; the two oldest sons were born in Lille only because their mother wanted to pass her period of confinement with her family.

The De Gaulles, in sum, were not at all "bourgeois" in the sense in which Flaubert—and, for that matter, Marx—understood the word. With a sprinkling of clerical nobility and military bourgeoisie in their ancestry, they were men of the pen: scholars, functionaries of the State, provincial writers, and clerks of the court. Threadbare and decent intellectuals, with an uncle who was a cavalryman and a cousin who

12

was a priest; people who knew grammar, Latin, and Greek, who went to mass and served the State without demanding too much in exchange—though silently regretting the necessity for putting their talents and virtue at the service of the Republic rather than at the disposition of the successor to "the forty kings who, in a thousand years, made France."

The real ancestor of the general is not Philip Augustus's squire, Richard de Gaulle (or de Waulle, or Dewaulle, which according to some means "the Frenchman" and to others "the rampart"); nor is it Jehan de Gaulle, who fought at Agincourt and is constantly quoted by delighted authors as having advised against doing battle there; nor Antoine de Gaulle, Marie Antoinette's "secretary for purchases"; nor even his grandfather, Julien-Philippe de Gaulle, the author of a "note on the life and work of M. Bidault, landscape artist." It is, rather, his grandmother, Joséphine de Gaulle (born a Maillot), an undaunted writer—eight pages of listings in the catalog of the Bibliothèque Nationale—author of novels with such old-fashioned titles as *Adhémar de Belcastel* and *Valérie de Montlaur,* of essays such as "The Consoling Year," dedicated to afflicted souls, and also of biographies of General Drouot (head of Napoleon's artillery), Chateaubriand, and the Irish Catholic hero, Daniel O'Connell. This lady of virtue was also editor of the *Correspondant des Familles,* an edifying little publication, but not so provincial that she would refuse to publish an article by Jules Vallès—yes, the Jules Vallès who was the firebrand of the Paris Commune—or a funeral oration (very subtly worded) of the socialist philosopher Proudhon. Chivalry, the republican army, Catholicism, "integral nationalism," the French revolutionary tradition . . . Could Charles de Gaulle be only a grandson?

Henri de Gaulle was both poor and a scholar, and

sufficiently the former to be forced to give up any thought of a military career and to resign himself, at first, to work in the Paris police headquarters—he left there in protest against an injustice done to one of his colleagues—and then to the position of a teacher in private schools. He taught literature, philosophy, and, for a time, mathematics in the Jesuit high school of the Immaculate Conception on the rue de Vaugirard.

He was a man of serious mien and delicate, bone-white hands, who wrote elegies in Greek and thought he would faint with emotion on the day the pretender to the throne visited the school. He defined himself politically as "a monarchist, beyond the time . . ."

An honest man, no doubt of that, and one of whom legend wills that he compromised his career by letting it be too clearly understood that he did not believe in the guilt of Dreyfus. A page on this subject, written by his son forty years later, gives the impression that in any case, no one spoke of the accused in this family in the way common to the majority of families who had any part in Catholic education during the last days of the century.

Madame de Gaulle: a provincial Roman matron, unbending on the subjects of religion and manners, carrying in her heart the army, the archbishopric, Alsace, and the *fleurs de lys*. A correspondent for *Le Figaro* reported that in the years just before the second war, when a friend congratulated her on the qualities of her sons, Madame Henri de Gaulle replied: "Yes, but they grieve me a great deal. . . ."—"Grieve you?" —"Yes." Leaning toward the friend, seeming highly upset, she whispered, "They are republicans. . . ."

Some of those who knew Charles de Gaulle around 1900 remember him as a skinny child with a fearless look—others term it insolent. Lower your eyes, his elders told him. He was also very sure of himself.

14

When he was ten, and playing like every boy of his age at sliding down the banister of the staircase, he fell. He was picked up and asked, "Weren't you frightened?"—"Frightened? Don't I have my star?" That same year, his father took him to see Rostand's *L'Aiglon* for his birthday. He was stunned by it. And since he passed his summers at the family property of La Ligerie, near Bergerac, he was literally nose to nose with Cyrano. A child of that age might have listened to his father read from Racine or Seneca every night, but it was Rostand he preferred. In his case, it was a taste which was to last beyond the stage of adolescence.

The Henri de Gaulles had five children—four sons and one daughter. At the family table, after grace, they improvised Latin themes on the subject of that day's soup. On Thursday afternoons, when the schools were closed, they went to meditate at the tomb of Napoleon or at the Arc de Triomphe; on Sundays, the father took the children to Versailles, and occasionally to the battlefield of Stains, where, as a lieutenant in the mobile guard during the siege of Paris in 1871 he had been wounded in the course of a sortie from the beleaguered city. The defeat of 1870 formed a dark background to the days of childhood, and lingered in memory. The first pages of General de Gaulle's *Memoirs* are devoted to this formation of the "certain idea of France" that thus took shape in his child's mind—one marked with banners and inscriptions carved in stone, with memories of glory and sacrifice, and echoed in Rostand and Detaille and the epic poems. The general is not being ironic. Let us be very careful not to imitate him.

The throne, the altar, the sword, and the Holy Water: the De Gaulles were people who held the right thoughts. And the matter of separation of Church and State, the inventories, the confiscation, were to be the climactic events in the adolescence of Charles de Gaulle and contribute almost as much toward the shaping of his personality as the stabbing memory of the lost province of Alsace. In 1907, the religious congregations were expelled from France by the anticlerical government: his father, in order to subsist, opened the Pension Fontanes, a "cram school" for students preparing for their baccalaureate; and he departed for Antoing, in Belgium, where he completed his studies with the same teachers he had always had. But it was in Paris, at the École Sainte-Geneviève ("Ginette") on the rue des Postes, where the Jesuits rounded off the education of their most brilliant students, that he prepared for the entrance examinations to Saint-Cyr. Georges Clemenceau was then prime minister for the first time.

The character itself was still hazy. From time to time, a gesture, a fragment of writing, defined its outlines. At the age of sixteen, he sent a kind of versified fable to the director of a provincial literary review which was conducting a poetry contest. This first effort of Charles de Gaulle—which, according to Alfred Fabre-Luce, was largely borrowed from the songwriter Gustave Nadaud—was titled *An Unpleasant Encounter;* in alexandrine meter, an outspoken crook fleeces a passerby too naïve for words.

Curious, this little text, in spite of its platitude: curious that a boy of this age should have written verses about a swindle rather than about the ladies. But even more significant was the gesture that accompanied this occasion. The review awarded him its first prize. He had a choice between twenty-five francs in cash and publication of his work. He chose publication. That much a man of letters, already . . .

But he did not content himself with writing bad poetry. He read a great deal, and not only Rostand. In those first years of the new century, intelligence went by the name of Bergson. A young man might have been urged by his father to mold his thought on that of Bossuet, but if he meant to assert himself as a member of his own generation he would have been reading *Matter and Memory* and *Creative Evolution*. Bergson represented freedom of the mind; he was the defender of that intuition which would be—along with "a certain idea of France" and the certainty of a great personal destiny—the arm and the standard of this young man who had already willed himself unique. In later years, as military theorist and practicing politician, his ideas and actions were to be characterized by a mobility, a kind of malleability, which stemmed directly from Bergson.

The "Charles, who acted as if he had fallen into an icebox . . ." as his older brother used to say, had found Rostand and his blaring trumpets to warm him. This gangling creature from the North, whom Léon Blum would judge to have been "carved from one block of stone," was rendered more tractable, more receptive to the subtleties of life, by the Bergson he encountered at eighteen. The doctrines of Bergson, and the praise of that "instinct . . . which guides us to the root of the order of things," were to be echoed in the first pages of *The Edge of the Sword*, in which he reproaches the General Staff of 1914 "for not having been Bergsonian enough." A rare complaint to be heard in an officers' mess . . .

But there was also Barrès: a Barrès who was already singing his swan song, but whose rhythms were more noble than those he had employed in his polemics against Dreyfus. It was not the aspect of his character that seemed no more than a sublimated Déroulède that struck and held a young man like Charles de Gaulle; it was the depth of his feelings regarding the unity of France—feelings that led him to talk of socialism, and not only to the workers in

17

the suburbs of Paris and the mines of Lorraine. Was Charles de Gaulle conscious of the artificiality of this "populist" approach? Probably not. And in 1947 he was to walk the same paths.

And then there was Péguy and the *Cahiers de la Quinzaine,* the Péguy who shifted from socialism to Catholicism, from the defense of Dreyfus to ardent nationalism. The lesson, in this case, derived from the combination of the intellectual adventure, the tragedy of rootlessness, and the specific manner of looking at France as an individual and at politics as a serious matter; but it also involved a certain intensity of tone, an animation, an emphasis. With Péguy, De Gaulle learned to beware of clericalism—at a time when the inventories and confiscations might have drawn him into it—and of militarism, in this climate of "revenge"; and, also, not to confuse noble sentiments with bad literature—though this was a lesson he sometimes forgot.

But no work of literature, no link with friends, would play a role in the formation of this odd and imperious young man comparable to that of his history books. From the battlefield of Alésia to that of Sedan, from the medieval laws on education to those of the nineteenth-century monarchy, from the intrigues of the Fronde's Madame de Longueville to those of the Restoration's Duchesse de Berry, from Colbert's reformation to the salt tax to the Convention's laws on the national wealth, he knew all there was to know. (To improve a naturally excellent memory, he practiced with his brothers, pronouncing words and names backward: elluag ed. . . .)

He was not yet twenty when he had absorbed, from fifteen centuries of French history, the two lessons which were to form his doctrine—as Bergson's thought was to form the base of his method—two of the rare ideas which he would never vary: first, that the history of France is an entity, and that so too is the French nation, from Philip Augustus to the socialist Blanqui; and second, that unless a man is a "separatist"—this is the only thing he will hold against the communists, but it is important—he is qualified for national service. It is for this reason that he will always display such a disconcerting contempt for "ideologies" and will always say "Russian" and never "Soviet," almost always "German" and very rarely "Nazi."

Even before he discovered Péguy, his certainty of French continuity permitted him to view the work of the revolutionary leaders on the same plane with the work of the cathedral builders. It may even have been this attitude which led him to the discovery of Péguy. And it was on this point that he parted company with the monarchist doctrinaire Maurras: to him, a mentality of sect or class is incompatible with the continued existence of the indivisible structure of the nation.

"I went to Saint-Cyr to take back Alsace, and also to dazzle Clarisse. . . ." This profession of faith, reported by Emmanuel d'Astier, was that of his future companion at the War College, Loustaunau-Lacau, and not of Charles de Gaulle, who seemed, thus far, to be unconcerned with any Clarisse. His sole concern, apparently, was still his manual of history—Turenne and Hoche, perhaps; they were his favorites.

"At that time, the French army was one of the greatest things in the world . . ." he wrote at the beginning of his *Memoirs*. So soon after the Dreyfus affair? True, of course, that Foch was teaching at the War College; Lyautey was in Aïn Sefra, preparing the way for his Moroccan proconsulate; and the General Staff had finally come around to equipping the troops with the Lebel rifle and the .75 millimeter gun. But at Saint-Cyr, where there had been two thousand cadets at the end of the century, there were no more than seven hundred in 1908. The army itself seldom left its garrisons, except when it was called out—disgustedly—to control the great strikes which marked the early years of the new century. The High Command, seemingly frozen in its tracks, did little to appease the thirst for new equipment made evident by the work of the military intelligentsia.

Under the terms of a regulation adopted shortly before, based on the relatively futile principle that a man cannot command without having first obeyed, each student appointed to the academy after the admission examinations had to begin by spending a year in an existing troop corps. So, in September, 1909, he was a soldier in the 33rd Infantry Regiment at Arras, playing the role of messenger boy and porter, trapped between tangles of packs and errands of sweeping-out. He detested this probationary period and was scornful of the idea behind it.

On October 10, 1910, when he arrived at Saint-Cyr, he was almost twenty. At this stage, a man began to emerge from the childhood of pious souvenirs and paper soldiers. The character hardened, took a stand, became annoyed—entered into a debate that was never to close.

Let us not think of him at Saint-Cyr as some fabulous adolescent, a kind of military Rimbaud. If he had any legend at this point, it was because of his height: he was not only known as "the double meter," but also as "the cock," and primarily as "Cyrano." The hazing inflicted on him by Lachouque, the upper-classman assigned to watch over him, was the order to climb up on a table and recite Cyrano's tirade on the subject of noses. At the annual academy show in 1911, he played the part of the husband in a village wedding. The following year, for the same ceremony, he was a clown in classic costume, with a pointed cap.

Under the direction of someone listed as Monsieur Loyal, who was actually his best friend, Jacques de Siéyès, he performed a routine of mounted gymnastics, accompanied by a female bareback rider—the future General Herreman. Was this gay fellow *le grand Charles?* Let's admit that he played the game—as he was to do, later, in other circumstances.

We know some of his friends of that period. He had little to do with Juin, future commandant of the graduating class, then Marshal of France, nor with Béthouart, who, from 1940, would be one of the "faithful." Did he know the four Chinese cadets who were in his class—a rather unusual occurrence, even if not particularly important? The graduating class was given the name of "Fez": it was 1912, the year of a treaty which was to link Morocco to France for half a century, and perhaps for a great deal longer.

We know that he tramped the fields and paths between Trappes and Chevreuse with his friends, endlessly discussing the nature of the new army. One of their topics was a statement of the director of the War College: "Aviation? It's a sport. For the army—zero!"

Europe was trembling again in those years when the German gunboat *Panther* dropped anchor off the coast of Morocco, when Serbia was attempting to escape from the Austro-Hungarian vise, when the eviction of pacifist Prime Minister Caillaux and the steady march of right-wing nationalist Poincaré toward the presidency of the Republic made it clear to anyone who could see that peace was no longer the "sick man" of a few years back, but already condemned. Writing the first pages of his *Memoirs*, forty years later, he was certainly making no attempt at trickery in stating that the army awaited "with serenity, and even with a secret hope, the approach of the moment when everything would depend on it." And these young men waited more eagerly than anyone else.

De Gaulle, Charles, left the academy with the number thirteen. Honorable, but no more than that. One of his instructors is said to have noted of him: "Average in everything, except in height." Hardly a definition of a flair for the military—perhaps because he was not particularly strong at either marksmanship or gymnastics. He could nevertheless have chosen the cavalry or the artillery. He asked to return to the regiment where he had "been hatched," the 33rd Infantry Regiment at Arras.

Did he know that a new commander had just been assigned to this regiment, a Colonel Pétain? Were the Saint-Cyr cadets of that time well enough acquainted with the army beyond their gates to know the name of an officer of this rank, even of one who had already established such a reputation for firmness, foresight, and competence? Perhaps the young Catholic officers had spread the story of this agnostic colonel who, when he was asked to designate those of his officers who attended mass, replied: "I stand in the first row at mass, and I am not in the habit of turning around."

Young men such as these, impassioned with their profession, could not help but know that Pétain's name was linked with an argument over fundamental doctrine. At the War College, he had found means of opposing his concept of the new primacy of firepower to the official theses of movement, attack, and the bayonet—less brilliantly, however, than Lanrezac, the "crack" officer of his generation and possessor of the only intelligence that could be compared to that of Foch. Had De Gaulle sensed in this glacial, Olympian officer a prefiguration of the heretic he himself would be? No matter; by whatever path it was that he came under his orders, he admired Colonel Pétain.

This first encounter of the colonel and the second lieutenant is the delight of essayists and biographers.

There are so many anecdotes that they fuse together, some of them seeming to stem from Plutarch and others from regimental gossip. Among them all, we might recall this one, which at least has the merit of recalling another such duo, that of the two most famous French strategists of the eighteenth century. The colonel was lecturing the young officers on the events of the siege of Arras in 1654 and describing the maneuver of Condé which threw one opposing general's forces into disorder and outflanked another. The second lieutenant leaped to his feet: "But Turenne was there, and made his presence known with the sound of his cannon. Arras was saved. . . ." If it is true—it will not be uncommon for De Gaulle to interrupt a "sermon"—the story is typically *gaullien*. It demonstrates the young man's shrewdness as well as his audacity: however odd its form, the tribute to the use of cannon was highly expedient when it is borne in mind that it was addressed to Colonel Pétain.

The zeal of Second Lieutenant de Gaulle irritated the other junior officers, who thought he was meddling in things which were "no concern of his." The troops, however, seemed to appreciate the tireless devotion to duty of this towering character, so steeped in the "social obligations of the officer" that he knew by heart the service record and background of every one of his recruits.

The two years Charles de Gaulle spent in this manner in Arras, on the eve of the war—and which, on this level, was to be prolonged through the years of combat—were of capital importance in the development of his mind and his reflexes. Although he had been born in Lille, he had been a "Parisian since the last century," as he put it himself, and a Parisian of the aristocratic quarters: from the Avenue Duquesne to the Place Saint-François-Xavier. But at this time, his every waking hour was spent with a troop made up of miners from the Pas-de-Calais, peasants from the Thiérache and the Tardenois, workers from Valenciennes and Charleville.

The foremost historian among his biographers, Paul-Marie de la Gorce, has strongly emphasized the role which this experience played in the relationship of Charles de Gaulle with the people he would one day govern: "Throughout his life, when he evokes the French people it is primarily the population of northern France he has in mind. When he addresses himself to the French it is the French of the North of whom he is thinking. . . ."

No matter how much he may have esteemed the people as a whole, it was this fraction of it which preoccupied him, not the Toulousains, the Avignonais, the Marseillais, or the *pieds noirs* of Algeria—the origins of some of his problems. The France of soccer rather than the France of rugby. Of cock fights rather than bull fights. Of coffee, rather than wine. But we also know his passion for national unity, and this is a more abstract force and therefore more total.

The war permitted him to measure that force. "The sacred union" of 1914 confirmed his dual certainty: that the nation is one, and that ideologies bear little weight when the fate of the nation is at stake. It was the socialist Viviani who led the nation into war. It was the socialist Péguy who lánced the most ardent call to combat—with the possible exception of the even more socialist Gustave Hervé. But the same phenomenon occurred on the other side of the frontier: neither Ebert nor Bebel even attempted to stem the nationalist fervor of the powerful German Social Democratic party.

It is worth pausing for a moment to study him as he left for the war he had awaited since early childhood, certain, as he was to write, "that France must pass through a series of gigantic ordeals, that the whole interest of life lies in rendering her, one day, some notable service, and that I will have the occasion to do it." ("The whole interest of life" and not "duty." Péguy would not have chosen those words. A gambler, and already something of a cynic. Speaking later of wartime action, he was to describe it as "the divine game of heroes." An echo of Lyautey, of the noble adventurer.)

There is a photograph of Charles de Gaulle dated October, 1914, when he was twenty-four years old. In it, this awkward giant of a lieutenant is leaning against a low railing set up before a photographer's backdrop of a forest, trying to appear at ease in an ill-fitting "government-issue" uniform of horizon-blue handed out to him mechanically by some quartermaster. His left hand, holding his gloves, rests on the knee with a weight that seems almost presidential. But there is something fragile in the silhouette, and beneath the soft cloth of the kepi the face has a languorous quality, one in which there is more of Proust than of Barrès: the eyelids slightly drooping, the nostalgic moustache, the chin drawn back into the collar. A terribly *fin-de-siècle* personage, closer to the world of *Remembrance of Things Past* than to a trivial present.

He was then a first lieutenant, having been promoted in October, 1913. He was also a young man of great intellectual curiosity, one who read *Le Temps* —to the astonishment of both his colleagues and the townspeople of Arras, where this newspaper was considered unduly stern and a trifle too "republican." He also carried in his field trunk several issues of Péguy's *Cahiers de la Quinzaine*. Trained in the art of command—at least in peacetime—and nurtured on as much history as it is possible to know at twenty, De Gaulle had already constructed for himself a set of personal ethics: a nationalism incorporating all

25

classes and beliefs; the certainty of an exceptional role to play, with priority given to intuition; and an awareness of technical evolution and the influence it will have on every form of activity, including the military. A brilliant apprentice, filled with noble animation and having no intention of looking at the approaching war with the disinterested gaze of Stendhal's Fabrice del Dongo at Waterloo.

But what would he be worth in action, in combat itself? The first experience under fire was decisive; it marked him so profoundly that thirty years later he spoke of it to his niece, Geneviève, on her return from deportation in Germany, as an experience comparable to that of the concentration camps. In *France and Her Army* (1938), he described it in one of his best pieces of writing, hard and sharp as glass: "The infantry has left the road. Deployed across the fields in a line of short columns, it moves toward the unknown drama. Silently, their throats constricted, watching their leaders, who force themselves to smile, the men move ahead, anxious but resolute. . . . The bullets are whistling now, rare at first, almost hesitant. . . . Less brutal than the shells, but frightening, because they wound and kill in silence. And then running, heart pounding, across the reaped fields of this end of the month of August. . . . In the space of a split second, it is apparent that all the virtue in the world is of no value whatever in the face of fire."

Neither fresh nor joyous, this war. And proving the gloomy Colonel Pétain to be right: it is firepower that counts.

Charles de Gaulle was wounded three times: at Dinant, on August 15, 1914; at Mesnil-lès-Hurlus (in Champagne), in February, 1915; at Douaumont, in March, 1916.

It would not be possible, without being lacking in

fairness to the character of the man, to pass over the Douaumont episode in silence. It is summed up in the citation awarded him afterward by General Pétain: "Captain de Gaulle, company commander, esteemed for his high intellectual and moral valor, at a time when his battalion was decimated by the effects of a frightful bombardment and the enemy had reached his company positions on all sides, led his men in a furious assault and ferocious hand-to-hand battle, the only solution he judged compatible with his sense of military honor. Fallen in the conflict. A peerless officer in every respect." It was the second of March, 1916. He was believed dead, and his parents received the announcement from a private source. He was actually seriously wounded and a prisoner.

Thirty-two months of captivity. He knew five internment camps. On his second attempt at escape, the German uniform he had stolen reached only to his knees and his elbows. On the third, he teamed up with a famous airforce pilot, Roland Garros. A wasted effort. After that, he was sent to Fort IX, the reprisal camp at Ingolstadt, which has been described by one of its inhabitants, the English Lieutenant Evans, in a book entitled *The Escape Club*. There, he was welcomed by Rémy Roure, who would later use his column in *Le Temps* to champion his cause; by Berger-Levrault, his future publisher; and by Major Catroux, who, on the eighteenth of June, 1940, was to ignore the fact that his new commander was also his junior officer. There was also a certain Tukhachevsky, who would command the Red Army before becoming a victim of the Stalin purges of 1937.

An intellectually fruitful period. He devoured the German newspapers, following the course of the war better through them than he could have in France, where the censorship was clumsier; took notes which were to become the source material for his first book, *Discord Among the Enemy;* and organized continual debates and conferences. After half a century, his companions in captivity still remember this effervescent intelligence, this astounding memory, this rage to learn and to teach—and also, emphatically, to be right. It was at this time, and by these men, that he was given the nickname "the Constable," which Churchill would rediscover twenty-five years later.

Curious sort of atmosphere, there in Fort IX. On his thrice-weekly tours of inspection, General Peter, commanding officer of a camp where water bombs exploded and mattresses burst into flames, would shake his head and grumble. *"Hier ist alles kriminal!"* That tall one who wandered unconcernedly through the constant tumult, holding a handkerchief to a long nose reddened by the cold, that was De Gaulle. "Why don't you go into politics?" he asked one of the friends who shared his barrack, a talented university teacher. "For myself, if I weren't a soldier . . ." And then added, "In politics, experience is the only teacher. . . ."

But the real "character" at Fort IX was Tukhachevsky. Twenty-three years old, handsome as a god, insolent, petulant, he talked of nothing but a new escape. How to get away? After the treaty of Brest-Litovsk, the Russian officers received permission to leave camp each day if they gave their word of honor as officers to return within an hour. Tukhachevsky had found his answer. As each man left the camp, he had to sign beside his own name on the register, so Tukhachevsky simply changed lines with a comrade: he signed next to Popov's name, and Popov signed beside Tukhachevsky's. That, they felt, released them from their oath. And so he left. In a last effort to hold him back, the French officers had said,

"You're the son of a noble family; if you go back to Russia now, you'll be shot." "Shot?" he replied. "I'll be a general by the time I'm twenty-five." At twenty-five he was a marshal. And shot at forty-three.

2

... Of a King
in Exile

Only half a war . . . Scarcely
liberated from Ludwigshafen, where he had been
sent from Ingolstadt, that is what he said. The Constable still thirsted for action, for more notable services. France dreamt of nothing but peace, but he
wanted to prolong "the divine game of heroes." In
the park of the family property at La Ligerie, just
after the war, he stood beside his three brothers, all
with the same moustaches, all wearing decorations,
and all laced tightly into the new uniforms which
marked the end of the campaign. Standing slightly behind the others, he seems even stiffer than they, more
conscious of the regulations; his height proclaims him
built for both battle and debate: the long silhouette
of a booted grenadier, the hard, lean look of a wolf.
He was about to leave for the East.

For more than a year, a Polish general named Hal-
ler had been busy in France recruiting volunteers to
fight against the Red Army, which had replied in
kind to Pilsudski's attempts at infiltration and was now
threatening the Curzon Line—the eastern frontier of
Poland established by the Allies. And against whom
would this young captain—Catholic, a stickler for the
rule of order, and deprived of the chance to take part
in the final hunt for the German—do battle more

willingly than against the army of the Soviets, the signers of the separate peace of Brest-Litovsk which had almost saved the day for the central powers? And where better than in Poland, helping the Poles, calling up a vision of Kosciusko and of the Poniatowskis, the most pro-Napoleonic noble Polish family— not to speak of Alfred Jarry's Père Ubu (he delighted in Jarry, whose knife-sharp humor would inspire him when the occasion arose).

April, 1919, found him on the banks of the Vistula. And not far away was another interesting personage (the lives of famous men frequently resemble the fourth act of a bedroom comedy): Tukhachevsky, ex-companion in captivity at Ingolstadt, soon to be a marshal of the Red Army and commander of the enemy forces.

Named to the rank of major by the Poles, Charles de Gaulle at first taught infantry tactics in the camp of Rembertow. He attempted to conduct his classes in Polish, but abandoned this relatively quickly— though not without having astonished his pupils by his linguistic virtuosity. His interpreter, Professor Wienewski, remembers his lectures as having been extremely brilliant, and followed with rapt attention. Some people thought him a little cold and vain, but he gave his Polish colleagues and students the impression of being "someone."

In June and July of 1920, when the Soviet forces launched their strongest offensive against Warsaw, the French instructors at Rembertow were assigned to Polish combat units. De Gaulle distinguished himself in the battles along the Zbrucz River and was decorated with the highest Polish award, *Virtuti Militari*. A fighter for their liberties, a French officer, and tall as a cavalryman: it required less than that in this romantic country to be pleasing to the ladies. According to legend—which in this case assumes the form of an elderly concierge—he was often seen in the Cafe Blikle, where the best pastries in Warsaw had been served for half a century, in the company of a tiny and charming young lady who might have been Princess Czetwertinska. (But the romantic imagination of the Poles must be borne in mind.)

A strong impression remained in his mind: that of a country in which France had a "presence" and a place in the hearts of the people. And also that of a military civilization which was to be of great interest to him (among the books in his library are the memoirs of Marshal Pilsudski, which he read in German and annotated himself); and the first contact, even though more remote, with the revolutionary army of the Soviets. There, it might be said, was a land and a people that concerned him.

A man can have a head full of new ideas, consider himself assured of a great personal destiny, and still behave like a character in a ladies' magazine story. At the annual Salon d'Automne in Paris, just after his return from Poland, a captain named Charles de Gaulle met a young lady from Calais named Yvonne Vendroux. Chance very probably played a negligible role in the meeting, since both captain and lady were members of highly respectable Christian families of the North and the Pas-de-Calais. But whether it was impromptu or not, their first conversation took place in front of a portrait of Maurice Rostand, poet-son of the author of *Cyrano de Bergerac*. From this, it was just a short step to a recitation of a fragment from the tirade on noses, a dazzled young lady, and a conquering captain. They were married six months later, on April 7, 1921.

Yvonne Vendroux's parents, who had business interests in Douai and Dunkerque—they manufactured tea biscuits—had several country properties, among them a chateau near Charleville called Septfontaines: there was a taste of Claudel in that. The young De Gaulle couple was to live in Paris, first on the Square Dupleix and later on the Place Saint-François-Xavier, but they would spend many summers in the Ardennes before buying a house of their own at Colombey-les-Deux-Églises, not quite so far from Paris. Calais, Dunkerque, Douai, Lille, Charleville: De Gaulle's roots were sinking deeper and deeper in the North—harsh winds, hard work, battlefields, flat horizons.

On the first of October, 1921, Captain de Gaulle was named assistant professor of military history at Saint-Cyr. Since it was no longer possible to become a commander in chief at twenty-seven, as the Convention had made Hoche, one might just as well talk about Hoche to boys of twenty. But knowing, and being completely engrossed by your subject, is not everything. It is also necessary to be able to express yourself, to convince your audience, and to avoid becoming a target for students' jokes. He would have to learn to master that great signal-tower of a frame, those choppy, sweeping gestures, that voice from the stomach, which climbs suddenly into the throat and emerges as a premature, almost mocking tremolo. He would have to train the awkward monster that was his body, transform his drawbacks into assets. Insofar as it is possible today to obtain reliable testimony, he succeeded.

The son of Professor de Gaulle was a teacher who was listened to. Even at this stage, he silenced all opposition with those abruptly changing rhythms of eloquence which were to make a microphone in London a weapon of war, and with the knowing gestures and expressions which the television screen would transform into millions of ballots for the President of the Fifth Republic.

In brief, he "chatted"—to use the word with which

Eugène Mannoni in *Moi, General de Gaulle* has summed it up. He chatted so well that he had to move back to the other side of the desk. The War College, inevitably, was the goal of every officer who wanted to play a part in the continuing function of the State, and he was certainly one of those. All of his study in those years had been concentrated on the ruinous excesses of German militarism, the specifically Prussian causes of the defeat of Berlin. It was at that time, in fact, that he was putting the final touches on his first book, which he had begun drafting during his captivity at Ingolstadt: *Discord Among the Enemy.* It is a very interesting little book, made up of five studies denouncing, one after another, the encroachments of military authority on the civil power in imperial Germany, and finding in those encroachments the fundamental reason for the collapse of the State at the end of 1918.

Charles de Gaulle was to publish better books. But this essay, written more simply than the prideful dissertations of the forties or the carefully polished *Memoirs,* has the merit of precisely setting forth the personality and ideas of this thirty-year-old officer in the aftermath of war. On the second page of the book, speaking of Von Kluck's disobedience to Moltke's orders in the first days of September, 1914, Captain de Gaulle wrote: "In war, aside from a few essential principles, there is no universal system, but only circumstances and personalities."

Empiricism, intuition, flexibility of mind if not of soul: on these points he was not to change. And the successive stages of his own career were to confirm him—in spite of himself?—in the other principle which the book makes clear: the necessity of utilizing the civil power to restrict the influence of the military, even in time of war. The account of Ludendorff's 1917 plot to overthrow Chancellor Bethmann-Hollweg and set up a military dictatorship is excellent: fast-moving and simply written. This "primitive" among the literary works of De Gaulle has a clarity of line, a sharpness of approach, which is often lacking in the majestic ornamentation—and even in the skillful omissions—of the later essays.

The book was not published until 1924. But in November, 1922, at the time when Captain de Gaulle entered the War College, he had already arrived at the two intellectual commandments of the historian and the wartime leader: there is no other strategy, in war, except that imposed by circumstances; and there is no line of conduct, for military men, other than that of preserving the equilibrium of power by respecting the rights of civil policy. Strategy, after all, is primarily a policy.

The War College gave him the occasion to put his ideas to the test of official doctrine, and to measure his character. The chair of tactics at the college—made illustrious by Foch—was held by a certain Colonel Moyrand, who is remembered as a scrupulous and competent teacher, but who was the most intransigent advocate of a strategy based on "compartmentation of the terrain." It is on a selected field that the action is constructed; and one holds there, sure of his ground, since everything has been prepared so that the enemy will impale himself on the trap. Basing themselves primarily on past battles, these were the lessons the masters of the college had drawn from the war of 1914-1918: superiority of the defense, preponderance of firepower, the danger of movement. Charles de Gaulle resisted: the enemy is no more stupid than we; he will do the same thing we do, and also try to find a favorable terrain! And since De Gaulle had a sense of the theater, he was to give dramatic form to the argument he supported.

It would be difficult to understand De Gaulle's

audacity in this period—no matter how certain he might have been that he was Hoche confronted with a government of old men, he was, after all, only a captain—unless we were to place the young officer in the framework which was temporarily his. His former colonel, Philippe Pétain, by then a marshal of France and the third ranking member of a phalanx of leaders still invested with incomparable prestige, had received him with kindness and understanding, and welcomed him into his home. The captain, in turn, sincerely admired the man who had so accurately foreseen the supremacy of firepower, even before 1914; and he had due respect for what might be termed the surgeon's role played by Pétain in saving both the army and public opinion from the confusion into which each had been drawn in 1917. He certainly made no attempt to draw comparisons between the clear talents of Pétain and the unique luster of Foch, a man of imagination and great brilliance. But having Pétain for a patron in the immediate postwar period was like having an ace in the hole. He was too conscious of the role he had to play to neglect it. With his back propped against the sturdy old oak, Cyrano was convinced he could defy the entire world.

And all the more so since he was not surrounded by timid men or conformists. Each week, he met at home with three other captains who were his classmates at the college and who were by no means mediocre companions. There was Georges-Picot, who belonged to a family with a long tradition of members of the Institut de France; Bridoux, whose father, a general, had been killed in combat; and Loustaunau-Lacau, the son of a Béarnais peasant and a chambermaid, and commandant of his class at Saint-Cyr. The first two, whose intelligence De Gaulle had valued, were to be opposed to him after 1940. With Georges-Picot, it was to be Syria first, then Algiers, and then

Paris. He would never forgive him for not having come over to his side during the crucial days in the Near East. The second, Bridoux, would be minister of war at Vichy, condemned to death *in absentia* by the De Gaulle government of 1945, and end as a military adviser to Franco. Loustaunau-Lacau, a sort of untidy d'Artagnan, a shrewd and thundering individualist, a good reporter and brilliant polemicist, in turn pro-Vichy and anti-Vichy, would negotiate behind the scenes with Gaullist emissaries, be deported by the Nazis, and die as a general and a deputy representing the right-wing parties. In short, Captain de Gaulle had chosen a good audience to try out his teeth on, and they were to grow sharper with assurance.

Luncheons with the marshal, debates with the three other musketeers, the uproar of school, work, and maneuvers—and at last came the time of examination and classification. The final exercise, called a "tactical field trip," took place in the vicinity of Bar-sur-Aube on June 17, 1924. Captain de Gaulle was put to the test: he was given an army corps to command. Throughout the day, he resolved the problems put to him, but did so by relating them constantly to an intuitive strategy and refusing to prepare his "compartment of the terrain," thereby giving proof of his complete disavowal of the official teachings. That night, when the time for the critique arrived, Colonel Moyrand, annoyed with his attitude, attempted to confuse him.

In an article published in July, 1960, in the review *Miroir de l'Histoire*, General Chauvin, who was a witness to the scene, tells this typically *gaullien* story: "Where were the combat vehicles of the left regiment of your right-hand division at that time?" the colonel asked. And De Gaulle, turning his head toward his chief of staff: "Chateauvieux, would you answer that?" The colonel, irritated: "But it was you I asked the

37

question, De Gaulle."—"Colonel, you entrusted me with responsibility for command of an army corps. If, in addition to that, I had to assume the responsibilities of my subordinates, my mind would never be sufficiently free to carry out my mission. *De minimis non curat praetor.* . . . Chateauvieux, please answer the colonel's question. . . ."

The result was not surprising: mentioned as "satisfactory," while in principle only the mention "very satisfactory" would open the doors to the lordly "Third Section" in which tactics and strategy were actually planned. The following reasons were given: "Intelligent officer, cultivated and serious; has brilliance and facility; good deal of worth. Unfortunately spoils incontestable qualities by his excessive assurance, his intolerance of the opinions of others, and his attitude of a king in exile. . . ."

Second stumbling block—after captivity—in the Constable's career. His patron was annoyed by it, and before De Gaulle left for his first postwar command in Mainz, the headquarters of the army of the Rhine, he was given reason to hope that a place would be found for him which would give him the opportunity for revenge.

In October, 1925, De Gaulle was appointed to the staff of Marshal Pétain, vice-president of the Supreme War Council, inspector general of the army, nominal chief of the French armed forces.

He was no sooner installed in the Invalides than he was assigned to preparation of a study on fortifications and the role of strongholds in the defense of France: irony of fate, or of his patron? The study was prepared in a month. At the end of the year it appeared in the *Revue Militaire Française*, to which De Gaulle had contributed an article on "The Orientation of our Doctrines of War" six months earlier.

Under the title "The Historic Role of French Strongholds," Charles de Gaulle, the future strategist of movement, inaugurated his career as official theorist of French national defense with a reluctant eulogy of concrete and the defensive, tracing the lines of fortifications sketched out by Vauban, which were to be the basis of the Maginot Line.

However, the new spokesman for the marshal recognized very quickly the risks inherent in his words, the interpretations that were being given them, and the conclusions that were being drawn. He did not give in on any basic points, and he remained generally unfavorable to a continuous line of defense, arguing instead for the maintenance of fortified points as bases of maneuver and movement.

His friend, Colonel Lucien Nachin—then a captain —had expressed anxiety about the possibility that an elaborate system of fortifications would induce an unwarranted sense of security in the French people, and in January, 1926, De Gaulle answered in these terms: "The defensive organization should not be a part of the plan of operations, as many people want it to be. A permanent necessity, linked to the geographic, political, and even moral conditions in which the country finds itself, it is a matter for the government. . . ."

A year later, still striving to maintain a balance between his own feelings and the duty of his office, which was to plead the cause of the continuous fortifications, De Gaulle called on an unimpeachable authority and wrote (again to Lucien Nachin) that the concept of the "squared field" and Vauban's concern with "barring the routes" had "seriously restricted the mobility of our enemies in the last years of Louis XIV's reign, and again in 1792-93." And he repeated with satisfaction a phrase of this same Vauban, quoted to him by his correspondent, and pointing out the advantage of having "few places, but good ones." This was quite different from the marshal's theses, which at that time were resulting in the construction of Maginot's enormous wall.

The Constable was beginning to realize that having a patron was not invariably advantageous. No matter how sure of oneself one may be, clothed in pride and armored in irony, it is impossible to escape altogether from the climate of adulation that surrounds a great man.

But he was about to harvest the fruits of his servitude: in the last days of 1926, he was inscribed on the promotion lists for the rank of battalion commander, although he was not actually promoted to it until ten months later. When Lucien Nachin congratulated him, he wrote, in pure *gaullien:* "It is pleasant to get ahead, but that is not really the question: it is a matter of making one's mark."

Making one's mark? His patron offered him the chance to do it, repaying him thus for his earlier deceptions: he was asked to conduct three conferences at the War College on the role of the leader. An almost unhoped-for revenge for the loser in the jousting match of 1924, the victim of Colonel Moyrand. Before a gathering of the entire school, teachers and pupils of both classes, he would propose (an odd word, applied to the Constable . . .) a philosophy for the man of war.

The first conference took place on April 7, 1927. Not content with having dictated the choice of the speaker, Pétain conducted him solemnly to the rostrum and, as presiding officer, introduced Charles de Gaulle to the paralyzed audience in these terms: "Listen, gentlemen, to Captain de Gaulle. . . . Listen to him carefully, because the day will come when a grateful France will call on him. . . ." (The last part of the phrase has been contested, but Colonel Nachin, who reports it, is a reliable source.)

The theses propounded by Charles de Gaulle before his audience at the War College, in the presence of Philippe Pétain, are, with very few variations, the material of his book *The Edge of the Sword:* the action of war and the leader—the theme of the first conference—of character, of prestige—the subjects of the two others. Those bits of eloquence captivated some and irritated others (naturally). A debate quickly resolved itself around the significance of this full-length portrait of the wartime leader. Some people considered it simply a self-portrait, others a homage to the marshal. And it is a fact that, of all the great military leaders then living, Pétain was the only one mentioned.

It was a debate without any object. As a good man of the theater, De Gaulle had built up his character in a series of layers. There was a background of Pétain, for the comportment and posture, for the conciseness and the method. But on this base of general's stars and of earned, established, tangible glory, the prodigious captain breathed his own spirit into the pale block of marble, into that polished, ceremonial figure.

Reading these texts today, and imagining them spoken in the raspy, emphatic tone which everyone remarked in Captain de Gaulle, it is not hard to believe that they must have "bowled over" his listeners. "You will have an intellect when you become a bishop," Stendhal's heroine, La Sanseverina, says to the young abbot she loves. And there was a great deal of intellect, and even greater assurance, for an officer who was still not wearing a fourth stripe. So many certainties, so lofty a style, and the declared patronage of the first personage in the military hierarchy: more than enough to have alienated from De Gaulle all those who refused to be captivated. The majority.

But Charles de Gaulle was to find a way around this wall of mistrust which automatically separates an

41

easy, confident speaker from the "mute masses." Thanks again to the good offices of the marshal, he was given the opportunity to express his views before a civilian audience. Repeating the conferences he had held at the War College in the great auditorium of the Sorbonne, not to soldiers this time, but to writers, professors, politicians, men and women of the world—to Bergson's audience—was no negligible satisfaction to the son of the teacher in the Immaculate Conception school, the grandson of Joséphine Maillot. And his success was greater than it had been among his colleagues.

His departure for Germany was not, however, quite as significant as Racine's retirement from the drama. Equipped with his fourth stripe, he was assigned to command of the 19th Light Infantry Battalion garrisoned at Trier. General Matter, chief of the infantry forces, stated to a friend of Charles de Gaulle: "I'm moving a future commander in chief into place."

1927. Along the pleasant banks of the Moselle, hemmed in by gentle, vine-covered slopes, it was very cold that year. So cold that an epidemic of influenza broke out, and the mortality rate among the troops caused a stir in political circles: thirty soldiers dead at Trier, "without counting the Vietnamese." The Poincaré government was questioned in the Chamber, and a commission of inquiry was appointed. Speaking before the Chamber, Colonel Picot, a member of the commission, made a point of discharging from any responsibility the chief of the 19th Battalion, "which is admirably commanded." The orator further specified: "When the soldier Gouraud, an orphan, died, the major himself wore a mourning band. There is a leader!" (loud applause). On the government bench, Raymond Poincaré, prime minister and paragon of all virtues, public and private,

42

nodded and cried, "Very good!"—the equivalent of a citation.

Major de Gaulle, who did not ordinarily dislike publicity, was annoyed by the incident, and considered those comments improper. He wrote to Lucien Nachin: "The 19th Battalion was not affected by the epidemic to anything like the extent Colonel Picot indicated. . . . This whole business is lamentable. . . ."

He worked. Although the chill which had recently developed in the marshal's attitude toward him had lessened his interest in the historical study he undertook while under his protection in 1925, he nevertheless made a great many notes and carried on a brisk correspondence with Lucien Nachin: "Force of circumstances is beating down what still remains of Europe's conventional and precious barriers. It seems self-evident that the Anschluss is near, then Germany's reclamation, by one means or another, of what was taken away from her and given to Poland. After which, they will reclaim Alsace. That seems to me to be written in the stars." That was written in 1928.

On a professional and intellectual level, this period in Trier brought him considerable satisfaction. But on the human level, he faced the worst ordeal which can confront a father: a third child was born to the De Gaulles, a daughter, Anne, who would never be normal and who was to live for twenty years. However reluctant one may be to approach such matters, it would not be possible to render an account of the life of this man—seemingly so completely protected by a hardness which, if not natural, was certainly deliberately acquired—without bearing in mind this secret, constantly bleeding wound. Before 1928, his claws had been sharpened only on pride; after 1928, a very personal suffering was to heighten his melancholy and cause him to react by biting and snapping. His most surprising letter to Lucien Nachin dates from this period—June 20, 1929: "Ah! All the bitterness that goes with wearing the uniform in these days! And yet it must be done. In a few years, they will be hanging on our coattails to save the country ... and the rabble, first of all. ..."

This is one of Charles de Gaulle's most widely discussed texts. The majority of historians, biographers, and memorialists give the following transcription of it: ". . . they will be hanging on *my* coattails to save the country. . . ." Which, of course, leads the reader to agree with their pessimistic prognosis on the mental condition of Major de Gaulle. "My" or "our"? (In French, *mes* or *nos?*) A careful reading of the manuscript text, which was phototyped in J. R. Tournoux's *Pétain et De Gaulle* (Plon), and a comparison of the first letter of the controversial word with the "m" of *mes* in the conventional form of courtesy at the end, makes it far more plausible to read the word as *nos*, "our." And after all, no matter how friendly he may have been with Colonel Nachin, or how firmly convinced of his own value and unconcerned with the habitual rules of the military hierarchy, it is still difficult to imagine that Major de Gaulle would have written to a senior officer he respected and announced that the fate of France would depend on him alone. Even though the image it calls up is odd, the phrasing *our coattails* is more credible. And not only more in conformity with the handwriting, but more eloquent about the spirit of "caste" that inspired Charles de Gaulle.

That it should be necessary to go to such lengths to arrive at this interpretation, that men who profess admiration or respect for De Gaulle should have accepted the customary reading, and that the general himself has never taken the trouble to resolve the controversy—all this says a great deal about the myth and its proliferation.

44

The German experience was fruitful, of course. But he had to broaden his horizons. He left for the Near East—more discreetly than Bonaparte.

Beirut was not a proper frame for him. That *trompe l'oeil* universe, all in silks and russet, did not sit well with the Constable; and all the more so since Colonel Catroux's transfer to Morocco deprived him of an incomparable guide and partner to the verbal fencing matches with archdeacons of the Church, horse trainers at the racetrack, and *condottieri* from the Lebanese hills. In his sarcastic manner, he would have appreciated them.

But there, as elsewhere, he "made his mark." His worried colleagues all saw in him one of the future masters of the military structure. And it is interesting to read this account of a "performance" of Charles de Gaulle in July, 1930, written by a witness who was to become one of the greatest critics of modern French poetry: "It was on the occasion of a distribution of prizes at a school. I saw a great devil of a major, uniformed in white and carrying an enormous saber, stand up and take a couple of steps to the front. We expected nothing from him except a doubling of our boredom. He began to speak and, instantly, all boredom vanished. We heard new and rare ideas, coming to us full-blown, every second, in a form so perfectly obedient and right that it was impossible to know whether they stemmed from the words themselves or from the force of the mind behind them. In the way he managed it, the structure of language lifted itself above contingencies and falsehoods, opened wide the realm of thought—free thought—and of human energy capable of influencing the enormous power of history. . . ."

Major de Gaulle visited Cairo, Baghdad, Damascus, Aleppo, and Jerusalem, but his usual enthusiasm for writing letters does not seem to have been stimulated.

From the disciple of Barrès, it would be reasonable to expect a lofty account. We get a bird's-eye view. After six months in the Near East, he wrote, again to Lucien Nachin: "My impression is that we are making scarcely any headway and that the people are as foreign to us—and we to them—as they ever were. It is true that we have adopted as a course of action the worst possible system in this country, trying to incite the people to lift themselves up by themselves . . . when nothing has ever been accomplished here— neither the canals of the Nile, nor the aqueduct of Palmyra, nor a Roman road, nor even an olive orchard —without the use of force. As far as I can see, our fate will be to arrive at that point, or leave. . . ."

The basic insight is there. This was the germinal stage of the feelings which were to form the basis of an "Algerian Algeria" policy: we have not "made any headway" with a civilization essentially different from ours, and these people are "foreign" to us; therefore, in an area where you do not "make your mark," why stay, why not disengage yourself?

He had taken the pulse of Germany, scouted Po- land, and measured the extent to which the Soviet revolution weighed on eastern Europe. And then he was brushed by the East. He could return to the General Staff, the broad highway to command, the exercise of power, the role of leader for which he had been sharpening his tools and toward which he was steadily moving with a terrifying simplicity and the awkward gait of some vertical dinosaur.

3
A Sword, for
What Purpose?

Charles de Gaulle was forty years old and attached to the general secretariat of the Supreme Council of National Defense. The army had made a secretary of him? He would write, but for the public—and a larger public, he hoped, than that which had heard him at the War College or even at the Sorbonne in 1927. The period from 1932 to 1934 was to see the publication of the two texts in which he declared himself and set forth his program, in which he unveiled his character—or rather, unveiled the statue he had spent twenty-five years modeling—and his objectives. These were his two most controversial books: *The Edge of the Sword* and *The Army of the Future.*

The Prince and *Mein Kampf?* Let's not exaggerate.

The Edge of the Sword was a new version of the trilogy of conferences held five years before on "the action of war," "character," and "prestige." To these, the author added two new chapters, one on the evolution of strategic doctrines and another on "politics and the soldier."

Because De Gaulle displayed a highly stylized cynicism (". . . evangelical perfection does not lead to empire"), because he emphasized the role of secrecy and dissimulation, his book was compared to *The*

47

Prince. As if Machiavelli had been as Machiavellian as those who make use of him! *The Prince* is a remonstrance to the prince, in which the Florentine secretary reminds him of the existence of the people and of the fact that the power of a leader can only be lasting when it is based on the consent of the governed. There is very little echo of this in *The Edge of the Sword.*

There are, of course, echoes of Clausewitz. On such points as the role of the leader and the influence of his combative will, as well as on the accidental character of the action of war, Clausewitz—who, at the time of the pact of Franco-Prussian "collaboration" after the battle of Jena said "no" to his king and went over to the Russian army to continue the struggle against Napoleon—was an inspirer of De Gaulle. "The will of the leader is the center from which everything in the military art branches. . . . All wars having their own character, and presenting, in their evolution, a great number of individual characteristics, each of them can be considered as a sea previously unknown to the commanding general. . . ." And what principle could have inspired Charles de Gaulle more than Clausewitz's famous dictum: "War is the continuation of political relations by other means. . . ."?

Nietzsche? Maurras? De Gaulle may have detested the first, and have written a preface to *Discord Among the Enemy* in which he holds the philosopher of the superman responsible for the madness and the consequent defeat of Germany; and he would later, in *France and Her Army,* denounce the spread of Nietzschean doctrines as a perversion of philosophic education in France at the end of the nineteenth century —but he had been exposed to their searing imprint. According to *The Edge of the Sword,* the leader is a superman tempered by the teachings of the Jesuits and the instructive disasters of the Empire. But he

48

is still an animal of great power, over himself and others; a man whose vision is so uncluttered by thoughts of God that action alone can raise him to "the divine game of heroes."

The neo-classic esthetic and the "realist" ethics expressed in *The Edge of the Sword* link its author with the cynical and most conservative Maurras, but it is not a Maurrassian book, since it pleads the cause of instinct against that of intellectualism. But this haughty text was published in 1932, just after the elections which had brought down the national front of 1928, at a time when the patriotic leagues were preparing the revenge which was to take the form of the riots of February 6, 1934. De Gaulle was not to be enrolled as a member of Maurras' Action Française. But it can certainly be said that the readers of Maurras were in possession of well-made keys to an understanding of him, and that he might have had an effect—especially on them—that was a trifle too stimulating.

Among others who are cited as his teachers, with better reason, is Captain Gilbert, the military essayist who was so greatly admired by the leader of French socialism, Jean Jaurès—Jaurès quotes him constantly in *The New Army*—and who published his best book in 1890, the year of Charles de Gaulle's birth. And above all there is Colonel Ardant du Picq, the theorist of "moral strengths" who was killed in 1870, after having published some very curious books: *On the Necessity, in Matter of War, to Know the Primary Instrument, Which is Man; On Ancient Combat; On Modern Combat;* etc.—books which are unknown to civilians who are not fortunate enough to have an intelligent military man for a friend.

Dry, sharp, lofty in tone, these little books written by an officer of the last century are ranked among the masterpieces of military literature. Consider a sampling of his style: "Combat at a distance is natural to man. All of his industry has been directed toward precisely this result. With the use of long-range weapons, he imagines that he will be forced to return to close combat: actually, he will just flee from a greater distance. . . ." And another passage, in which he is a direct precursor of De Gaulle: "Armor has always been the prime source of confidence of the horseman, and more so today than ever before. And heart, spirit, speed, have another value than that of numbers. . . ."

For those who might doubt that Ardant was a source of inspiration to De Gaulle, it might be pointed out that after having been ignored for many years, his books were collected into volumes and published in a fully annotated edition in 1930 by Lucien Nachin, the longtime confidant and friend of the author of *The Edge of the Sword*. The thoughts of the two writers mingle—aristocratic, proud, but neither militarist nor totalitarian. Ardant du Picq is more stark, more direct than De Gaulle. Of the two, he is the twentieth-century writer.

But this is of relatively little importance. *The Edge of the Sword* remains an essay which has tone and spark, which reveals a personage and confirms a writer. The man who wrote it quite obviously took himself for another—for several others at once—but did it deliberately, defining as his own objective that formidable silhouette he had projected on the wall. De Gaulle was playing at frightening himself, confusing himself, with this fearless, secretive, almost inhuman giant he had fashioned with his own hands; and he ended by becoming completely captivated by him, drawing into himself the energy he had manufactured. This is the first revelation of that strange duality of the historian and his hero, of the observer "I" and the actor "I," of the clear conscience and the march of history. He was preparing himself to discuss General de Gaulle.

The conferences at the War College had caused annoyance. The "chats" at the Sorbonne had been successful. The book created no impression at all. But it attracted the attention of a small number of intelligent men, both civilian and military, who were preoccupied with these problems and who were to form a sort of Gaullist cell and participate, throughout those decisive years, in his quest for a concrete program and his efforts to put it into effect. From this point on, the Constable, the great individualist, was to form part of a team, "his" team. It was no longer the quartet of argumentative captains from the War College; it was a kind of studious circle which gathered sometimes at Major de Gaulle's home on the Place Saint-François-Xavier, sometimes in the apartment of the noted legist Paul Grunebaum-Ballin on the Boulevard Beauséjour, and sometimes at the Brasserie Dumesnil, just across the street from the Gare Montparnasse. Charles de Gaulle spoke at these gatherings in his loftiest tones. But there were also times when he listened, when he accepted advice. It is worth pausing to consider such a privileged moment. . . .

It was the faithful Lucien Nachin—a former enlisted man who had become a talented officer—who played the role of "manager" for the champion. It was he who had gathered around Charles de Gaulle a coterie whose guiding spirit was an astonishing man —perhaps the only man aside from André Malraux to have exercised a direct influence on the life and mind of Charles de Gaulle—Lieutenant Colonel Émile Mayer. A former friend of Taine, he was already a man of over eighty; but he had lost nothing of the agility of his mind, and while he took part in the discussions with Major de Gaulle he also carried on an assiduous correspondence with the future Nobel prize winner of literature Roger Martin du Gard and with many others.

How did it happen that so brilliant and cultivated and officer, a comrade of Joffre's at the Lycée Charlemagne and a schoolmate of Foch at the Polytechnique, had never attained a higher rank? As early as 1895, his superiors had been annoyed by his proclamation of faith in the innocence of Dreyfus. This "folly" might have been forgotten. But in the first years of the new century he had published a brochure entitled *No More Army, No More War,* which caused a scandal. No more army is bad enough; but no more war! And in 1917, when his friend and protégé, Lucien Nachin, was a prisoner of the Germans, Émile Mayer had thought to influence his jailers in his favor— and perhaps even to obtain his release—by writing him a letter in which he heaped praise on the greatness of spirit of the German people. Needless to say, the letter never reached its destination. It was intercepted by the French censors, and its only effect was to bring discredit on this singular officer who had made the mistake of being good-hearted at a time when he should have been "thinking right."

With his career thus shattered, Émile Mayer then became one of the most widely read military critics of the time. He had qualifications for this other than his courage and generosity. In 1903, he had predicted that the next war would be a combat between men in trenches, since firepower would render movement and offensives impossible: in essence, the same thesis as that supported—with less spirit—by Colonel Pétain.

When Lucien Nachin introduced him to De Gaulle, the old philosopher-at-arms at once developed a deep attachment for this unique personage. Of their meetings in the apartment of Mayer's son-in-law, Paul Grunebaum-Ballin, we know little except for the essential: the idea of the professional armed force (The Army of the Future), which was to serve as the Constable's standard, was born of these discussions. To be

De Gaulle was all very well. But to what purpose?

He was convinced of the preeminence of the political over the military. And in military matters, he was convinced of the importance of economy of means— the doctrines of Louvois and Carnot—in the action being conducted. "One does not go to war to get killed," Marmont, Napoleon's marshal, had said; "one goes to conquer the enemy." And Ardant du Picq, more profoundly, and adapting his lesson from the old Chinese military masters such as Sun-Tze had also said: "Man does not go into combat for the struggle itself, but for victory. He does everything within his power to suppress the first and assure the second." Suppress the struggle? At Ulm, and at Jena, through maneuver and movement, Napoleon had made any effort on the part of the enemy useless: he was already trapped. Now it was necessary to "unearth" war, get it out of the trenches, restore the mobility which could make of it the terribly innocent art of the gladiators who had fought with nets. And what is mobility if not the machine? Émile Mayer and Charles de Gaulle—the former emphasizing the role of aviation, and the latter the future of the tank—were approaching the crux of their idea. They were seeking, and on the point of defining, a basic justification for the man with the sword.

At this point in their collective meditation, legend has it that the decisive impulse came from a third party: even better, from an anonymous third party. In an issue of the *Journal des Enfants de Troupe* which carried a highly flattering article about *The Edge of the Sword*—probably written by Lucien Nachin—De Gaulle noticed an essay entitled "Ideas of an Amateur," in which the ideas he and Émile Mayer had been discussing for months were formulated with remarkable acuteness.

This anonymity is disconcerting. And so is the accidental manner in which the article came to light. But in any case, the text itself is curious. This "amateur" suggested that body armor had disappeared not only because firearms had made uncertain the protection it was intended to assure, but also because it had become too costly for large masses of individuals. This lack of personal protection, he added, could no longer be tolerated by the fighting man. It stemmed from this that there was a need for multiplication of armored machines; but their number would also be limited by their cost, and their maintenance would require that they be handled by specialists. Since soldiers functioning outside of these protective shells would become increasingly rare, and since there would be only limited numbers of the machines themselves, the conflict to come will be restricted to a battle between professionals, essentially different from the citizens' war which had been brought into being by the mass conscriptions of 1793 and the strategy of Moltke.

A month after publication of this article, De Gaulle wrote to one of the members of his "team" that he had found in it ". . . approached indirectly, but in an original manner, certain concepts which are henceforth my own." Then he added, "I am, in fact, now at work developing them into a new book." Inspiration or plagiarism?

In his continuing campaign for the professional army, De Gaulle himself had underlined the fact that he could refer to precursors of every nationality. The pioneers in the field were indisputably the English (because this concept of strategy and these "means" were directly inspired by maritime strategy. Machines, technics, high-velocity weapons—we are closer to the fleet than to the army . . .). It was at the battle of Cambrai, in March, 1917, that the Royal Tank Corps had engaged for the first time in an autonomous tank

54

action. This initiative of the earliest precursors was subsequently the origin of a whole body of "avant-garde" literature on the subject, including studies by Generals Fuller and Morell and the inevitable Captain Liddell Hart.

On the French side, the inventor was General Estienne, who, at Corbény on April 17, 1917, had employed tank units created as a result of his own efforts and sent them into the battle in advance of the infantry battalions they had previously been intended to support and cover. In a speech delivered at the School of Arts and Crafts in Paris in 1920, this same general had suggested the creation of an army of 100,000 men capable of covering fifty miles in a single night, the striking force of which would be 4,000 tanks manned by a shock troop of 20,000 men.

In Germany, specialization and motorization were, in a sense, a by-product of the treaties. Since the German armed forces were limited to 100,000 men, the objective of their organizer, Von Seeckt, could only be the creation of "an army of 100,000 captains," whose effective strength would be doubled by the use of machines. In his book *A Soldier's Thoughts,* published in 1929, the commander of the Reichswehr gave an account of his work: the creation of a genuine professional army, the hard core of the future Wehrmacht. But the real pioneer of the Panzers—as history was to prove—was Captain Heinz Guderian, who had brought himself to the attention of his superiors as early as 1924 in the course of maneuvers that were focused on the theme of motorized strategy and conducted by the future commander in chief, Von Brauchitsch. In 1931, Guderian was given command of the first motorized battalion: the cannons were made of wood and the tanks were armored with laminated plywood . . . but the spark had been struck. Guderian, however, was to be confronted with the same skepticism that met De Gaulle in France. When Hitler came to power, the situation changed, and Guderian was listened to. In 1935, he was given command of the 2nd Panzer Division. He would lead his tanks far and fast.

Was he inspired, for a time, by De Gaulle's ideas? In his book *A Soldier's Memoirs*, he mentions his French rival only once (in connection with the 1940 battles), citing him as the propagator of his ideas "in France." He also designates the source of his thesis: the Austrian general, Ritter von Eimmansberger, author of *Kampfwagenkrieg (The War of the Tanks)*, which was published in 1934—at the same time as *The Army of the Future*—but was available in manuscript to the military leaders of the Third Reich a good six months earlier. It is true that De Gaulle had published the essential points of his ideas in an article which appeared in May, 1933. But it is worth noting that from 1932 to 1937 the reports of the German military attachés in Paris never mentioned either De Gaulle or his books.

In De Gaulle's case, there were four ideas that seemed to form the basis of his doctrine. First, as we know, this disciple of Bergson was a devotee of movement, initiative, imagination. Ever since the days of the "discussion groups" at Fort IX in 1917, he had talked of "detrenching" warfare and restoring maneuverability.

And for the historian who lived with thirty generations of Frenchmen—dining with heads of medieval guilds and interviewing Jacobin leaders—the corps of specialists he envisioned, and termed "the masters," was not an aristocratic chivalry but an elite group of guilds or corporations destined to mold a peasant population to the uses of mechanics and techniques. The Nuremberg one glimpses here is that of Hans Sachs, the good artisan of the *Meistersinger*, not that of Hitler. An industralism, a technical modernism, was taking form; and it was to take other forms after 1958.

Above everything else, De Gaulle is a historian. But he is also a dramatist, and not always a first-rate one. What was the ultimate purpose of this force he wanted to create? To "create the event," to tie up the threads of the drama, to transform combat into a fourth act of Corneille. Pathos, thunder and lightning, decision. The style of the communiqués would help to do it.

Fourth idea, and perhaps the principal one. A military man, De Gaulle saw himself as a political man. From Louvois, builder of Louis XIV's army, to Hoche, young leader of revolution *"levée en masse,"* his ideal was a balance between the citizen-soldier and the cabinet minister-colonel. "If I were not an officer, I would go into politics." There was nothing to indicate that he intended the weapon he wanted to forge as a legion of praetorians to support his pronunciamentos. But everything indicated that he saw it as an instrument of diplomacy, of a policy embracing great areas and active alliances. A weapon of speed for a diplomacy of movement. The political thought rapidly outstripped the military argument.

One night in November, 1932, Émile Mayer persuaded Lieutenant Colonel de Gaulle to throw down the gauntlet by outlining the new doctrine in an article for mass consumption. The Constable set to work with all the ardor of an ambitious specialist who is certain of his facts. But the article would soon take on a wholly new significance: on January 30, 1933, Hitler came to power in Germany.

De Gaulle was to make many mistakes in the political domain. But everything we know of his reactions at this time makes it clear that he never deluded himself on the subject of nazism, of its fundamental perverseness, or of the mortal threat it contained within itself. (In 1922, in fact, the author of *Discord Among the Enemy* had denounced Ludendorff, who was later to become a source of inspiration and support to the man in the brown shirt.)

The May 10, 1933, issue of the *Revue Politique et Parlementaire* carried the article in which he outlined, in a dozen pages, the basic theses of his later book, *The Army of the Future*. It should be noted that he ascribed the need for a profound military reform not only to the "exigencies of the techniques of war," but also to "international developments."

The crusade for armored divisions had begun. And it was to reveal a new personage.

For months on end, the Constable made the circuit of editorial reception rooms, sitting in dingy corridors, waiting until some military editor consented to receive him and read his "copy," and sometimes inviting to lunch such specialists as the correspondent of *Le Temps*, Edmond Delage. This phase of Charles de Gaulle's life should not be forgotten. There is no mention in the legend that he was ever subjected to an actual rebuff or an affront. But the door-to-door odyssey of the maker of articles, the salesman of prose, was an experience whose bitterness could easily have colored an individual's relations with an entire professional group. . . .

But the-great-devil-of-an-officer-who-is-waiting-to-see-you was not always kept waiting. He very rapidly enrolled three renowned journalists as members of the "team": on the right, André Pironneau, editor in chief of *L'Écho de Paris* and, later, director of *L'Époque;* at the center, his ex-companion in captivity, Rémy Roure, who at that time was signing his articles for *Le Temps* with the pseudonym Pierre Fervacque; and on the left (relatively speaking) Émile Buré, of *L'Ordre*. From this beginning, the offensive spread into various political circles after publication of *The Army of the Future.*

There is no point in dwelling at length on theses that have been analyzed a hundred times or on an exposition that has often been praised. The beginning of the book is disconcerting, coming as it does from the man of intuition, from a man who had never ceased fighting against an a priori doctrine and insisting that the military art is made up only of "contingencies" and flexible situations. From the moving portrait he drew of France, quoting Napoleon ("The policy of nations is in their geography"), it would be easy to believe that the writer was a faithful disciple of Colonel Moyrand, the master of "compartmentation of the terrain." There are echoes of the 1925 advocate-in-spite-of-himself of the Maginot Line.

But this was done so that the idea of protection through movement would be more impressive. Only maneuver, and rapid maneuver, could protect the vast gaps which the northeast frontier of France offered to the invader. This rapidity could only be achieved with the machine, which demands highly specialized technicians; and it could only be assured by an armed force constantly on the alert, a status which could be demanded only from men acclimated and dedicated to their task.

The force of reasoning became irresistible; and it is a source of constant astonishment to the reader that on this point De Gaulle did not sweep away all opposition, since he linked the mobile force he wanted created to the very future of French diplomacy, the policy of alliances in the East, collective security, and defense against nazism.

The Maginot Line strategy entailed diplomatic as well as military immobility. The whole policy of guarantees founded on the Russian alliance and the Little Entente collapsed at the moment the French armies rooted themselves in the soil and made the concrete wall in the northeast the limiting point of their action. Fortification, or ghetto?

With a title that struck an immediate spark, a conclusion that took the form of a challenge (*The sword is the axis of the word, and grandeur is indivisible*), and a set of theses too tempting not to be as double-edged as his own sword or the saber of the typical French common man, Monsieur Prudhomme—"that was good for defending order or for smashing it"— the third book of Charles de Gaulle could not fail to irritate some people and disturb others. The counteroffensive was led by everything the military profession could drum up in the way of symbols—from Ministers of War Maurin and Daladier to Marshal Pétain, and from General Weygand, who had inherited the mantle of Foch without deserving it, to Colonel Fabry, counsel for the "competent" parliamentary committee.

On June 15, 1934, one month after publication of *The Army of the Future*, Minister of War Édouard Daladier delivered a speech in the Chamber of Deputies which was both an apologia for concrete walls and an indictment of the offensive. In the *Revue des Deux Mondes*, General Weygand, chief of staff of the army since 1931, emphasized that the sole objective of French strategy was to "hold" the line of fortifications in the northeast, allowing any assailant to shatter himself against it; and that the projected force of professional troops could only result in dividing the army. He concluded: "On no account, two armies!" Marshal Pétain threw the weight of his authority into the melee by writing, in a preface he contributed to a book entitled *Is an Invasion Still Possible?*, that neither tanks nor airplanes had altered the known qualities of any future war and that the security of the nation depended entirely on its fortifications. And side by side with the hero of Verdun appeared the shade of Père Ubu, from whom one anonymous reviewer of *The Army of the Future* quoted a phrase that, ironically, does honor to the prophetic military genius of Ubu's father, Jarry: "When we get back from Poland, we'll use our knowledge of physics to dream up a wind machine that will transport the entire army."

Pétain, Père Ubu, the Daladier radical party? De Gaulle resumed his door-to-door journeying, this time carrying his message into the Palais Bourbon, and from the popular Club du Faubourg to the inner circle of the Action Française.

The Edge of the Sword had fascinated the champions of "integral nationalism." In May, 1934, Charles de Gaulle agreed to deliver an address at the Cercle Fustel de Coulanges, a group inspired largely by the doctrines of Maurras, and listing Marshal Lyautey as one of its sponsors. But just as the former proconsul in Rabat had kept his distance from the parties of the extreme right by refusing to lend his name to the reactionary operations of February 6th, so De Gaulle —a daily reader of *L'Action Française*—refused to allow himself to be outwitted by this group.

The Constable at the Club du Faubourg? It is difficult to imagine him in this stormy arena, debating the matter of the "pigheads" in the army with communist speaker Paul Vaillant-Couturier. But there he was, with his friend Colonel Mayer, a regular attendant at the meetings of the club, and with Colonel Gérard, who had been Jean Jaurès' adviser at the time when Jaurès was writing *The New Army*. For the offspring of a monarchist family, the disciple of Barrès, the philosopher of history steeped in Richelieu and tempted by Maurras, this was a curiously revulsive atmosphere.

And he was also present in the corridors of the

Chamber of Deputies. At one of the gatherings in the Grunebaum-Ballin apartment in June, 1934, he met the son of one of Émile Mayer's innumerable friends: Jean Auburtin, a young lawyer with contacts in high places, who was instantly captivated by this prodigious colonel and introduced him to his friends, the moderate right-wing leader Paul Reynaud and his aide, Gaston Palewski. It was with these two that De Gaulle would form his first political alliance. Reynaud sensed the fertility of his ideas and was subjugated by the force of his personality. On the fifteenth of March, 1935, the ex-minister of finance took the rostrum in the Chamber of Deputies to defend the ideas expressed in *The Army of the Future*—and did it with precision and competence, since De Gaulle had edited his speech on all of its essential points. The government was asking the Chamber to pass a bill calling for a compulsory two-year period of military service, and Reynaud linked his assenting vote to an amendment calling for the creation of "a specialized corps of six divisions of the line, and one light division . . . made up of soldiers serving under contract, and to be put on a footing of complete readiness by April 15, 1940, at the latest. . . ." (The date is an interesting one: two weeks before the Nazi push began.)

The effect of Reynaud's intervention can be measured by the account given of it by Léon Blum. Six months earlier, writing about De Gaulle's book in *Le Populaire*, the socialist leader had stated that he was against the creation of a professional army. But now he said: "Reynaud told us that the army, as conceived by Colonel de Gaulle, was the effective instrument of collective security. . . . I remember murmuring, rather emphatically, to the friends who surrounded me, 'On that point, he is right!' "

While the ideas and prejudices of the most subtle and the most liberal of the parliamentarians of that period were thus vacillating, the commander in chief of the French army was also prey to an ever-increasing anxiety. In 1936, and again in 1937, Gamelin—who assures us in his *Memoirs* that he had been a partisan of autonomy for armored units as early as 1932—was to place before the Supreme War Council the question of creation of an armored corps. He too was lucid, but he too was vacillating; so how could he have hoped to overcome the stubborn resistance of the "Weygand party," or of conservatives as influential as General Georges.

However, on March 7, 1936, Hitler reoccupied the Rhineland and was met by nothing more tangible than Albert Sarraut's historic phrases. The first German "Panzers" had appeared on the scene, as De Gaulle pointed out in a letter to Reynaud on July 16th. To alert the country, it was imperative that both Parliament and the press be shaken up. The campaign undertaken by De Gaulle at this time was characteristic of his concepts. It was not to the Right that the aristocratic, solitary, and imperious hero of *The Edge of the Sword* turned in search of support. The nation, always the nation, from the Capetian kings to revolutionary regicides . . . There was, of course, Jean Le Cour Grandmaison, the ex-naval officer who had for years been pleading with the Commission for National Defense for establishment of a program whereby the land forces would train voluntary recruits as highly technical specialists, just as the navy did. And there was Paul Reynaud. But we must here try to place ourselves in the perspective of the times. The little man was then—in conformity with the Gaullist ideal—linked to no single party or faction. A financier of the Right, but a diplomat of the Left—a determined partisan of the Russian alliance, of the doctrine of collective security, and of resistance to any form of fascism.

The Constable's other allies were even more significant: Philippe Serre, guiding spirit of *La Jeune République,* left-wing Catholic group, and partner in the Popular Front then being formed; Léo Lagrange, devout pupil of Léon Blum, and a future socialist cabinet minister; and especially Marcel Déat, who had left Blum's party two years before and had not yet become an adherent of nazism. It was Déat— this stocky, earthbound Mongol, this philosopher of action and brilliant dialectician—who most interested De Gaulle. He was fascinated by the man. But the ex-minister for the air force, though tempted by De Gaulle, was to choose Hitler. . . .

In January, 1937, Philippe Serre took up the baton passed to him by Reynaud. Quoting Henri de Jouvenel, who had formulated the slogan "Police forces, but no more armies!" he emphasized the fact that the constantly increasing specialization of airmen, sailors, and mechanics had opened the path toward creation of a corps of technicians; denied that De Gaulle's project would minimize the importance of the inducted troops; and called for creation of an army which would be both "that of Jaurès and that of Louvois"—that of the masses and that of a trained military elite.

At the end of September, 1936, Émile Mayer opened the doors of the new prime minister to his friend: Léon Blum wanted to meet the Constable. Blum has left us this account of the first meeting of the two most widely disparate personalities in the France of that time: "I saw a man whose height, breadth, and carriage had something of the gigantic about them. . . . He came in with a calm, even placid, air of assurance. . . . The man who presented himself in this fashion, who studied me so quietly, who addressed me in those slow and measured tones, could clearly be concerned with only one idea, one belief, at a time;

but then he would give himself to it completely, without permitting anything else to weigh in the balance. . . . Clemenceau is the extreme type of this temperament, which an often contemptuous misanthropy prevents from believing that any single action whatever can have a useful result, but who nonetheless is committed to act, because action is a vital necessity. . . ."

In the version of the interview which he gives in the first volume of his *Memoirs*, De Gaulle appears in his usual garb of sarcastic prophet and appropriates to himself the magisterial tone of a placid giant faced with a fragile chief of state. What seems uppermost in his memory of this dialogue is that the possessor of executive power in the Third Republic was neither capable of concentrating on any serious matter, nor in a position to make himself obeyed, nor even aware of the extent of his rights and his duties. The last phrase which he reports himself as saying to Léon Blum—"National defense is the responsibility of the government" (one of his continuing themes)—was undoubtedly charged with all the irony inherent in the fact that a military man should have been recalling this truth to a socialist prime minister.

Lieutenant Colonel de Gaulle had by then been named to the Center for Higher Military Studies. From the point of view of action, the blow was obvious. Paul Reynaud's proposal for an amendment to the draft law had been defeated. But the proponent of the professional army did not retire definitively from the political arena after he had taken the measure of its ambushes and tasted its poisons and sensed its possibilities. Rebel that he was, he had been enabled to weigh the vices of the parliamentary world against those of the General Staff, and there was no doubt in his mind that the second was first in overall shabbiness of character. With only about three or four exceptions, it was among civilians that he had found his few defenders. And his political adversaries—a Daladier or a Flandin—had not treated him with the meticulous animosity of the conservative generals. A damnable profession; but for the man who knew how to make use of it, a splendid lever . . .

He was now forty-seven and a colonel, with a checkered but brilliant career. The Popular Front was undoing itself in hesitancies, technical controversies, and the doctrine of nonintervention. The Anschluss, which he had expected, had come. Munich was approaching. Who, at this point, was De Gaulle?

An officer who had acquired exceptional notoriety for one of his rank. And it was because of this that the army did not like him; he was a "journalist," a "politico." He wrote well? Splendid; he could succeed Weygand as a member of the Académie Française and one would be rid of him. There were a few generals, however, who regarded him highly— such men as Doumenc and Hering, partisans of armored units for the army. He had faithful friends and some disciples in military circles. And in certain political circles, he had built himself a kind of legend. But a very narrowly circumscribed legend; at the beginning of 1939, a young deputy as alert to his times as Pierre-Olivier Lapie, future minister of education, could still ask, "Who is this officer who chose such a splendid pseudonym?"

The man had become no more tractable on matters of basic importance to him. No matter how amiable he might have appeared to a journalist whose help he wanted or to a parliamentarian he was attempting to convince, he could quite suddenly become hard and cutting as a sword. Following shortly after the death of his father, he lost his old friend, Émile Mayer, the counselor, the wise man—dead at his desk while correcting the proofs of *France and*

Her Army, on the day he had written on his calendar, "Today, my death." He bought a house at Colombey-les-Deux-Églises, in the *département* of the Haute-Marne. The doctors had told him that the climate there would be good for the sick child, Anne, his second daughter. He had lost the first battle of his life, and he sensed the approach of war.

His political ideas were in a state of flux. In 1934, he had been close to the doctrines of Maurras, or at least to monarchism. But listen to him at this time: "Maurras is a man who is right to the point of having gone mad with it!" In spite of his parliamentary disappointments, he was slipping away from the fringes of the Action Française, and toward the Christian Democratic circles: thus, in 1938, we find him at the table of Daniel-Rops, the noted Catholic historian who was looking for talented authors for his collection "Presences": it was here that the colonel who had brought in the manuscript of *France and Her Army* met a young journalist who signed his articles in *Temps Présent* André Sidobre, but whose name was really Maurice Schumann, and who was to be the noted spokesman of the Free French in London.

This evolution toward what was then the Left—or, more accurately, toward anti-fascism (a word which had not yet lost its meaning)—became more pronounced after an incident that was of some importance in this career which, for so long a time, had been buttressed by a great public figure: the rupture with Marshal Pétain.

It was a trifling affair. In response to a request from Daniel-Rops, De Gaulle offered for publication his historical studies of the French soldier, undertaken in 1925 when he had been on the marshal's staff. He wrote to his former patron, asking permission to use this work since it had been done at his request and under his aegis, if not under his direction.

The marshal refused, unless it was to be made clear in the dedication that he had been the originator of the work. De Gaulle rebelled, refused, suggested an epigraph which was no more than a vague acknowledgment of debt—and was turned down.

In short, pride against pride, creation against tradition. But De Gaulle judged that possession was nine points of the law when it was a matter of one's own work, ignored the refusal, and by signing his name to *France and Her Army*, broke with the marshal.

When one of his friends on the Left talked to him about a government headed by a moderate socialist, Paul Boncour, which "is brewing," and suggested that he might become undersecretary of state for national defense to a minister of defense who would be Pétain, De Gaulle emphatically declined, and added: "Beware of him; he is a man of redoubtable duplicity."

Beyond the literary quarrel, it is possible to make out the political background of the affair—though neither of the two men was as yet completely aware of it. The colonel, as we have seen, was by then a member of the anti-fascist camp, which was described by *Gringoire, L'Action Française*, and his erstwhile friend Marcel Déat, as "the war camp." The marshal was somewhere else. Having for a long time been considered a "republican officer," he claimed to be annoyed by the campaign being conducted by the former socialist Gustave Hervé in *La Victoire* in favor of an "authoritarian republic," under the rallying cry of "Pétain is the man we need!" But he did not disavow it.

In 1934, on the occasion of the funeral of Marshal Pilsudski, the marshal had had a long meeting with Goering. A year later, on November 22, 1935, the members of the Supreme Council of National Defense took part in an extraordinary scene. Seized with a kind of intoxication with truth, Pierre Laval, the new prime minister, "let the cat out of the bag" and revealed the basis of his policy: an end of the British alliance and of assistance to eastern Europe, and closer ties with Germany. In his *Memoirs,* Gamelin, then commander in chief, reports that after he returned home he wept; he also adds that Marshal Pétain greeted this profession of faith with total serenity. And in 1939, the old marshal accepted the post of first French ambassador to Franco's Spain with a somewhat surprising display of pleasure.

It can be seen from this that the quarrel over *France and Her Army* was not a purely literary one. Even this early, it was Vichy and London which were facing each other, and opposed to each other.

At the time when he returned to the actual practice of the profession of arms, Colonel de Gaulle was, therefore, a personage who signified something more than just a specialty, a talent, a character, a "literary coterie." During those months when the thunderclouds were gathering, it was one of those rare men who is conscious of the tides of history who took command of the 507th regiment of tanks at Metz. Half in irony, half in admiration, he became known as "Colonel Motor." Often wearing immaculate white gloves, which in the midst of all this machinery were an affront to both common sense and regulations, he set about the business of shaking up his men—drivers, gunners, mechanics—and imposing a regime of rigorous testing of the equipment. One inspection team mentioned his activities, and not kindly. But he made "the 507th" into a unit which was talked about. The general commanding the army corps in Metz congratulated him publicly on the occasion of the July 14, 1938, parade, even though he detested him; the general's name was Giraud.

But the congratulations were addressed to the "stringbean" colonel who had formed his men into a

69

crack unit and kept his machines in a state of gleaming perfection, not to the theorist of the war of movement. In the course of divisional maneuvers, "Colonel Motor" proposed launching his armored unit in an autonomous movement. Giraud intervened, irritably: "So long as I am alive, De Gaulle, you will not impose those theories here. . . ."

To say that he foresaw the outbreak of war would be saying very little indeed. As a historian, as a specialist in his field, and as a militant pessimist, he had been living in a state of war for months. When it came, he had just left Metz and the 507th to assume command of the tank units of the Fifth Army, stationed in Basse-Alsace.

In Poland, the *kriegspiel* described in *The Army of the Future* was becoming tragic fact; and while the Wehrmacht overwhelmed its ally in two weeks, the Franco-British army did nothing. But it was not simply a matter of strategy or technical capabilities. "Colonel Motor" confirmed, once again, the fact that war is primarily a form of policy, and stated that if France did not even attempt to make Hitler pay the price of Polish agony, it was because many people in government circles "were inclined to see Stalin as the enemy, far more than Hitler . . . and were concerned with striking at Russia . . . more than they were with coming to grips with the Reich."

In Alsace, he welcomed a group of visiting British parliamentarians in these terms: "Gentlemen, this war is lost. . . ." (A long, very long silence. Bowler hats and umbrellas bob and wave, reflecting consternation.) ". . . So we must prepare for and win another war: with machines!"

In January, 1940, De Gaulle was in Paris. Paul Reynaud, now minister of finance, asked him to dine with Léon Blum. The socialist leader has reported the colonel's proposals in his *Memoirs*: "I am playing my part in a state of total mystification . . . the few dozen light tanks attached to my command are just a grain of sand. . . . If we don't react in time, we are going to lose this war, miserably. . . ." Blum then goes on to relate De Gaulle's comment as he accompanied him back to his home: "If you are in a position to act, in agreement with Paul Reynaud, do it, I beg of you!" A few days later, he received a memorandum signed by Colonel de Gaulle. "And it was then," Léon Blum wrote, "that I learned, that I understood everything. The mechanized army had to be organized, at any price, and with no further delay. . . ."

Léon Blum was just one of the eighty military and civilian leaders who had received Colonel de Gaulle's memorandum, dated January 24th and entitled "The Advent of Mechanized Power." It was both a condensation and an additional chapter of *The Army of the Future,* but it was charged with an eloquence born of the recent events in Poland:

In the present conflict, to remain inert is to be beaten. . . . At no cost must the French people succumb to the illusion that the military immobility which exists today will be characteristic of the war to come. It is the contrary which is true. The motor has given modern weapons of destruction a power, a speed, and a range of action such that the present conflict will sooner or later be marked by movements, surprises, attacks, and pursuits whose speed and scope will infinitely surpass those of the most shattering events of the past. . . .

Let us make no mistake about it! The conflict which has now begun may well become the most extensive, the most complex, and the most violent of all those which have ravaged the earth. The political, social, and moral crisis of which it is the result runs so deep and is so widespread that it will inevitably lead to a

71

complete unheaval in the situation of peoples and the structure of States . . .

The visionary was, first and foremost, an observer. It was readily apparent that the lucidity of the author of *The Army of the Future* had been augmented by the lessons drawn from the Spanish and Polish campaigns. The man who in 1934, and in spite of the advice of Émile Mayer, had allowed his faith in tanks to blind him to the place of air attack in the war to come had "corrected his aim." The 1940 memorandum accorded due place to all forms of mechanized weapons.

Despite its inflammatory content, this text did not even provoke a scandal in a universe where everyone was congratulating himself on having won a "white Marne" simply by having slept through the winter. But the defeat of Finland in March brought on the fall of the Daladier cabinet and the elevation of Paul Reynaud to the post of prime minister. The ideas of "Colonel Motor" were now in power, and his friend called him to his staff as military adviser. He left Alsace and his tanks and returned to Paris. Scorned as a writer, would he now be accorded the revenge of possessing effective power? No. Reynaud was subjected to pressures on every side and forced to parcel out his remedies in doses which were largely governed by the conservatives. On the twenty-first of March, De Gaulle was present at the "frightful" (as he was to describe it) session of the Chamber in which the Reynaud cabinet succeeded in pulling together a majority vote—thanks to the efforts of Léon Blum, who was not a member of the cabinet. This new parliamentary experience, in time of war and following the deceptions of 1935-37, should not be forgotten in considering the Constable's behavior when he will confront the parliaments of Algiers and of Paris.

Under pressure from his predecessor Daladier and the group that no longer believed in victory, Reynaud abandoned his intention of appointing De Gaulle to the post of secretary general of the government's War Committee. The colonel was about to return to Alsace, embittered and disillusioned, when Gamelin, the head of the General Staff, summoned him to his "cloister" in Vincennes and entrusted him with command of the 4th Armored Division, which he had just decided to create, and which was to be formed as of the fifteenth of May.

But both men were caught short: in the early morning of the tenth of May, the Wehrmacht began its passage across the Ardennes and hurled itself at Sedan. In three days, the front was broken and the horde unleashed by Von Manstein was racing toward the mouth of the Somme. For their part, the best of the Franco-British forces were hastening to Belgium.

As early as the eleventh of May, Colonel de Gaulle was being pressed to enter the field with the division whose scattered elements he had been assembling for the past two weeks. On the fifteenth, General Doumenc ordered him to counterattack in the Laon sector to save the Sixth Army.

The colonel went directly to Laon and was greeted by firing along the Sissonnes canal; first contact with the enemy was established. But before he had an opportunity to employ, at last, this "mechanized power" of which he considered himself the prophet, Charles de Gaulle was able to measure its devastating effects. To reach the front lines in May of 1940 was to receive the full shock of the debacle like a hard blow to the face. "If I live, I will fight, wherever necessary, whenever necessary, so long as it is necessary, until the enemy is defeated and the national honor washed clean. Whatever I have been able to do in the

73

succeeding years, it was on that day that I resolved to do it."

After the two decisive experiences of his youth—that of first coming under fire in August, 1914, and that of captivity in 1916—here was the test of maturity: the experience of defeat. He came out of it hardened, more intolerant than ever. Ready to seek a quarrel with the entire world.

On the seventeenth of May, elements of Colonel de Gaulle's 4th Armored Division clashed with General Guderian's XIXth Corps along the Serre river. The man of *The Army of the Future* face-to-face with the man of *Achtung Panzer!* It must have occurred to him that this was some medieval tournament, a kind of judgment of God. But for more than fifteen years Guderian had been forging the armored units he was now leading forward at the lightning pace Hitler had announced at a meeting on the sixth of March. De Gaulle could confront him with only scattered fragments of the major unit he supposedly commanded.

One of his officers, Lieutenant Galimand, has described the state of disorder and unpreparedness in which the 4th Armored was forced to fight—with young officers, fresh from Saint-Cyr, taking their place in a tank for the first time, and completely lacking any communications equipment. Even so, De Gaulle's young men fought well, retaking Chisvres and Lislet from the Germans and being halted only at Montcornet, after having penetrated the line at that point. It was the massive intervention of Stuka dive-bombers which forced them to draw back. De Gaulle was compelled to order a regrouping around Sissonnes.

On the nineteenth, the colonel resumed the offensive and again attempted to cut the invasion route of the XIXth Corps on a line extending from Crécy—yes, Crécy, one of the worst disasters in French military history, five centuries earlier—to Pouilly. Once

74

again, it was enemy aviation which paralyzed him. In spite of the appeals of General Touchon, commanding the Sixth Army, he was ordered to break off contact with the enemy and pull back across the Bruyères range. The retreat was to be a painful affair. For De Gaulle, the battle of Laon-Montcornet had been at least a partial failure.

It is interesting to note here a passage from Guderian's *A Soldier's Memoirs:* "We were told of the presence of Colonel de Gaulle's 4th Armored Division, which had been making itself felt since the sixteenth. . . . De Gaulle was faithful to the rendezvous on the following days, and on the nineteenth, with a few isolated tanks, managed to reach a point two kilometers from my advance command post. . . . I lived through a few uncertain hours, until these uninvited guests were turned away."

Ten days later, however, at a time when the French army was no longer anything more than a torn and shattered body, the armored units were called on again, this time to stem Guderian's race to the sea in the Abbeville sector. De Gaulle, promoted on May 25th to the temporary rank of general, had received reinforcements of armor—he now disposed of 140 tanks—and of artillery. He was given the assignment of hurling the Germans back from their Abbeville bridgehead. On May 28th, he attacked to the north, to seize the Camp of Caesar (obviously . . .), which commanded the bridges of the city. In three days of bitter combat, the 4th Armored succeeded in broaching the enemy positions, taking approximately four hundred prisoners, and destroying several dozen tanks and cannon. But on the thirtieth, De Gaulle had to pull back his forces—reduced to half of their effective strength—to the region of Marseilles-en-Beauvaisis. Not, however, before he had received a warm citation from the new commander in chief, Maxime Weygand.

His conduct in this engagement has been commented on both widely and diversely. In 1955, General Perré, an old specialist in armored tactics who had commanded a company of tanks as early as 1918 and who was in command of the 2nd Armored Division, on De Gaulle's flank, in 1940, wrote an article on the subject for *Écrits de Paris,* a pro-Vichy review which was not benevolent toward him. In it, Perré stated that De Gaulle "could scarcely be said to have acted like an innovating theorist," that "nothing is more classic than [his] order of battle," and that he "fell into the most obvious error of French procedures: that which consists of underestimating the density of vehicles necessary to break through a defensive front. Where the Germans envisage the use of seventy to one hundred tanks per lineal kilometer, our system timidly sanctions the use of twenty to fifty, and the commanding officer of the 4th Armored actually employed thirteen. Obviously, he was limited in his equipment, but to a very considerable degree he had control over the breadth of front of the attack."

And Lieutenant Galimand, who was then on his staff, judged him brave enough, but a "ham actor," and recalled that after the general's departure for Paris the division gave an equally good account of itself, notably on the Loire. Philippe Barrès, then a faithful Gaullist, described him standing fearlessly "beneath an apple tree, smoking like a locomotive, calm, utterly calm, dressed like his mechanic, in an old leather vest with no insignia." Would the wartime commander ever have been the equal of the philosopher of action, the writer, the statesman? This brief experience does not make it possible to give a positive answer. Although possessed of a physical courage attested to on dozens of occasions, an almost inhuman composure,

76

and proverbial energy, Charles de Gaulle does not seem to have shown on the terrain of battle the qualities of invention and speedy decision that make a Condé or a Rommel—whether he has a thousand men at his command or three hundred thousand.

But no matter how deceiving they might have been for the author of *The Army of the Future*, the two episodes of Laon-Montcornet (May 17-19) and Abbeville (May 28-30) sufficed to make of De Gaulle—along with Prioux in Flanders, de Lattre at Rethel, and the valiant young soldiers of Saumur—one of the men (they are more numerous than is generally believed) who saved something that perhaps was the honor of the French army in that spring of 1940. In the face of such a disaster, it was not sufficient just to have foreseen it; it was also necessary to have demonstrated that you could fight, if you were provided with the means to do it.

And it was not only as a part of the Franco-German conflict, but also as a turning point in Charles de Gaulle's debate with himself, that those days were of prime importance. The decision that had been born of a long habit of psychological insubordination and brought to full maturity in the shame and anger aroused by the debacle of May 16th was to be made possible by the brief period of success in the field. To have been one of the few commanders who had not fled from the enemy was a factor that would play its part in the "different" behavior of Charles de Gaulle on the eighteenth of June.

On June 5th, when Paul Reynaud gathered all military powers into his own hands and asked the new general to become a part of his government, it must have seemed that he had just returned to his old job; "Colonel Motor" had fought well, but it was clearly on other fields that he could best assert his originality and give a true measure of himself. The following day, a strange figure descended the steps of the Hôtel Matignon, behind a platoon of graying politicians with faces permanently marked by the ceaseless round of electoral banquets—a great, solitary wolf, awkward and morose, two stars on the army kepi, a flinty eye, a disdainful cigarette, a pair of white gloves in one hand: the Constable had become undersecretary of state for national defense.

First mission: London. He was charged with obtaining from the English a promise that the RAF would be committed to the combat in France and that the Allied forces rescued from Dunkerque would be promptly returned to the front.

On June 9th, he was received by Winston Churchill. Captured by the extraordinary vitality and talent of the British prime minister, De Gaulle drew from this first interview one of the most striking portraits in a famous gallery: that of the "great champion of a great enterprise and great artist of a great History." But he failed completely in his mission—fortunately. Did he really believe that he was acting in the best interests of the common cause? Committing the British air forces to continuance of the battle on the continent, when it was already becoming apparent that this island would soon be the last bastion of liberty, would have been ruinous for everyone; British egoism had suddenly become the most precious trump in the hand of the Allies.

And yet this attitude, which could certainly have been qualified as regionalism and which would inevitably have led to the destruction of the last weapon of liberty, the RAF, was typical of the blundering militancy displayed at the time by the new undersecretary of state. It would be another week before he could lift himself, after June 15th and almost alone, to a level of world strategy.

On the morning after his meeting with Churchill,

he took part in the deliberations of the War Committee for the first time and learned of the failure of his mission to London. The committee was debating the arguments of the commander in chief and the marshal—who was absent that day—in favor of halting the struggle. A brief dialogue between Weygand and De Gaulle ensued (given here in the version of the latter, who was not in the habit of attributing the best role to his opponent): "We will have to capitulate."—"There are other prospects!"—"Do you have something to suggest?"—"The government does not make suggestions, it gives orders!"

The dispatches which flooded in from everywhere on June 10th told of nothing but disasters, and Mussolini declared war. The government left Paris for Tours. "A day of agony," De Gaulle was to write of it. At midnight, several hours after the departure of the other members of the cabinet, Reynaud and the general left by automobile for Orléans. De Gaulle had only one word on his tongue: Africa. The struggle would have to be continued from there. . . .

On the eleventh, Churchill came to Briare to meet with his French colleagues; it was clear from this point on that the British considered France conquered, and no less clear that they did not consider themselves included in the defeat and that they intended to pursue the combat. In the three days that followed, from Cangé to Chissay and to Tours, along the banks of the Loire—where, after the defeat of Napoleon III Chanzy had continued the struggle against the same enemy seventy years before, it was only the modalities and the itinerary of the disaster that were disputed among the Allies—Allies no longer, really, but simply partners with separate spirits. During the meeting of the Inter-Allied Council at Tours on the thirteenth, Churchill, to De Gaulle's indignation, accepted the idea of a French request

79

for an armistice. In exchange for releasing Paris from the engagements taken in common on March 28, 1940, he asked only that the French fleet not fall into the hands of the conquerors.

The French ministers, for their part, no longer argued over General Staff maps but over Michelin road maps: where to flee next? To Quimper? To Bordeaux? To Algiers? De Gaulle, who was thinking primarily of Algiers, announced himself in favor of Quimper and was ridiculed. At that stage of deterioration of the French armies, the project of a "Breton redoubt" was absurd. He has maintained that, to his mind, moving the government to Quimper would have sealed it up in a dead-end street and made an embarkation for Africa inevitable. But the various measures he proposed on the seventh, the ninth, the twelfth, and even the fifteenth of June, as the government moved from Rennes to Brest, would make it seem that he believed in the "redoubt" in spite of everything. Charged with tension, stubborn, out of step with his colleagues, he flailed out in every direction just to remain standing erect.

On the twelfth, in any event, he extracted from Reynaud a promise that the government would be transferred to Africa. But after having agreed to meet him in Algiers, the prime minister moved only to Bordeaux. On the night of the thirteenth, the undersecretary of state for national defense decided to resign his post. The energetic Georges Mandel, minister of the interior, dissuaded him: "We are just at the beginning of the world war. You will have great tasks to fulfil, General. . . . Your present position could make things easier for you." A prophet always finds others more prophetic than he.

Bordeaux represented the final collapse of the fight-to-the-bitter-end campaign he had conducted for the past ten days, his own defeat within the larger defeat.

He paused there on the fourteenth, and went to see Marshal Pétain for the last time. Of this taciturn, icy, interview, he would later write—without citing Chateaubriand: "Old age is a shipwreck." It is a formula he was to repeat many times, but not very often in later years.

On the fifteenth, the head of the French Navy, Admiral Darlan—to whom, as they drove together from Tours to Bordeaux, Marshal Pétain had casually offered the post of "first consul" in the new regime— told Paul Reynaud that General de Gaulle's project of transporting 900,000 men to North Africa within the space of ten days "doesn't make sense." In the meantime, the undersecretary of state for national defense was returning to England by way of Brest.

The spirit of June 18th was already present in his mind. On the deck of the ship which was carrying him to Plymouth, he turned suddenly to the captain and demanded: "Would you be prepared to fight under British colors?" And a few hours later, he would make a decision which was to place the simple undersecretary of state outside the framework of the State and on an inter-Allied plane, and which was also to place De Gaulle, the nationalist, on a level where the nation is of less importance than global ideology and strategy: he ordered the *Pasteur*, which was carrying a large cargo of arms from the United States to France, turned back into an English port.

When he arrived in London on June 16th, French Ambassador Corbin, Jean Monnet, one of the future architects of European recovery, and René Pleven, who was to become his closest civilian aide, presented him with the strange idea of a total Franco-British union—surely the most anti-Gaullist idea that has ever crossed the mind of man—and De Gaulle, ignoring his philosophy of history in favor of the immediate strategy, saw in it the occasion for a psychological

81

shock great enough to restore courage to those in France who still favored continuing the struggle. He persuaded Churchill, whose government accepted the plan immediately; then he telephoned the text of it to Reynaud, who was to propose and defend it to his. But toward the end of the afternoon of June 16th, the little prime minister would be forced to concede defeat to a majority led by Vice-President Chautemps, Pétain, and Weygand, who (like the majority of Frenchmen) at this time had only one idea: to be finished with it.

De Gaulle left London still hearing the echo of a telephone conversation in which Churchill and Reynaud had agreed to fight to the end for the project of Franco-British fusion. Was there to be a new birth of hope? He landed at Bordeaux during the night of the sixteenth and learned that the prime minister—his chief, his friend—had resigned and voluntarily transferred his powers to Marshal Pétain—gaudy symbol of the policy of armistice. It was as if he had been struck by lightning.

In this Bordeaux, where there were only a handful of castaways of the Republic and a few die-hard, eloquent opponents of capitulation—such as Raphael Alibert, future minister of justice at Vichy, who proclaimed himself "the marshal's nanny"—and where the first gesture of the Pétain government had been to order the arrest of Georges Mandel (an unbelievable measure, for which the marshal had later to apologize humbly to his victim)—in this Bordeaux the flamboyant Constable was no more than an anguished phantom from the past. Apparently concerned that he might be arrested himself, on Weygand's orders, he planned to sleep aboard an English cruiser in the harbor, indicating that he might already have taken the decision to break with the legality of disaster. But he was acting as if he were in a kind of hallu-

cinatory trance, in which he was led rather than followed by the delegate Churchill had sent with him,
Sir Edward Spears.

Who, at this point, was the man who tomorrow
would claim, as did Racine's Mithridate, that Rome
was no longer in Rome, but wherever he might be?
Before taking his own place in History with a few
spoken phrases, he was, as we have seen, a man of
many histories. In this mercurial career, June 18th was
neither a miracle nor a cataclysm. It was certainly
not what the crossing of the Rubicon had been to
Caesar, or the 18 Brumaire to Napoleon—those were
gestures which had expressed the inevitable shock of
a force against a mass. But with relation to the times
and the system—that of the senescent army of a tired
Republic—the Constable had, for years, been in a
position of intellectual and moral dissidence.

Let us reconsider the stages of this dissidence.

1924. At the War College, in contradiction to the
official teachings of Colonel Moyrand, which were
based on an a priori theory of tactics, Captain de
Gaulle advocated a set of theses inspired by "the circumstances." He preached this Bergsonism applied to
combat with an arrogance that extended even to details. The unfavorable rating he was given as a result
surprised only himself. In the courtyard of the school,
as they were saying good-bye, his friend Chauvin described it to him thus: "In the past two years, you
have planted enough banderillas in their hides to
warrant being put to death." To which he replied,
furiously: "I won't come back to this filthy hole until
I'm its commander!"

1927. He came back to the War College as a simple
captain and confronted the elite (supposed) of the
French army with the theory that disobedience forms
a part of the panoply of the leader (a leader he
situated outside time and place, and who might be

a Teutonic knight, a condottiere, or a samurai). In an "officer factory" De Gaulle affirmed support for a hero who would be an "enemy of laws."

1934. Not content with publishing *The Army of the Future*, a doctrinal work which brutally contradicted all official teaching, Lieutenant Colonel de Gaulle stimulated and prolonged the quarrel—opposing Pétain, Daladier, Weygand, and the highest-ranking officers of the army, and unleashing a politico-military guerrilla warfare in which he mobilized nonconformist parliamentarians such as Paul Reynaud, Popular Front deputies such as Philippe Serre, and "heretic" officers such as Lieutenant Colonel Mayer.

1938. The publication of *France and Her Army* caused an altercation between Pétain and himself in which the colonel refused to give an inch when he was recalled to order by his former patron, the dominant figure in the French army. It was not simply a question of a literary argument or of an author's vanity; it was also a matter of military tradition, of professional ethics. On a general moral plane, as well as on that of right of ownership, the "old man" was evidently wrong. But not on the level of the customs of the service. Since when did a vassal demand his rights when faced with his suzerain? The traditions of military discipline dictated obedience. He faced the marshal, and cried: *This is mine!* and refused to yield. Hardly commonplace.

January, 1940. In the midst of war—or, at least, in the midst of a state of war—a colonel distributed tracts inciting the elite of the nation to disobedience. It was the affair of the memorandum on "The Advent of Mechanized Power," which summoned the principal personalities of the country to force the General Staff to adopt a strategy it did not believe in, and to provide the organization and the means of putting it into effect in order to avert catastrophe. The extraordinary merit of this text has been recognized, but it must be agreed that the initiative for it is singular, to say the least. Clemenceau had acted in the same way, from 1914 to 1917. But he was an ex-prime minister who had returned to journalism. De Gaulle was an officer on active duty who, in the face of the enemy, cried out to the nation: *Your leaders are inept, and we are disarmed!*

In sum, a fine career as a rebel, clearly shaping into that of a famous insurgent . . . On the eighteenth of June, De Gaulle was not uprooted by his destiny and forced to become a character alien to himself. On the collective and mythical plane, he remained the personage he had never ceased to be: the superior man who recognized himself as such; who burdened himself with no hierarchy; who believed himself so completely attuned to the national interest that he could find a justification for every one of his acts (although they would also have to be sanctioned by success; he would return to this, often); and who was prepared to consider any method that might be of a nature to insure success of his theses—since they were legitimate, since he was thinking for France.

If a man lives constantly in the company of kings, knights, and statesmen of French history, he ends by considering himself their permanent delegate on earth, the spokesman of France, the repository of national legitimacy. And faced with this legitimacy, of what weight would be an order, an order from a troop of solemn old men, ministers without a capital and generals in flight?

The dispute raged within him. Circumstances were bringing to a bursting point elements which had long ago begun to ripen. The whole past history of this touchy nationalist, this patriot in combat, this prophet preaching in the desert, would have led him to refuse to admit defeat with the haughty serenity of a

Marshal Pétain. But his refusal was directed at something beyond just defeat. What he had seen since he had become involved with strategy—or, in other words, with policy—was the disintegration of a State which, to his historian's mind, had been and must become again the incarnation, the crowning achievement of everything he held most dear: classical thought, French rationalism, the Jacobin spirit.

For many years now, he had been contemptuous of the refusal to adopt military theses—his own—whose basic soundness had now been proven by events, and of the stubborn conservatism and caste mentality of the chiefs of the General Staff. But what he had seen in 1934-36, at the time of the great debate on the professional army, then in March and April of 1940 on the occasion of the formation of the Reynaud cabinet, and finally, during the frightful weeks of May and June, 1940, was a State with no central axis, torn into factions, into a patchwork of mediocre and antagonistic interests and feudalities.

For De Gaulle, June of 1940 represented not so much the insolvency of the army—he had taken its measure years before, and saw in its performance only a foregone conclusion—as the collapse of the State. Having placed all of his hopes on Reynaud, the fact that he should have been reduced to impotence was, to De Gaulle, a yardstick for the measurement of decay. If the Constable took to the sea, it was not only because a decision had been made at Bordeaux which was contrary to what he believed to be the interest and the honor of the nation, but because he sensed falling away beneath his feet everything that made up the ideal of his life: a State that expressed and served, through the most diverse paths and ideologies, the unalterable, incorruptible French nation.

This rebel-by-inclination nonetheless went through some harsh hours of doubt, a doubt of which his

86

Memoirs carry only a faint trace. In 1948, he read the first chapters of them to André Malraux. The author of *Man's Fate* remarked to him that this polished text gave scarcely any account of the debates that must have gone on within. "People will want to know what was happening at the time in the heart and the mind of the man of June 18th. . . ." Then De Gaulle, speaking in the voice that seems to come from the depths: "But, Malraux, it was horrible. . . ."

On the eve of the great decision, he wandered through a Bordeaux that seethed with intrigue and was empty of action, speaking to almost no one, appearing suddenly in an office of the prefecture, glancing briefly around, and then dashing back outside to materialize from behind a pillar and confront the British ambassador like Banquo's ghost. When he encountered the chairman of Parliament's Foreign Relations Committee, Jean Mistler, he stated with terrifying calm: "Well, it's clear; the Germans have lost the war. Now the battle must be resumed!" And on the morning of the seventeenth, with his aide-de-camp Geoffroy de Courcel and Sir Edward Spears, his host, he suddenly boarded a plane for London—a plane that would not come back.

4
Charles-
the-Alone

Locminé, late afternoon of
June 18, 1940: a market town in Britanny, drenched
in sunlight, dust, and shouting. A dazed and bewildered crowd was gathered in the square, surrounding
their priest—who supported an old lady on his arm, a
fragile, emaciated figure. German motors rumbled
and growled through the streets, heading west, indif-
ferent to the stunned population. Then they were
gone, and the French soldiers who were beginning to
flood in from every corner of the front could only
shake their fists at the dust and curse. Among them
was artillery captain Xavier de Gaulle, searching for
his mother and his daughter, Geneviève.

A few minutes passed. A young man came out of
his house, running toward the square, shouting: "It
isn't over . . . not yet. There's a general who just made
a speech on the radio . . . he says we have to go on
fighting. . . ."—"What general? Weygand?"—"No, his
name is De Gaulle. . . ." The old lady released the
priest's arm, stood motionless, her hands clasped as if
in prayer, and cried: "It's my son!" Twelve days later,
the old lady was dead. And the gendarmes of Locminé—resistance members before their time—escorted
the mother of General de Gaulle to her grave with full
military honors.

This story is not probable, and it has been a long time since the printmakers of Épinal became aware that they were coloring their naïve pictures of French legend too highly. And yet, this story is true: it must be remembered that it took place in the heart of the forest of Brocéliande, cradle of Celtic romanticism. An adventure like that of Free France required such moments to grow, to survive, and to triumph. A man is not De Gaulle without a great deal of luck, without recourse to magic and to a sense of the fabulous. A man is not De Gaulle if he does not know how to "make use of dreams to lead the French." The words spoken in London would become the nocturnal voice of dreams. The splendid white moustache of the marshal would never be more than a daytime symbol of security.

Charles de Gaulle had landed in London in the early afternoon of June 17th, two hours after Marshal Pétain's broadcast appeal from Bordeaux: "It is with a broken heart that I tell you today that combat must cease. . . . Last night, I sent a message to the adversary. . . ." Cease combat, against someone who is now the "adversary" and no longer the enemy, before having the slightest knowledge of Hitler's intentions?

And yet, there was a degree of reticence to De Gaulle's welcome in London. Churchill was acting against the advice of the Foreign Office, which was not at all favorable to an initiative that might have further aggravated relations with the Bordeaux government, when he received him and announced that he was putting the broadcast facilities of the BBC at his disposal. Why? First, because these two great carnivorous animals had established between themselves—at first sight, and again at Briare and Tours —a ravenous complicity, which would not exclude, as they were to grow more accustomed to each other, a kind of hatred. And also because Spears, who possessed a high degree of credit with the prime minister, had persuaded him that De Gaulle was the forerunner in London of a "legitimate" Reynaud-Mandel government, for which the paths must first be cleared.

Hitler had two objectives: to allow a French government to be established, so that he could then saddle it with the responsibility of turning over everything he had promised himself to extract from that country in the way of materiel; and to avoid the possibility of Darlan's fleet joining the English. For the first, as for the second, he had to avoid imposing the intolerable. The intolerable? He had measured, with disturbing insight, the degree to which the "tolerance" and the sense of honor of the French had been softened by the debacle, and the degree to which the flight from Dunkerque had already shaken the Franco-British alliance. And he was to win on every count: secure the government's guarantee of armistice, neutralize the fleet, set France against Great Britain—with whom he had never ceased hoping to make some kind of arrangement, with whom he was even at that moment sounding out on such a possibility through the intermediary of the Swedes.

De Gaulle did not know all of this when he arrived at the BBC in the late afternoon of June 18th. He knew only invasion, disaster, the collapse of the State and of the army, the call to surrender. Had he been able to foresee the surprising diplomatic competence of the surprising strategist of the French campaign, he still would not have been capable of moving so much as an inch from his position. His "very nakedness," as he would say, forced him to appear as the "inflexible champion of the nation and the State" and adopt a policy of "intransigence" which, under the given circumstances of the armistice, was both unjust and blind, and which would be revived, when he faced the Allies, as a policy of boasting and obstinacy.

But nothing was so important to him as the sense of history, and a consciousness of the irreducible part played by morals and justice in every historic debate.

It was eight o'clock in the evening, on that eighteenth of June, 1940. Seated before the microphone, between an elderly French announcer, Thierry, and Gibson Parker, the English broadcast supervisor, Charles de Gaulle, very pale, his dark brown hair glued sweatily to his forehead, began to read from two sheets of paper propped up on a sort of lectern. His voice was hollow, firm at the beginning, and then a trifle unsteady:

The leaders who, for many years, have been at the head of the French armies, have formed a government. This government, invoking the defeat of our armies, has entered into relations with the enemy, to bring a halt to the battle. . . . But has the last word been said? Must hope disappear? Is the defeat a final one? No. . . . France is not alone! She is not alone! She is not alone! This war is not limited to the unhappy territory of our country. This war is not decided by the battle of France. This war is a global war. . . . Overwhelmed today by a mechanized force, we can conquer in the future, with a superior mechanized force. . . . I, General de Gaulle, today in London, invite all French officers and soldiers on British territory . . . engineers, specialist workers in armament factories . . . to join forces with me. No matter what may happen, the flame of French resistance must not, and will not, be extinguished. Tomorrow, as I have done today, I shall speak on the radio from London.

Let us open the *Memoirs* for a moment: "As I heard the irrevocable words come forth, I felt within myself that one life was ending, the life I had led within the framework of a solid France and an indivisible army. At the age of forty-nine, I had become

91

an adventurer, a man whom destiny had plucked from the line and made unique."

Yes and no. We know that he had not crossed his Rubicon, the English Channel, without anguish, and that he had some reason to feel himself "alone, and stripped of everything, like a man on the brink of an ocean he has claimed he will swim." But this text of June 18th (which has often been confused with later statements in which this first denunciation of the armistice and its advocates is amplified into vengeful polemics, and also with that of the poster which appeared in July on the walls of London: "France has lost a battle, but France has not lost the war") nonetheless took its place in the direct course of an existence which had already been "made unique"; which had always been in conflict with "the leaders who, for many years, have been at the head of the French armies," and which had been a constant struggle for the advancement of those "engineers and specialist workers" from whom the author of *The Army of the Future* expected the creation of the "superior mechanized force" which would one day be the instrument of victory for France. No matter how its author may describe it, the broadcast of June 18th was the conclusion of a very specific career as an officer, as well as the preface to an uncertain adventure as a statesman.

First, just to exist. Gather together men and strength, maintain a form of State, obtain recognition and support from abroad, and primarily from Great Britain. For the men, there were few who came. Those who were already in London or who arrived in the days just after the armistice—Ambassador Corbin, Jean Monnet, André Maurois—left. Those who did come were not well known; or if they were, like Pierre Cot, former leftist minister of the air force in the Blum cabinet, they were embarrassing.

Did De Gaulle really want to attract the major military and civilian leaders to London or to place himself under their authority? There is no reason to doubt the sincerity of the appeal he addressed to General Auguste Noguès (in his second broadcast to the French people, on June 19th, he linked this name with those of other famous colonial rulers, Bugeaud and Lyautey), and he knew at the time that Noguès, as resident-general of Morocco, had informed the Bordeaux government of his readiness to continue the struggle. But on the other hand, it would be wrong to underestimate the validity of the arguments used by Noguès to justify his decision to remain with the Vichy government once he knew that the armistice provided an opportunity to save the fleet and preserve the North African "sanctuary" and the army of Africa. In July and August of 1940, a German attack based in Spain (with or without Franco's agreement) could very probably have destroyed all of this.

The debate has been resumed a hundred times. In defense of Pétain and of Noguès, General Georges—this old adversary of Gaullist theories—has cited Winston Churchill as saying, in 1943, that from a strategic point of view the decision made in Rabat and in Vichy was useful to the Allies. It is an inexhaustible dialogue between immediate utility and historic significance.

But it must be observed that if France was not totally occupied at the time and handed over to the administration of some *gauleiter,* it was less because of the efforts of a handful of good shepherds than because of the fact that Hitler preferred this solution, finding it—as of June 18-20—better suited to his objectives, more economical to Germany, and more costly to the English. Harsher terms might have resulted in the fleet's going over to London, and Africa's responding to the appeals of De Gaulle or—as would probably have happened in such a case—of Weygand and Noguès.

There were, however, some who heard De Gaulle's appeal and listened—Catroux, for instance, the former comrade-in-captivity of Ingolstadt whom he had so greatly admired ten years earlier in the Near East. Having been removed from his post in Saigon by the Vichy government, he came to join De Gaulle's cause and place himself under his orders; and when he arrived in England in September, while De Gaulle was in Africa, he flatly rejected the propositions of a British cabinet anxious to substitute an amenable and noted general of the army, whose worth they had had an opportunity to judge for themselves, for a stubborn and still relatively unknown brigadier. And from various corners of the Empire came such men as General Legentilhomme, Colonel de Larminat, Commodore d'Argenlieu, Major Brosset, and Captain Philippe de Hauteclocque—the future Leclerc.

Béthouart, his classmate at Saint-Cyr, arrived in London at the head of the Foreign Legion brigade, which had been sent to Norway. When he departed for Morocco, he left behind him a half-brigade of the Legion commanded by Colonel Magrin-Verneret, the future General Montclar—who had as assistants a certain Captain Koenig and a Captain Dewawrin—who was to set an example for members of his effective but very controversial intelligence network by adopting as a pseudonym the name of a Paris metro station: Passy.

In the last days of June, an odd personage arrived in London from Gibraltar: Admiral Émile Muselier. This sailor, who was as possessed as his commander in chief, Darlan, with a passion for politics, had had a checkered career strewn with ambushes, conflicts, and plotting; nothing about it would change, from London to Saint Pierre and Miquelon and to Algiers.

There was less difficulty in recruiting "civilians."

René Pleven, Professor Cassin, Georges Boris, Pierre-Olivier Lapie, Jean Oberlé, Jean Marin, were among the first civilian associates of General de Gaulle. Maurice Schumann, his colleague of Paris Christian Democrat groups, arrived on June 30th, and was cordially welcomed by Charles de Gaulle as a friend from the literary days of *Temps Présent*. Fifteen years later, in an article for *Réalités*, Schumann, then leader of the Mouvement Républicain Populaire, recounted the astounding statements made to him by the leader of Free France in the course of their first meeting in London. Hearing them, who would not immediately have become a Gaullist, even though he reserved the right to change his mind in the future?

If Hitler had meant to come to London, he would already be here. . . . I think that Russia will come into the war before America, but they will both come in. . . . Hitler is thinking of the Ukraine. He won't be able to resist the temptation to settle things with Russia, and that will be the beginning of his downfall. . . . In short, the war is a terrible problem, but it is already decided. What remains to be done is to bring all of France over to the right side.

Stupidity, as everyone knows, is not his strong point. A vision of the day after tomorrow, for objectives that vary from those of the day before yesterday to those of today and tomorrow.

As of June 28th, General de Gaulle had been recognized by the British government as "leader of the Free French." On August 7th, letters were exchanged between him and Winston Churchill, supplemented by an agreement in which His Majesty's prime minister adopted the general's propositions concerning the formation and conditions of eventual employment of a corps of French volunteers. In a letter added to these texts, and kept secret at the time, Mr. Churchill

95

stipulated that although he had publicly engaged himself to assure "the integral restoration of the independence and greatness of France," this expression "does not, strictly speaking, include the matter of territorial frontiers." But, the prime minister added, "We will do our best." To General de Gaulle, the English "best" was not necessarily synonymous with the French "good." He mentioned the subject in his reply, also dated August 7th, and kept secret: "I hope that circumstances will one day permit the British government to consider these questions with less reserve."

Everyone had considered the French fleet, the "Darlan fleet," as the pivot of the June negotiations between France and England, and then of those between France, Germany, and Italy. On the twelfth of June, at Briare, Churchill had grasped the admiral's arm and barked at him in his best ferocious-bulldog manner: "Whatever happens, don't turn over the fleet!" The admiral made a horrified protest, invoking his honor. In his *Memoirs,* De Gaulle seems to feel that Darlan attached at least as much importance to his "private empire." These two aspects of the matter were so clearly contiguous that the Führer concentrated his attention on it for the entire period of June 17th to 22nd with a caution which, in this particular case, amounted almost to genius. He was determined that the naval units commanded by Admirals de Laborde, Godfroy, and Gensoul should not arrive in British ports.

As late as the twenty-fourth, both Churchill and De Gaulle were obviously badly informed, so that they denounced—almost carelessly for such a serious matter at such a time—the surrender of the fleet to the Axis powers. By the twenty-fifth, and in spite of the relative security inherent in the text of the armistice, the cabinet in London had made its decision: destroy the fleet, rather than leave its fate uncertain. Behind the obvious strategic motives—which are understandable enough on the part of men in a desperate situation—many observers have felt that there was another, more insidious, temptation: destruction of French naval power for a considerable period of time.

It was called "Operation Catapult," but one of the British officers who carried it out termed it "Operation Boomerang." The repugnance of Admirals North and Somerville, and of officers such as Commodore Holland, is apparent in every line of their published accounts of the destruction of the fleet at Mers-el-Kebir. If the men who were responsible for the security of the British Isles felt that it was a vital necessity to remove the threat posed by Hitler's utilization of French warships, they might at least have left Admiral Gensoul an avenue of escape to the French West Indies. The catastrophic misunderstanding which resulted had its origins in the frantic haste of the London cabinet to settle the matter once and for all, and in Darlan's orders to the fleet commanders to reject any discussion of it.

De Gaulle was caught between the two arms of a pair of pincers, wanting to preserve what still remained of French armed might, but helpless against the cynical determination of men for whom he was not just an ally, but also a guest and a protégé. Even so, he used the microphones loaned to him by the same people who were responsible for Mers-el-Kebir to express the "grief and anger" of the whole of the French people and to warn the English against "representation of this odious tragedy as a direct naval victory." But in an attempt to clarify London's reasons for the action, he made the statement that the Pétain government had agreed to "turn over our warships to the discretion of the enemy." To the "discretion of the enemy" in the ports of North Africa, which the

Rethondes agreement of June 22nd had finally selected as the places of their internment? It was an attempt to excuse a defensible crime by an untruth.

The Mers-el-Kebir affair gave pause to a large number of Frenchmen who might then have come over to the cause of Free France, but it was a smaller number than either De Gaulle or his associates had feared. Although the affair itself was horrible, it clarified relations between the Gaullist forces and the British, relations which now, according to the general, could only be those of *one power to another*, even though one of those powers was minute. The same man who, on June 15th, had asked the captain of a French destroyer if he would be willing to serve under British colors, was now determined to raise his own flag. De Gaulle recovered from the "hatchet blow" of Mers-el-Kebir all the more rapidly because he saw in it a confirmation of his theses on the continuance of national egoisms over and above any ideological groupings or alliance of interests. The test that was still to come, at Dakar, was far more cruel. Here, he would see that unity of Frenchmen, which was the prime object of his faith, shaken to its roots, and in circumstances which were beyond the direct control of the Nazis.

He had, however, approached the subject cautiously. Although major segments of French Equatorial Africa, from Fort-Lamy to Douala, had rallied to the Free French cause, Dakar had answered his appeals first by evasion and then by a direct refusal from Boisson, who had been made high commissioner for French West Africa by the Vichy government. But the capital of Senegal was one of the keys to the battle of the Atlantic. From the point of view of Free French prestige, as well as that of Allied strategy, it was essential to dispose of the problem of Dakar. As early as the beginning of July, General de Gaulle had been studying a plan which centered on a landing at Conakry (in French Guinea, south of Senegal), to be followed by a gradual investment of Dakar, which he judged difficult to conquer by simple persuasion and costly to take by force of arms. He broached the subject to Churchill, who announced himself in favor of the direct approach: a Franco-British squadron, drawn up in full view of Dakar, but not firing a shot.

On the twenty-third of September, an Anglo-French fleet anchored outside Dakar. General de Gaulle was aboard a Dutch transport, the *Westerland,* which he would describe—because he was aboard it—as "carrying the fortunes of France." Unfortunately, the spectacle of the fleet at anchor envisaged by Winston Churchill was ruined because the fleet was hidden behind a solid English-style fog. No one in Dakar was even aware of the visual shock he had had in mind. The emissaries sent into the city, Commodore d'Argenlieu and Captain Bécourt-Foch (grandson of the marshal), were refused admission and forced to return to the gig that had brought them in. As they pulled away from the wharves, there were two long bursts of fire from a heavy machine gun: d'Argenlieu was seriously wounded.

In the city itself, a delegation of pro-De Gaulle citizens of Dakar was attempting to convince Boisson to welcome the fleet; and in Rufisque, a little city close to Dakar, Boislambert was attempting to convince the mass of the people. At three o'clock in the afternoon, the shore batteries opened fire against Admiral Andrew Cunningham's fleet, and his ships replied. On the following morning, De Gaulle demanded that the operation be halted. It was a failure, and it must not be drowned in blood. Cunningham carried on for a few hours longer, but without conviction. Dakar remained in Vichy hands.

When Churchill had consulted him about the operation, Roosevelt had had his reservations, but in the end he had said: "All right—but be sure it succeeds!" Even though the prime minister was humiliated by the defeat, he did not turn against De Gaulle, and on the following day he paid tribute to him in the House of Commons. But De Gaulle's position with relation to Roosevelt was permanently altered, and—as other writers have noted—the seeds of the November, 1942, imbroglio in Algiers were sown in Dakar. Convinced that it was indiscretion among his own people—if not an actual case of betrayal by certain Free French agents—which had brought about the failure of the plan, the Americans continued to use it as an argument for keeping De Gaulle uninformed about major Allied operations.

For De Gaulle himself, this was the worst moment. In those last days of September, 1940, the man who had never doubted himself, his destiny, or his country, was helpless, prostrate, wounded in both his pride and his most basic certainties. He had ordered Frenchmen to fire on Frenchmen. And Frenchmen had fired back, in full view of the African people in whom he had placed his hopes—and of the English. One of the men who knows him best has said: "After Dakar, he was never the same man. He was never happy again."

French West Africa was closed to him, but not all of Africa. Up until the end of July, the "Empire" had wavered between armistice and resistance. Boisson's adherence to Vichy was a cruel blow to the cause of Free France. On July 30th, De Gaulle decided to speak directly to Africa. Since the leaders had refused his leadership, he would appeal "if need be, to the people themselves." A risky maneuver, from a long-term point of view . . .

From the twenty-fourth to the twenty-eighth of August, men who were loyal to De Gaulle were to assume control, successively, of three African cities:

Fort-Lamy, Douala, and Brazzaville. It was a decisive operation, first, because the Third Reich saw in it the creation of a magnetic pole which would make it necessary to treat North Africa with caution, since the possibility now existed that it would go over to Free France (in this sense, De Gaulle was covering and consolidating—in spite of himself—the tricky game Weygand, high commissioner in Algiers, was playing in the area); and secondly, because it put a parcel of "French" territory beneath the feet of Charles de Gaulle. A blessing for the Constable, who remembered Danton's sentence: "One cannot bring away the earth of his country sticking to his shoes . . ."

So it was in Brazzaville, capital of French Equatorial Africa, and now capital of fighting France, that General de Gaulle, with no word of warning to London, created the Council for Defense of the Empire, on October 22, 1940—Brazzaville, destined to be the birthplace of Free France, before becoming the cradle of decolonization. The feeling of being again in a land where France was still sovereign gave him a new voice; he spoke as a leader. The caution, the reservation, of the end of June were far behind.

De Gaulle was no longer the solitary precursor asking help from better-known names, no longer the commando parachuted in to prepare the way for a proper government. He presented himself as the legal guardian of France: "I will exercise my powers in the name of France." And he added, with a foresighted prudence which made Churchill aware that he was dealing with a statesman: "I engage myself to consult with the representatives of the people as soon as possible. . . ."

Decidedly, this Charles who was no longer "Charles-the-Alone," who had ceased to be "Charles Lackland" since the New Hebrides, Tahiti, New Caledonia, and the French cities of India had rallied to his cause, was

101

not just some adventurous captain. And it is possible that, sometimes, the Allies regretted it. If not, why should some of them never have ceased supporting a competitor, a possible alternative: from Catroux (who flatly refused, as we know) through Muselier, to General de la Laurencie—Vichy's military delegate in Paris, whom U.S. agents would attempt to convert to open resistance—to Darlan and Giraud and even to Édouard Herriot?

In short, this was the De Gaulle of the time: the victim of Mers-el-Kebir, the desperately wounded man of Dakar, the solitary voice of the BBC, the leader of an organization that had already become a political system, the general of a few regiments scattered from London to Douala—and already taking himself for France.

5
War with Whom?

Neither Vichy—obviously—nor Washington, nor Moscow, nor London, nor even the majority of fighting men on the territory of France, were entirely taken in by this visionary egocentric with the perpetually arrogant manner. But he existed.

If he was to assert his position vis-à-vis the Axis Powers and the Allies, his enemies and—even more importantly—his friends, it was still necessary, however, to assemble some kind of force. It was necessary to "be present in the battle, in order to be a part of the victory," so that France would not be simply a witness to her liberation, so that she would not just *submit* to the most dramatic period of her history— the period whose foremost protagonist was General de Gaulle. It was this necessity which resulted in the formation of the Free French Forces, from the little group formed in London around Montclar, Muselier, and Valin, to the divisions which would take part in the campaigns in the Near East, the operations in North Africa, and the landings in Europe in the summer of 1944.

In the use he made of those forces, which became trump cards of some importance after the Libyan campaigns of 1942, the hard core of Gaullist thought was constantly apparent: the utilization of force for political ends—less for the conquest of a piece of terrain or destruction of an enemy position than as a base for a diplomatic initiative, a new round of negotiations and claims. Leclerc at Koufra, Koenig at Bir-Hakeim, Pouyade on the Russian front—each of these was a card in the hand of Charles de Gaulle.

And it was through sacrifices like these that he was able to improve the hand until, in September, 1941, he could face the reticent English and the displeased Americans with creation of the French National Committee. The English would recognize it, at first, only as the "National Committee of the Free French"; they had no desire to change their 1940 recognition of a "movement" to recognition of a truly national organization. But De Gaulle no longer depended on London only. Things were moving in France.

"The Army of the Night" in France was not formed entirely as a result of Charles de Gaulle's appeal. Many of those who had refused to capitulate in June of 1940 had done so without hearing the London radio. And among those who began to gather together in groups of their own at the end of the summer of 1940—socialists, trade unionists, anti-fascist intellectuals—the London team aroused suspicion: they were militarists, reactionaries. . . . Some men of the Left, such as Lapie, Cot, Labarthe, and Louis Levy, had joined De Gaulle in the early days; but the first was sent to Africa, the second brushed off, and the others remained uncommitted for a time and then went over to active opposition. Moreover, the first contacts between London and the Resistance had been made by British agents who were less concerned with reestablishing democracy in France than with collecting intelligence information.

As early as the beginning of 1941, three Resistance networks had assumed national importance in France:

Combat, created by Henry Frenay; *Libération,* founded by Emmanuel d'Astier; *Franc-Tireur,* set up by Jean-Pierre Levy. General de Gaulle had not foreseen the birth of these forces when he spoke, on June 18th, of "the flame of French resistance"; he was thinking only of the presence of French fighting men at the side of the Allies. The grand strategist of the movement had accorded no place in his estimates for the work of the men of the *maquis,* saboteurs, and night raiders. It is striking to observe how briefly he considered this aspect of the combat in his *Memoirs* —up until the beginning of 1943. We shall see why his viewpoint changed at that time.

In the autumn of 1941, a young man named Jean Moulin arrived in London. He was not yet a factor of any great importance, and he could claim nothing more than an intermittent association with Frenay. But he had been prefect of Chartres, so he was, in a sense, an envoy of that "State," of those "notables" whose support De Gaulle was seeking; and he explained that the members of the Resistance within France could render important strategic services beyond the scope of simple gathering of information.

In the preceding three months, the whole problem of the effectiveness of the Resistance had been altered by a single event: Germany's invasion of the U.S.S.R. had brought into the Resistance movement the whole organization of the French Communist party, of which only a few members had previously refused to accept the implications of the 1939 German-Soviet pact. It was a decisive shift of balance, but also a supplementary cause for mistrust between London and the Resistance forces in France. From this point on, General de Gaulle—very prudently—would attempt to establish closer relations with fighting elements on the mainland.

In 1942, this "reconciliation" was to be marked by

105

several important missions: Jean Moulin's return to France (actually in January, 1943), by parachute, charged by General de Gaulle to attempt to unite all of the various forces hostile to Germany and to Vichy; the visit to London, in March, of Christian Pineau, the representative of *Libération-Nord* and of the trade unions; and the arrival in England, in July, of André Philip, the socialist deputy and noted scholar, who shortly afterward was named to the French National Committee as commissioner for the interior. This newly created post was intended to coordinate relations between Free France and the Resistance, the scattered components of which task had previously been directed (and would continue to be, heroically) by Pierre Brossolette, another socialist teacher.

De Gaulle had three complaints about the men working on the mainland. The first was that the various networks worked with the English, made use of Major Buckmaster's communications and transport, and on occasion accepted weapons and funds furnished by His Majesty's Government; and the man of June 18th considered this a breach of national unity. The second was that the members of groups such as *Libération* and *Combat* existed on their own, not identifying themselves with the broadcasts from London and, while basically accepting De Gaulle's military directives, not feeling themselves bound to obey him on a political level. The third was that for De Gaulle and his companions in London the objective was the reestablishment of French greatness, not the restoration of a regime on the order of the Third Republic, while for the men of the Resistance, primary emphasis was on the resurrection of democratic liberties.

Several episodes of the time bear witness to the extent of these difficulties. Christian Pineau arrived in London in March, 1942, charged by the unions, by companions such as Cavaillès, and by leaders of several of the Resistance networks—d'Astier and Frenay among them—to obtain from General de Gaulle a message to the French people defining the "democratic goals" of Free France. De Gaulle welcomed this first important emissary of the Resistance warmly and with interest, but was astonished that anyone should want to extract such an engagement from him. It was to require hours of negotiation before Pineau, with the help of his fellow trade-unionist, Adrien Tixier, would obtain from the general an agreement to forego his practice of condemning the Third Republic as severely as he did the Pétain regime. And it was not until he was about to board the plane which was taking him back to France, on April 28, 1942, that Pineau received from the hand of a breathless motorcyclist the text of the declaration he had hoped for, bearing down harder on the men of Vichy than on their predecessors, and going into such matters as the liberties to be reestablished, social objectives, and economic planning. It was at this point, and almost in spite of himself, that De Gaulle became the leader of the Resistance: the Constable was now the symbol of the Popular Front.

Three months later, André Philip arrived in London. To make it very clear that he had not come "at the orders" of the general, he defined his position in a radio interview before he had even seen him. "What do you think about General de Gaulle?"—"I don't care a thing about the general. . . . I came to join forces with the undersecretary of state for national defense of the last free—and therefore, the last legitimate—government of the Republic." De Gaulle heard the broadcast and was delighted by it. The arguments put forth by this professor of law followed exactly the direction which he wished, and provided an answer to the objections relative to his "legitimacy" —his status as a representative of the French people

107

—with which the Anglo-Americans were constantly confronting him. The general welcomed Philip with open arms, and they spent an entire evening walking together. The socialist leader later described their long promenade: "In the space of three hours, De Gaulle delivered a perfectly prepared thesis on the State and the Nation. As soon as he had finished, I said, 'General, as soon as the war is won, I shall part company with you. You are fighting to restore national grandeur. I am fighting to build a socialist, democratic Europe....'"

In November, a few days after the Allied landings in North Africa, it was Henri Frenay—who had already made one trip to London the preceding year—who faced De Gaulle across his desk. The general attempted to obtain his adherence to the National Council of the Resistance, which Jean Moulin was working to set up in France. "General," Frenay said, "there is a risk in this. Such an organization, made up of political personalities, is sure to have a policy of its own. Since its situation is not the same as yours, what would happen if this policy were different from yours?"—"I would give an order."—"General, on a military plane we don't dispute your orders. But things are not quite the same in the political domain." And then, De Gaulle: "In that case, Frenay, France will choose between you and me!"

This matter of the National Council of the Resistance was at the heart of the disagreements between De Gaulle and the Resistance, as is evidenced by the caution with which it was approached by a man like Frenay. Why should the leader of *Combat* have been opposed to the creation of the CNR (Conseil National de la Résistance)? Because he saw in it a resurrection of the old political and trade-union forces; he saw in it a return to the past—the substitution of a spirit of restoration for the spirit of resistance. And he

108

foresaw that of all of the old organizations only the communists would profit from it: firm in their doctrine, solidly organized, strengthened by struggle and sacrifice, they would easily dominate a conglomeration of exhausted, compromised, or divided parties.

Buy why should De Gaulle have been insisting on the constitution of a group which was just a holdover from the Third Republic and which could, conceivably, open the path to a "people's democracy"? Because in the debate which had again been brought to the surface by the Allied landings in North Africa—with no Gaullist participation whatever—it was vitally necessary for him to affirm his status as representative of France and to demonstrate to London, and especially to Washington, that he was not just an untractable individual but a man who had behind him both the French republican elite and the leaders of the working classes. Since he had been made the leader of the Popular Front, he might as well exploit the advantages of that fact for diplomatic ends.

The CNR would be established, on paper at least, but with certain abstentions: Frenay, for instance, remained on the sidelines, and *Combat* was represented by Claude Bourdet. A few weeks later, Jean Moulin was arrested by the Gestapo and tortured to death. But the organization itself would already have been in existence long enough to insure De Gaulle's success in the confrontation with the Americans in Algiers.

A remark of one of the Resistance emissaries to London is worth bearing in mind: "De Gaulle gave the impression, in London, of warring against the English more than against the Germans." The English, in any event, were closer at hand; and his "vigilance" was never lacking in items calculated to sustain it. From Madagascar to Djibouti and the Near East, London made it relentlessly clear that the law of the jungle was still in effect between old colonial nations.

The affair of Syria and Lebanon nakedly reveals both British greed and the exasperated mistrust of the leader of the Free French. On the one hand, there was a digestive system, and on the other, a nervous system. In other words—perfectly normal allies.

The battle of the Mediterranean, to use the title of General Catroux's book, was of prime importance to the cause of Free France because it was the only one in which she could have taken a military step that was on a really "political" level, either by replacing Vichy in the Levantine countries, by gaining a foothold in Algiers, or by participating in Allied victories in Libya, Tunisia, and Italy. It was approximately this that De Gaulle had in mind in the spring of 1941: "I flew toward the complicated East with simple ideas. . . ."

When it is remembered that General de Gaulle was dealing with an ally, his behavior in this instance would appear to have been inadmissibly brutal and arrogant. But it must be borne constantly in mind that this ally, tempted by the devil, would have taken any other attitude for agreement with its policy—and the mechanisms at work in the formation of British policy were leading it implacably toward eviction of France from the area, regardless of any prior engagements or texts.

The operation in the Levant, which had been considered by Catroux and Churchill as early as September, 1940, was made abruptly urgent by the concessions Darlan made to Hitler in the course of his visit to Berchtesgaden in May, 1941: the admiral had agreed to put the Syrian airdromes at the disposition of the Luftwaffe. As a result, Nazi military power would have bases in the very heart of the Allied strategic position, at a point from which it could lend support to Iraq—already in revolt against London—

threaten the Suez Canal, and strike directly at the Soviet Union on its southern flanks in the Crimea and the Caucasus.

De Gaulle and Catroux had hoped that the expeditionary corps in the Levant, formed by Weygand at the beginning of the war as a watchdog unit on the flank of the U.S.S.R., would rebel against leaders attempting to implement agreements which constituted an act of military collaboration with the Reich. But De Gaulle was no longer harboring any illusions on this subject when he cabled Catroux, on May 3rd: "In case events should lead our British allies to move into the states of the Levant which are 'under French mandate,' it is necessary that we take part in their operations in the name of the rights and interests of France, and by reason of French participation in the war."

On the tenth of May, German planes landed in Syria. On the nineteenth, Catroux attempted to bring Archibald P. Wavell into a joint operation against Damascus, but the British commander in chief in Cairo decided that the matter could wait. Was Catroux then to march with only the little division of General Legentilhomme, the only one then at his disposition? On the twentieth, De Gaulle cabled him from Brazzaville: "We must push on to Damascus, even with a single battalion on trucks. The psychological effect will do the rest." Subsequent events would show that such an action could only have been a derisory Operation Suicide. Before coming over to the cause of Free France, Colonel Collet had warned Catroux that the Vichy forces would defend Syria against him. When London then decided to follow De Gaulle's advice and undertake the operation, the leader of the Free French knew that to "assure the presence of France" in this phase of the war he would be forced to fire on other Frenchmen. What he had

111

not been able to support at Dakar he would have to undertake at Damascus.

Catroux and he did not do it without having expanded the psycho-political bases of the operation by issuing a proclamation, on June 8, 1941, stating that France recognized the "mandate states" of Syria and Lebanon as "free and independent," and that if the Free French were entering their territory it was in order "to free it from Hitler's forces and insure respect for the rights of the people as well as for those of France." It was a promise which would see many setbacks before its final accomplishment—and one which General de Gaulle would have been better advised to equate immediately with the time of accomplishment he had in mind: the end of the war.

As for the battle, it took place less on the ground—Dentz, the commander of the Vichy forces, was so "intoxicated" by a few audacious Gaullist feints that he believed himself confronted with a far superior force, and thereafter confined himself to a series of withdrawals which caused relatively few casualties—than around the conference tables. And less between adversaries of the campaign—the armistice of Saint-Jean d'Acre, signed on July 14th, quickly settled the question of withdrawal to France of the Vichy troops —than between British and Gaullist allies.

Catroux had represented Free France in the course of the negotiations—sitting beside General Maitland Wilson and across the table from the Vichy government's General de Verdilhac—but he had not been invited to sign the texts. As soon as De Gaulle learned the details of the Saint-Jean d'Acre convention, he rejected it as an agreement which, according to him, did not sufficiently emphasize the rights of Free France, since it did not make her the official trustee for the national interests in the Levant.

On July 21st, in Cairo, the chief of the Free French

called on Captain Oliver Lyttleton, British minister-resident for Middle Eastern Affairs, and declared that he was "reassuming full and complete control over Free French forces in the Levant." Three days later, after an audacious feint of leaving the scene entirely— an announced flight to Brazzaville, where he was prepared to denounce British duplicity to the other members of the alliance—De Gaulle extracted from his opponent an "interpretative arrangement" of the Saint-Jean d'Acre text, accompanied by a pact of collaboration between the British authorities and the "Free French" in the Middle East. Both texts recognized the assumption of British command in those areas in which it disposed of the superior force, but affirmed the preeminence of the Free French authorities in Syria and Lebanon in conformity with "the particular obligations of France in the States of the Levant."

Thus, the British government had been brought to recognize that in the Levant General de Gaulle was the heir and trustee to the rights held by France under mandate from the League of Nations. It was an unquestionable diplomatic success, at least for the moment, and one which provides a measuring rod for De Gaulle's bargaining abilities when he is confronted with better-armed adversaries. But incidents continued to occur, in places as far separated as Jebel ed Druz and Aleppo, showing that, as Churchill put it, "England did not fight in the Levant in order to substitute the Gaullists for Vichy."

It was at this point that General Sir Edward Spears, who had been waiting in the wings for months, returned to the stage. Having failed in London in his attempts to establish himself as guardian of the chief of the Free French whom he had brought there, he now, in Beirut, wanted to be the man who would pay off the French mortgage on the Levant. Both Syrian and Lebanese political leaders had at first been enchanted by the June, 1941, promise of independence, and were greatly deceived by De Gaulle's subsequent statements, putting its application off until a later date; and Spears made good use of this in his untiring efforts to set them against Catroux, urging them to demand "elections, immediately."

In August, 1942, having made up his mind to demand Spears's recall to London, De Gaulle flew to Cairo, where Churchill was at the time. He was received by Richard Casey, the successor to Oliver Lyttleton, and Casey also committed the imprudence of advising him to arrange for elections in the Levant. "Elections? Are you holding elections in Egypt? And don't you think that the British authorities in the Middle East have more urgent tasks than influencing policy in nations administered by France? Beating Rommel, for example?" Casey, infuriated, reported the remark to Churchill, who flushed angrily: "General Spears will remain in Beirut." Catroux, in recounting the affair, concluded: "And so, for my sins—and also, perhaps, for those of France—I kept Spears."

A few weeks later, on September 30, 1942, having reached a common agreement to "drain the abscess" of relations which had become more and more tense, Churchill and De Gaulle met in London, assisted by Anthony Eden and René Pleven. The two great wild bears let out their claws:

CHURCHILL: Why do you refuse to permit elections in the Levant? England has given its word to the Arabs that democracy will be respected.

DE GAULLE: We are not bound by England's promises.

CHURCHILL: You want a Frenchman in command of inter-Allied forces in the Levant. But it is England that assumes the preponderant responsibilities in the region.

114

DE GAULLE: The De Gaulle-Lyttleton agreements stipulate that command in any sector shall be exercised by the representative of the nation whose effective forces there are most numerous.

CHURCHILL: All of the difficulties between us stem from your excessive concern with prestige. . . . After all, are you France? In the course of events, other groups of France may be called on to assume more importance than they do today. . . .

DE GAULLE: If I am not France, why are you discussing this with me?

CHURCHILL: I can only conclude, once again, that General de Gaulle is attempting to improve his personal position by creating difficulties for Great Britain.

DE GAULLE: If I had been thinking of my personal position I would have remained in Vichy, where I would be chief of Pétain's General Staff.

And yet, in those decisive hours for the future which would begin with the landing in Algiers, De Gaulle would appear to Roosevelt as Churchill's "protégé." The violent collisions between the prime minister and the general were of a strategic, political, and historic nature; but the two men spoke the same language, and if they came to hate each other they did it on a common level of "spirit" if not of force. Between Roosevelt and De Gaulle, a clash of character would swell into a philosophical contradiction; between them there would never be anything more than a dialogue between the deaf, constantly hovering between mistrust, misunderstanding, and outright refusal.

The affair of the Levant sums up relations between De Gaulle and London; the affair of Saint Pierre and Miquelon forms a microcosm of those between the leader of Free France and Washington: it reveals, with crystal clarity, the confrontation of an overwhelming physical power with a taut and naked will.

In the course of the summer of 1941, a story (which

was never verified) penetrated the highest official circles in London, Washington, and Ottawa: German submarines were taking on food on the island of Saint Pierre, one of the two tiny French possessions off the coast of Newfoundland, still administered by the Vichy government and regularly broadcasting Admiral Darlan's propaganda from its transmitter. It quickly reached De Gaulle's ears that the American government had decided to entrust the Canadians with the mission of neutralizing the Saint Pierre radio. According to Robert E. Sherwood's *Roosevelt and Hopkins,* this suggestion "angered the redoubtable and incorrigible Free French leader, General Charles de Gaulle, who felt that such an action would be an insult to French sovereignty unless it were taken by French forces under his command. He accordingly sent Muselier to Canada to study the situation."*

In fact, the armada of Free French naval forces that sailed for Halifax had a larger objective in view: De Gaulle and Muselier (who were still in agreement at that time) had planned to complete the recovery of Saint Pierre by a similar take-over of the French West Indies. Muselier judged it advisable to consult the Canadian government in Ottawa on the matter, and the Canadians, following the lead of the London cabinet, declared themselves favorable to the Free French operation. But Roosevelt was opposed to it, feeling that such an initiative at this time would alienate Admiral Robert, the Vichy governor of the Antilles, with whom Washington had recently concluded a pact. On December 17th, Roosevelt received a cable from London in which De Gaulle stated, according to Sherwood's book, that having been informed of the objections of the President of the United States, he had postponed the operation against Saint

* Robert E. Sherwood, *Roosevelt and Hopkins.* New York: Harper & Bros., rev. ed. 1950, p. 479.

Pierre. It should not be forgotten that on December 7th the Japanese had attacked Pearl Harbor, and the United States had come into the war the following day. Roosevelt was a man with a great many things on his mind. . . .

A few days later, however, at the "Arcadia" conference, Roosevelt, Churchill, and the Canadian prime minister, Mackenzie King, were going to have to resolve, among other, more considerable, problems, the matter of a serious crisis between Washington and Free France. The participants were informed that as of December 18th De Gaulle had given Muselier "the order to proceed with the retaking of Saint Pierre and Miquelon, without informing the foreigners." His cable concluded thus: "I take full responsibility for this operation, which has become indispensable to the safekeeping of French possessions."

The operation, well prepared and conducted by Muselier, received the approval of the local population; consulted by a referendum in which they were not asked to choose between De Gaulle and Pétain but between Free France and the Axis powers, they voted 97 percent in favor of the newcomers. But once again, De Gaulle was going to learn the difference between an immediate success and a long-term advantage.

Echoes of the violence of Roosevelt's reaction can be found in *Roosevelt and Hopkins:* "De Gaulle's action in this matter was plainly outrageous and inexcusable, even though it was in conformance with Allied military policy, and sound policy at that. . . . It was a demonstration of the arrogance and recalcitrance as well as the courage and fierce devotion to the cause of French sovereignty. . . ."* A note addressed to President Roosevelt several days later by

* Sherwood, *op. cit.*, p. 480.

Secretary of State Cordell Hull (who had publicly stated his irritation with the action taken by "the so-called Free French") reproduced a cable from Admiral William D. Leahy, the United States ambassador to Vichy, which quoted Darlan as having stated that this operation would serve as a pretext for German action against French Africa. Hull then added, for his own part: "This fact leads straight to our plans about North Africa and our omission of De Gaulle's cooperation in that connection."*

Was the leader of the Free French aware that he had gone too far in subjecting Roosevelt to an affront at the very moment of Pearl Harbor and in alienating so formidable a personage at a time when his relations with London were already being affected by the crisis in the Near East? He negotiated an agreement which would have permitted Washington to improve its relations with Admiral Robert and with Vichy, and turned over the defense of Saint Pierre to the Canadians, evacuating Gaullist forces and maintaining there only an administrator for Free France, Alain Savary, as a sort of personal contact. A concession on the part of the Constable? If the agreement was not carried out, it would be Vichy, not he, who bore the responsibility.

But it is Cordell Hull's phrase regarding North Africa that should be remembered. This was the decisive matter, and De Gaulle knew it very well. This was the decision that had to be weighed. The price he might pay for the keys of Saint Peter could mean temporary eviction from Algiers.

General de Gaulle's real objective in this decisive year of 1942 was not, as it happened, to land in North Africa and set up a government there; it was to set foot again on the soil of France itself. He states this

* *Ibid.*, p. 485.

118

on several different occasions in his *Memoirs,* primarily in the period beginning in the month of August, seeming to belittle the difficulties of the enterprise and attributing to American timidity the fact that Operation Torch—the detour through Africa—was preferred to Operation Sledgehammer—a direct assault on Europe.

As early as April, 1942, he and his chief of staff, Colonel Billotte, had drawn up a plan for landings in Brittany and Normandy and proposed that it be carried out at the end of the year. The Dieppe raid in August—when De Gaulle, after a recurrence of a malignant fever contracted in Syria, was close to death—did not discourage the General Staff of the Free French forces. Under Mountbatten, Kieffer and his commandos had attained the major part of their objectives: for several hours, they had controlled the sky and a tongue of occupied territory. But the losses were heavy.

On the 27th of July, in London, General de Gaulle at last met with Generals George Marshall and Dwight D. Eisenhower and Admiral Ernest King. Pleading for the rapid opening of a second front in Europe, he met with embarrassed silence—although the able American ambassador in London, John Winant, had welcomed the Constable's offer to serve as a "military adviser" to the Allies.

Well aware that Roosevelt was in no hurry to invite him to Washington, De Gaulle dispatched various emissaries: Adrien Tixier at first, as a permanent delegate in the American capital; then Emmanuel d'Astier; and lastly André Philip, "commissioner for the interior." He felt that those were the men who could convince Roosevelt of his leadership of both the Resistance and the masses of the people of France.

Few meetings have been such total failures as that between the President and André Philip. Having left

London on October 6th, Philip was forced to wait in Washington for more than a month before he was received at the White House. More specifically, he was forced to wait until the day after the North African landings on November 8th, since Roosevelt had firmly decided that no Gaullist adherents should share in the secret of the operation. The socialist leader carried with him a message from De Gaulle to the President of the United States—a long argument for the defense, which the general had written himself, and in which he spiritedly and simply disclaimed any aspiration toward dictatorship or confiscation of national sovereignty for his own profit: "Yesterday, no one else bringing with him either a group of Frenchmen or a corner of French territory came forth. . . . I was alone. Should I, because of that, have remained silent? Tomorrow, after the odious experience of personal power now being carried out by Pétain with the connivance of the Germans . . . who would be so foolish as to imagine that he could establish and maintain personal power in France?"

This eloquence found no response in Roosevelt. As Philip talked to him about the aspirations of Free France, the President cut him off: "As far as I am concerned, there is no France, politically speaking, until such time as elections can give her representatives. . . ."

"But until such elections, and in order to organize them?"

"We are in the process of training a corps of politico-military specialists, which will guarantee the administration of France in the period until democracy can be reestablished. . . ."

"Mr. President, to the French people, a foreign occupant is still an occupant. . . ."

"I," Roosevelt said, "am not an idealist like Wilson. I am interested primarily in effectiveness; I have

120

problems to be solved. Those who help me in solving them are welcome. Today, Darlan gives me Algiers, and I shout: Long live Darlan! If Quisling gives me Oslo, I'll shout: Long live Quisling! . . . And if, tomorrow, Laval gives me Paris, I'll shout: Long live Laval!"

Recalling that meeting today, the socialist leader adds: "After a few minutes of listening to him, I found myself thinking: this is all very well, but Léon Blum is in another class. . . . Ten minutes later, I thought: no, it's really Herriot that he reminds me of. And after half an hour, I came to a conclusion: yes, decidedly, it's Laval. . . ."*

The effect such a report must have had on De Gaulle can easily be imagined. But while André Philip was taking a course in comparative politics in the Oval Room of the White House, Operation Torch had already shattered relations between the United States and De Gaulle, who found himself again, as he had been in London in June, 1940, Charles-the-Alone.

On the evening of November 7th, Mr. Bogomolov, the ambassador of the U.S.S.R. to the governments-in-exile in London, gave a reception in honor of the anniversary of the Soviet revolution. Jan Masaryk, minister of foreign affairs of Czechoslovakia, took René Pleven by the arm, and murmured, "It's for tonight. . . ." It was in this manner that General de Gaulle learned that the forces of General Eisenhower were preparing to land on what was still French soil.

Billotte was officially notified at one o'clock on the morning of the eighth. He decided to wait for dawn before confronting the storm. At six o'clock, De Gaulle, in pajamas, received him, listened to him, and then: "I hope the Vichy people throw them into the sea!

* From a personal interview between André Philip and the author.

You don't go into France like a pack of burglars!"

When he received Soustelle at eleven o'clock that morning, while the radio was broadcasting retransmissions of Roosevelt's appeal to the French, Pétain's reply, the statement of Giraud—who was still in Gibraltar—and an account of episodes which were clearly not what the Americans had hoped for, the leader of the Free French suddenly said: "If there should be a great battle, God knows what the consequences may be for France. It may be better if we don't meddle in it. . . ."

Don't meddle in it? This is a new side to De Gaulle. But one hour later, he had organized his thoughts for a meeting with Churchill. The prime minister, in one of his most jovial moods, assured him that even though the Americans had insisted that De Gaulle be kept out of the operation, and were now depending on Giraud, London would do everything in its power to maintain him "at the center of the political action." "Regardless of that," De Gaulle replied, "we will urge the French to fight beside the Americans."

At eight o'clock that evening, the leader of fighting France spoke again on the radio: "Now, at last, the great moment is here! This is the hour for courage and good sense. . . . Frenchmen of North Africa, let it be through you that we return to the line of battle from one end of the Mediterranean to the other, and the war will then be won because of France."

The improbable floundering about that took place in Algiers from the eighth to the tenth of November— extending even beyond the cease-fire Juin extracted from Darlan, the "oblivion" of Giraud in Gibraltar, and the investiture in power of Darlan himself by the Americans—served to increase the prestige of General de Gaulle, whose absence suddenly became more of a problem than his presence.

The phase which began for De Gaulle in this manner was perhaps the most significant of his life. It was at that time that his individual personality was clarified, acquired density, took on that hardness and brilliance which a jeweler, speaking of a diamond, would describe as belonging to a stone "of the first water." Not just because within ten months he would outwit and eliminate the unfortunate General Giraud —who in this case was no more than an artichoke to be eaten leaf by leaf by a rival who had sharpened his teeth on tougher foods—but because he, this supposed Machiavellian and disciple of Maurras, would symbolize the irreducible part played by morals and faith in any great political movement. And not, certainly, through his actions or his propositions, which would continue to seem cynical and often brutal, but because he would symbolize the man for whom there exists, in all matters of state, an absolute, a categorical imperative, a system of values.

In a sense, it is disturbing that this man, who had given so many proofs of the slight importance he attached to men, should have demonstrated with naked simplicity that when it is a question of liberty and national integrity a Darlan could not be substituted for a De Gaulle, a Laval for a Jean Moulin—no matter how "useful" such substitution might have seemed. It is even more surprising that in this particular tournament it should have been the Anglo-Saxon puritan, Franklin Roosevelt, who wore the colors of cynical pragmatism, of "the temporary expedient," and De Gaulle who carried those of men who were willing to die because, if "Paris vaut bien une messe," as Henri IV said, it must not be just any mass. The former, of course, spoke as a man responsible for enormous enterprises. The latter, isolated, was almost without responsibility. But the situation does not explain everything. De Gaulle's clarity of vision, here as in the summer of 1940, reforged statesmanship, though leaving him free to forget it later.

De Gaulle, faced with "expedients," was obviously not Joan of Arc before her judges. Antigone kept Creon's objectives constantly in view and made a trump of virtue. But where, in public affairs, does the argument of utility end? Let us listen for a moment to De Gaulle, speaking to Churchill, on November 16, 1942: "It is a strategic error to act in contradiction to the moral character of this war. . . . Today, we are making war with the soul, the blood, the suffering of peoples. . . . If France should one day be forced to recognize that—because of the Anglo-Saxons—liberation has come to her in the form of Darlan, you might perhaps have won the war from a military point of view, but you will have lost it morally, and in the final analysis there would be only one winner: Stalin."

Actually, De Gaulle was not so completely excluded from Algiers as he appeared to be. Professor René Capitant, his colleague on the General Staff of the Fifth Army during the winter of 1939-1940, had gathered together a little group of Gaullist partisans there and made it into a North African antenna for Frenay's *Combat* network on the mainland. Even before the first waves of American assault troops had arrived on the beaches and in the harbor, this group had carried out a model *putsch*, occupying several public buildings and neutralizing Admiral Darlan, whose presence in Algiers was a surprise to the Allies (he was there, by chance, as a result of the mortal illness of his son, who was stationed in the city). Capitant, and other Gaullist sympathizers—José Aboulker, Guy Calvet, Commissioner Achiary, Colonel Jousse, and Van Hecke, the director of the Vichy-founded but Resistance-controlled youth movement—were unable to carry through with this first phase of their enterprise. But even though they were ousted now by Darlan's neo-Vichy authorities, they bided their time and set about assembling the means to carry out their purpose.

The leader of Free France was not entirely removed from the heart of other things, either. The meeting with Roosevelt, which had been "in the air" for three months, was finally set for the twenty-sixth of December. And the British government showered him with marks of sympathy. In his *Memoirs,* De Gaulle quotes Churchill as telling him, "For you, the situation is magnificent. Giraud has been liquidated politically. And in the long run, Darlan will be impossible. You will be the only one left. But don't clash head-on with the Americans. Be patient. They will come to you because there is no alternative."

In the meantime, the Anglo-Saxons continued to find fault with the statements of Charles de Gaulle, who bluntly removed himself from any part in the dealings with Darlan. But De Gaulle obtained Eisenhower's authorization for one of his aides, General d'Astier, to see the admiral. The brother of the leader of *Libération* attempted to convince Darlan that he should now bow out; and when he returned to London on December 24th he informed General de Gaulle that the admiral "senses that the ground is shifting beneath his feet, and will give up his post very shortly."

This was the day on which all of the Algiers conspiracies came to a head in a whirlpool of intrigue led by Robert Murphy on the American side, by Jacques Lemaigre-Dubreuil for the adherents of Giraud, by General Bergeret for the Pétainists, by Abbé Cordier for the royalists, and by José Aboulker for the Gaullists. At three o'clock in the afternoon, Admiral Darlan was assassinated by Fernand Bonnier de la Chapelle, a young and militant royalist. De Gaulle wasted no time on pity. Noting briefly that Darlan's tragic end provided a form of reprieve for faults which, though due to an ambition to be absolute master of the navy, must be attributed primarily to the "long infirmity of the State," he decided—Creon was never very far away—"to take advantage of it."

He proposed to Giraud that they meet immediately to establish a provisional central power, now made urgently necessary by the dramatic events in Algiers —an offer which was promptly rejected because of the "unfavorable atmosphere." And thus began the long combat with Giraud. Against De Gaulle, what could a man like that do—that good, tradition-steeped officer who "as a colonel, was brilliant," according to Catroux's ironic definition, but whom the malicious hazards of the military career had made into a general of the army; that proconsul in Africa whose policy there would soon be summed up in a famous slogan: "The Jews in their shops, the Arabs at their plows"? There can be no doubt that the "civilian and military commander in chief" had the unqualified support of the Americans, or that there was a very large section of French public opinion which was eager to dissociate itself from Vichy—that is to say, from the approaching defeat of the Germans—and happy to find in Giraud a Pétain sponsored by the conquerors. But against a duelist as clumsy and rigid as that, De Gaulle was a virtuoso, and there could be no doubt of the eventual winner. Giraud was only an alibi. De Gaulle was a force—a force capable of using every available means to rally the strength of a people for whom liberation from nazism was not just a matter of "expediency," but a revolution.

Since the spring day when General Giraud had succeeded in escaping from Koenigstein and returning to France, De Gaulle had attempted several times to secure his cooperation. On what plane? Since the time when he had served under his orders in 1938, the author of *The Army of the Future* had had no great regard for Giraud's talents; and Giraud, as we have seen, detested him. But the figure of the former governor of Metz was well enough known for him to be of interest as an advocate of fighting France, and for De Gaulle, there was no military command that took precedence over political authority. Giraud, however, had been told by Lemaigre-Dubreuil in May that he would have the support of the Americans, so he never deigned to reply.

Nevertheless, with Darlan removed from the scene, he now had one point of terrible vulnerability in any debate concerning a sharing of tasks and responsibilities in the struggle against the Axis. On May 4, 1942, in order to avoid being returned to a German prison, he had signed a letter to Marshal Pétain (of which there was a copy in London) which read: "I give you my word as an officer that I will do nothing which might, in any manner, embarrass your relations with the German government or interfere with the work you have charged Admiral Darlan and Premier Laval with accomplishing in your name. My past is a guarantee of my loyalty." A document which hardly pointed him out as the ideal military leader of a coalition directed against the Reich.

General Giraud did not consent to meet De Gaulle, however, until the day when Roosevelt and Churchill asked them to come together at the Casablanca conference. In De Gaulle's reservations about accepting the offer, as well as in the attack on Giraud with which he prefaced the meeting (in his eyes, Giraud was guilty of having accepted an invitation from *foreigners* to a meeting on *French sovereign territory*— a statement which was bold, to say the least, when it is remembered that the meeting took place in the

Moroccan protectorate) there was evident again that character, at once grandiose and ridiculous, which seemed to reflect the chauvinism of Déroulède and the passion for etiquette of the Duc de Saint-Simon. (We can almost hear Saint-Simon: "Monsieur de Gaulle had no equal in his arrogance of place, and being seated next to a prince who was not of the blood royal was an affront so grievous to him that it was likely to make him ill.") But this hair-splitting conceit was also a strategy. And because the chairs had to be moved around to suit his whim, De Gaulle would leave Casablanca a larger figure, and Free France would share in the new image.

At last, Charles de Gaulle found himself face to face with Franklin Roosevelt. There are only a few vague reports on the meeting. Harry Hopkins says almost nothing about it except that the general was constantly watched by a dozen bodyguards armed with submachineguns—which struck the American presidential adviser as being extremely funny. According to De Gaulle's account, Roosevelt made no attempt to conceal from him his determination that since the United States would henceforth be furnishing the principal war effort, the peace was going to be an American peace, in France as elsewhere. "We assaulted each other with good manners," De Gaulle writes, with the somewhat heavy-handed irony which is a part of the charm of his *Memoirs.*

But the President obviously could not obtain his agreement to his plan—which had been endorsed by Churchill and Giraud—for creating a directory of three generals, presided over by the latter and seconded by De Gaulle and Georges. The leader of the Free French, for his part, proposed the constitution of a provisional government in Algiers, with himself as president and Giraud as commander in chief. After a Churchill-De Gaulle meeting, which was, according

128

to the general, "the roughest of their encounters," and two further meetings between De Gaulle and Giraud, the conference broke up on a note of almost total disagreement. But not before De Gaulle, haughtily, and "to please the President," had consented to clasp Giraud's hand briefly for the benefit of American cameras. A draw? Apparently.

By demanding too much, had Charles de Gaulle obtained nothing? No. In the future, he would have a delegate in Algiers—Catroux—whose superior abilities would rapidly assert themselves in the conflict with Giraud. And in spite of the annoying, deceptive outbursts of Casablanca, he had managed to impose his presence, even though he had been forced to wait to impose his ideas. From this time on, in their secret correspondence Roosevelt and Churchill would refer to him as "the bride"—a figure who might be laughable, but without whom the ceremony could not go on.

Algiers, after this, resembled the slow swinging of a pendulum from Giraudism to Gaullism. All of the mechanisms which played a part in the renewal of political life were at odds with Giraud's neo-Vichy ideas. Although he decreed the arrest of the Gaullists who had carried out the *putsch* of November 8th, he was forced to release them almost immediately. If he retarded the abolition of the anti-Jewish laws, he caused temperatures to rise. If he consented to it, it was a concession of defeat. *Combat*, with René Capitant as its leader, became the dynamo of the embryonic regime, while the communists, as soon as they were released from prison, revived their propaganda and set to work to reform their organizations. The most intelligent of Giraud's partisans, from Jean Monnet to Maurice Couve de Murville, recognized the situation for what it was: without De Gaulle, the theater of Algiers was a theater of shadows.

But it was primarily in France, now entirely occupied by the Germans, that the evolution was decisive. The arrival of the Wehrmacht and the Gestapo in parts of the country previously unoccupied radically altered the character of the Resistance and incited the various different networks to coordinate their efforts: the surge of popular emotions swung the pendulum in favor of the man of June 18th. On May 27th, Jean Moulin informed London that the National Council of the Resistance, in its first full meeting, had called for the constitution of a provisional government in Algiers presided over by General de Gaulle, "the sole chief of the French Resistance."

It was on this day that De Gaulle, who had been invited ten days earlier by Giraud to come and "form with him the French central power," decided to leave London for Algiers. The move was dictated by developments in the struggle against nazism on the soil of France itself, not just acceptance of a call from a colleague installed in his position by the Americans. But his own relations with the Allies had scarcely been improved. On May 8th, Roosevelt had written to Churchill: "The conduct of the bride is becoming more and more unbearable. He is installing his venomous General Staff of propagandists in Algiers in order to create discord there. . . . De Gaulle may be an honest man, but he is a victim of a Messiah complex. When we go into France, we are going to have to consider it as a military occupation. . . . As for De Gaulle, I don't know what to do about him. Perhaps you would like to name him governor of Madagascar?"

On the thirtieth of May, the leader of the Free French landed in Algiers, and was met at the airport by Giraud.

"*Bonjour, mon général . . .*"

"*Bonjour, Gaulle . . .*"

Regardless of the protocol, the soldier with the splendid moustaches was no longer anything more than a member of the supporting cast. Naturally, the French Committee for National Liberation, created on June 2nd, had two presidents. But no one was deceived by this, and on the next day it was to De Gaulle that Peyrouton—on request from Colonel Jousse, one of the earliest Gaullists—handed in his resignation as governor-general of Algeria. He was replaced by Catroux. Giraud had not even been informed of it, and his reaction was sharp. To even the score with his rival, he named Admiral Muselier prefect of police for Algiers, knowing full well that Muselier had broken with De Gaulle immediately after the Saint Pierre and Miquelon operation. It was a wasted effort.

In the following month (until his departure for the United States, where he had been invited by Roosevelt) the naïve "co-president" found himself being gradually stripped of his majority in the councils of the French Committee for National Liberation (the CFLN) and of his civil responsibilities—a prelude to loss of his military prerogatives. And all of this in spite of the efforts on his behalf made by Churchill on June 5th ("I was afraid," he wrote to De Gaulle, "that you might have swallowed Giraud at one gulp"), and by General Eisenhower on the nineteenth. It is worth considering the tone—variously pitying, sarcastic, and almost contrite—in which De Gaulle reported his victory: "I would rather not have had to pluck the poor man. But what other means did I have?"

On July 31st, Giraud returned from his trip to the United States and took part in the meeting of the committee which plunged him into total obscurity: General Juin was appointed commander of the French expeditionary force for Italy, and the post of titular commander in chief was no more than a fiction. Giraud, who was no longer even asked his opinion by Robert Murphy and General Mark Clark, resigned himself to being what he was—but not without having played one last trick on De Gaulle: the capture "by stealth" of Corsica, a privateering adventure completely in the manner of this warrior who had missed his proper century. On August 29th, when London, Washington, and Moscow recognized the CFLN as the provisional government of France, it was De Gaulle alone who was its master.

So now he was really in power. In three years, Paul Reynaud's undersecretary of state for national defense had become the leader of the only governmental organism in a position to represent France in this city of Algiers to which he had wanted to lead his colleagues of the time. It had been a long detour, filled with cruel vicissitudes. But he was now at the head of what remained of the State, and he intended to lead it directly toward full restoration, and participation in the final campaigns of the war. But how did he exercise this power when he was compelled to measure it against an opposition which was diffident at first, then firm and sometimes bitter—the Consultative Assembly, inaugurated in Algiers on November 3, 1943?

The man who for so many months had been Charles-the-Alone in London found it difficult to detach the idea of power from the idea of secrecy, of arbitrary decisions, of a continuing test of strength, of the techniques of gathering intelligence, of bureaus and of courts—one might almost say of the seraglio, although the Algerian atmosphere had little effect on this haughty sultan. One of the most curious aspects of this Algerian regime was the extent to which the center of power was separated from a society whose extraordinary contrasts would only become apparent later. From the Villa des Oliviers in the city to his little house in Kabylia, De Gaulle lived in Algiers as Rommel had lived in the desert, as a nomad. A few collaborators, such as Louis Joxe, made his contacts for him. He would not really discover Algiers until 1958. . . .

France, as seen from Algiers, was the Resistance. And the Resistance was not only (if one can use that word) heroic little groups of exceptional men who had voluntarily entered into a merciless adventure; after November, 1942, it was also an underground army drafted—sometimes thoughtlessly—by patriots whose capacities were not always on a plane with their intentions, or by *condottieri* heedless of risk or of any central planning. But those were considerations which could not depreciate the military importance of these forces at the end of 1943—an importance which Eisenhower recognized openly when he paid tribute to the men involved. But what of Charles de Gaulle? Did the man in whose name so many others gathered together at the risk of their lives always weigh his responsibility to them? Did he give to their endeavors the same thoughtful care he devoted to taking precedence over so-and-so at such-and-such a diplomatic reunion?

The gap that separated the men who were making the revolution in France and the men who were preparing for the restoration of the State in Algiers can be glimpsed in dozens of accounts of the Resistance, from that (highly partisan, of course) of Charles Tillon, communist leader of the FTP, to the evocation of the drama of Vercors by novelist Alain Prévost, son of Jean Prévost, a noted writer who was one of the leaders of the *maquis* in that region. And even though he occupied a position of great responsibility in Algiers, Emmanuel d'Astier occasionally gives indications of the same situation. His efforts to obtain arms for the Resistance from Churchill—first at Marrakech, and then in London in 1943 and again in 1944—sometimes appear to have been a personal initiative, rather

133

than the carrying out of directives received by the minister of Charles de Gaulle.

It must, however, be noted that when a communist newspaper in Algiers accused the provisional government of having done nothing to aid the Resistance fighters in the Vercors, De Gaulle demanded that Fernand Grenier, communist deputy who was then minister of the air force, choose between a written apology to his colleagues and resignation from the government: this representative of the Communist party in the cabinet preferred to sign the honorable reparation dictated to him by Louis Joxe, under the mocking eyes of the other ministers.

Some of the problems which would be storm centers of politics in later years were already cropping up in Algiers—among them the matter of political purges (Pucheu, a former minister of the Vichy government, would be shot in spite of the guarantee of safety Giraud had given him) and of decolonization. The government was actually in the colonies, and as early as November, 1942, immediately after the Allied landings, Ferhat Abbas published his "autonomist" manifesto. De Gaulle would never forgive (as would be seen in 1960-62) this Algerian politician for having attempted to obtain from the Americans something which, in his eyes, only France had the right to grant. Monsieur Abbas would shortly find himself under house arrest in an oasis south of Oran. The Algerian "long march" had begun. And in January, 1944, Charles de Gaulle was to preside over a conference in Brazzaville in which he would attempt to win acceptance of the idea of individual emancipation of the colonized peoples, through education and self-help, rather than through a large-scale liberation of nationalities.

The nation whose custody he had assumed was

being reborn, both on the battlefields and in the diplomatic councils.

In December, 1943, after having contributed an expeditionary corps to the Allied forces in the invasion of Italy, France was invited to take part with the United States, Great Britain, and the Soviet Union in the work of the Consultative Commission for that country. It marked her "reentry" on the world stage. But De Gaulle himself was not invited to the conference at Teheran, at which, that same month, Stalin obtained Roosevelt's support against Churchill's plan to direct the next Allied landings against Yugoslavia and Greece and then strike up at Vienna and Central Europe—a plan which would have created obstacles to the occupation of the eastern European states by the U.S.S.R. The president of the CFLN was annoyed that he was still being kept in a kind of quarantine, but his presence at the conference would have altered none of its essential conclusions, since he too was opposed to the Churchill plan. In his impatience to see France play a vital role in the last days of the war, he was willing to see her become a field of battle.

And the hour was approaching for a final settlement of accounts with the Nazis on the European soil they had conquered, but which now was beginning to burn beneath their feet. In 1942, to the vast disappointment of General de Gaulle, the Allies had decided on Operation Torch instead of Sledgehammer—the circuitous movement through Africa and then through Italy, instead of a frontal attack on western Europe. Now, the plans for Sledgehammer were dusted off and transformed into Overlord: western Europe would be liberated through a landing in France.

But how would France herself be freed? What authority would be substituted for that of the Reich? De Gaulle remembered André Philip's meeting with Roosevelt in November, 1942, and therefore knew the

American President's intentions only too well: to impose on the French a regime of military occupation—AMGOT (Allied Military Government of Occupied Territories). For months now, Americans had been attending classes at Charlottesville, Virginia—classes in which, in the space of sixty days, they were expected to learn not only the French language but the art of becoming prefect of Rennes or subprefect of Langon. . . . The chief of the Free French would never have tolerated the power of these "sixty-day wonders"; much less would the president of the CFLN—which, on May 15, 1944, became the "Provisional Government of the French Republic."

But General de Gaulle accepted the invitation of the chief of the British government, who wanted him in Great Britain at the time of the landings in France. And after having received a new invitation from Roosevelt to come to Washington, he landed in London on June 4th. He was just in time: a trifle later and he would have repeated—aside from the reversal of residence—the humiliating experience of November 8, 1942.

A few hours later, accompanied by Pierre Viénot, a former undersecretary of state of Léon Blum who was now the provisional government's ambassador in London, and by General Béthouart (who had become chief of staff after narrowly escaping a firing squad in Meknès), De Gaulle was greeted by Churchill in the headquarters the prime minister had set up in a train about twenty miles outside of Portsmouth. With his passion for history and drama, and a memory rich in the climactic moments of the last war, Churchill had recreated the atmosphere of the railway car in which the armistice was signed at Rethondes. Anthony Eden and Ernest Bevin were with him.

In a tone befitting a herald of Henry V, Churchill began describing what the landings would be like. As a connoisseur of this sort of thing, De Gaulle was properly admiring. But suddenly the prime minister was discussing political problems, suggesting that Roosevelt's agreement be obtained for the installation of an administrative and military regime for liberated France. With cold brutality, General de Gaulle cut him off:

Do you think I have to submit my candidacy for the government of France to Roosevelt, or to you? The French government exists! I have just been told that the troops taking part in the landings have been provided with a so-called French currency, printed abroad—and the government of the Republic absolutely does not recognize it! . . . I shouldn't be surprised if Eisenhower were to announce tomorrow that he is taking France under his authority. How do you expect us to come to any agreement on such a basis?

Approached in this manner, Churchill replied in kind: "I want you to know, General de Gaulle, that every time we must choose between Europe and the open sea we will choose the sea. . . . Between you and Roosevelt, I will always choose Roosevelt!" Bevin put in a word to indicate that this was not the point of view of all the British political leaders. Having thus contributed—or so he thought—to easing the tension, he attempted to bring the discussion back to the problems of administration in France. De Gaulle was furious, and cried: "We are here to discuss only military matters! Policy and administration are French affairs, and only French affairs. . . . And don't let me hear any more about your counterfeit money!"*

At Eisenhower's headquarters on June 5th, De Gaulle was briefed on the details of Operation Over-

* From a personal interview of the author with General Béthouart.

lord. In a rare display of modesty, he did not point out that the project bore a strong resemblance to the one he had outlined with Billotte in the spring of 1942. Returning to Carlton Gardens that night, he handed the file on the earlier plan to his chief of staff, and made a sound resembling laughter: "Well, this might at least have helped to inspire those people. . . ." In his *Memoirs*, he states that the only point of disagreement between Eisenhower and himself at the time had to do with the proclamation prepared in Washington for the supreme commander, since this did not even mention "the French authority which has maintained and directed the war effort of our people for years, and which has done General Eisenhower the honor of placing under his command a large part of the French army." It is true that the debates on cardinal points of strategy and the employment of major French units had taken place six months earlier in connection with the Italian campaign.

On December 27, 1943, in a discussion in Algiers with the Anglo-Americans, De Gaulle had threatened to withhold all of his forces unless he was allowed to select the division which would be sent to reinforce the First Army in Italy; unless he was given assurance that another division (Leclerc's) would be reserved for the liberation of Paris; and unless there was a formal engagement to launch Operation Anvil—the landings on the Mediterranean coast of France—shortly after Overlord. He had won on all of these points.

For his part, General Eisenhower wrote in *Crusade in Europe* (Doubleday, 1948) that from the American point of view it was impossible to grant De Gaulle in advance the thing he wanted immediately, namely clear and definitive recognition as the only person who "had the right to give orders to the French

138

population in directing the necessary co-operation with the Allied forces. . . . We worked hard, within the limits of our instructions, to win De Gaulle to our point of view, but although after the campaign was started he co-operated with us effectively, he did not meet our requests at the moment."

Charles de Gaulle is not easily made happy. The closer the hour of liberation drew, the sharper his humor became.

He was more strongly resolved than ever to make life difficult for his hosts. When Mr. Charles Peake was detached from the Foreign Office to serve as a liaison officer with De Gaulle's staff, De Gaulle learned the news, as he wrote, "with great pleasure for myself, and some commiseration for him." And in fact, he promptly stirred up another storm by refusing to speak on the BBC after the rulers of the other occupied countries, and especially after Eisenhower, since he did not want to appear to endorse what the supreme commander was scheduled to say. He disapproved of it.

This time, Churchill's fury was on a plane with his genius: he dictated, on the spur of the moment, a letter in which he called on General de Gaulle to leave British territory. . . . But the unhappy Mr. Peake would not be compelled to carry lightning to Prometheus: Eden, in agreement with the French ambassador, Pierre Viénot, suppressed the message, and nothing more was heard of it.

6
The
Sacred Rites

And then it was dawn of June the sixth. With every hour that passed, freedom returned to another corner of French soil. De Gaulle remained completely silent until six o'clock in the evening. Not until then would he issue his summons to the nation: "For the sons of France, wherever they may be, whoever they may be, the simple and sacred duty is to fight the enemy with every means at his disposal. . . . The orders given by the French government and by the French leaders appointed to this task by the government must be followed to the letter." De Gaulle contradicted Eisenhower on two points: (a) far from calling for calm among those who were not immediately involved in military operations, as the supreme commander had desired, he called for a general uprising; (b) he spoke of discipline only in connection with "French" leaders. Were the risks involved in such a program on a level with the political and moral satisfaction he expected to derive? He also ordered the administrative liaison officers to have as little as possible to do with the Anglo-Saxons and not to "contribute to any usurpation"—of French sovereignty, obviously.

It was not until after a week of acrimonious bickering, which Eden and Viénot did their best to smooth over, that he judged the conditions were fulfilled for a visit to France by the president of the Provisional Government of the French Republic: on the thirteenth of June, De Gaulle boarded *La Combattante* at Portsmouth. Very early on the morning of the fourteenth, he set foot on a beach between Sainte-Mère-Église and Courseulles, accompanied by Viénot, d'Argenlieu, Béthouart, Billotte, Palewski, Boislambert, Courcel, Teyssot, Coulet—who would shortly be named Commissioner of the Republic for the Liberated Areas—and Chevigné, the military commandant of the sector.

For De Gaulle, this was the major test: he was the Dauphin confronting Joan for the first time. Would the people of France "recognize" him, as the maid had recognized her king? The films which were made on this tremendous day are extremely revealing. Against a desolate background of stricken villages, the man of June 18th seems a timid interloper surrounded by an equally timid people. But each of them is measuring the other, adjusting to each other, "considering" each other. He walked with a step that was a trifle uncertain; he did not yet have that air and that assurance of an old champion (which he was to assume later) making his way, unperturbed, through the popular turmoil. He was still a temporary leader, and "the laurels of the gods" did not yet sit upon his brow. Normandy, to tell the truth, was not the promised land of wartime Gaullism (the men of the 2nd Armored Division were to learn this later, and be resentful).

The countenance was surprising; the gait, the height, the look of this personage disconcerted the children, the priests, and the gendarmes of Bayeux and Isigny—because they had been made to be disconcerting—but the name spoke to all. The crowd gathered around him, still surprised, but more and more attentive, becoming warm. The sharp-angled

141

voice of the man who had stood proxy for the nation, the nocturnal, demanding voice was the voice of this giant in an earth-colored jacket who strode through their midst, surveying the ruins of his country with an air that was at once sad and proud.

The plebiscite had not yet been held, but an option had been taken. And in the same way that he had learned to deduce the results of a presidential election by a glance at the returns from the state of Maine, Franklin Roosevelt knew that day that General de Gaulle was destined to govern France. On the fifteenth of June, immediately after his return to London, the president of the Provisional Government of the French Republic received a visit from Anthony Eden, who, as the general writes in his *Memoirs*, informed him that President Roosevelt "is only waiting for you to come to Washington to revise his position."

So De Gaulle went to America. In a surprising psychological turnabout, he made no attempt to conceal the pleasure he derived from the trip. One of his closest and most constant companions states that he had never seen Charles de Gaulle in such an equable, happy frame of mind as he was during this visit among the Americans.

And this time, the Roosevelt-De Gaulle meeting would not be a scene from a spy novel, as it had been at Casablanca. The general knew that he was the guest of the most powerful man in the world, and the President knew that he was talking to the most powerful man in France—at a time when his armies were venturing into that country like fish into an unknown sea. De Gaulle refrained from expressing indignation when Woodrow Wilson's successor outlined his dream of a universe governed by four "great powers"—the United States, the Soviet Union, Great Britain, and China. After all, this man was—as he writes in his *Memoirs*—a "great spirit," an "artist"

142

whose "idealism . . . cloaks a will to power," and a man who had "a very real love" of France.

Curiously enough, the theories of this man whose political philosophy was diametrically opposed to his own neither moved nor irritated him; they served only to confirm him in his old ideas: "In matters affecting nations, logic and sentiment weigh very little in comparison with the realities of power; the important thing is to take it and to know how to hold on to it." The general himself must have shown proof of a light and agile mind, since Roosevelt closed the interview—according to De Gaulle's account—with these words: "In the matter of serving France, it's true that nothing could replace the French people." The people . . .

But this apparently harmonious interview, related in De Gaulle's *Memoirs*, was to have an echo that sounded a false note. A few days later, the general received a photostat of a letter addressed to a member of Congress in which Roosevelt commented on the attitude of his guest: "When it is a matter of future problems he seems completely 'manageable' from the moment when France is considered as a world power. He is highly sensitive to anything concerning the honor of France. But I think that he is essentially an egoist." It is a remark which permitted De Gaulle to close the matter with one of the passages in his *Memoirs* of which he himself is most fond—and which sums up one of the problems the man in the White House would not be the only person to ponder: "I will never know if Franklin Roosevelt thought that, in anything concerning France, Charles de Gaulle was an egoist for France, or simply for himself."

After Washington, it was time for a surprise sidetrip. The stocky little mayor of New York, Fiorello La Guardia, a character who seemed to have stepped out of a Frank Capra film, greeted the Constable with a

completely Sicilian display of affection. They stood together on the steps of City Hall, waving to the crowds,
looking like Mutt and Jeff. But the thing that was
strange was the mass of people that pressed around
him, cheering and applauding when he spoke a few
words of friendship in his awkward English. In his
automobile later, he said to Pierre Mendès-France,
then his assistant: "So my partisans here are the poor,
the immigrants, the Jews, the Negroes, the Puerto
Ricans?"

It was here, rather than in Normandy, that he
would learn that even for a Constable the pursuit of
a certain policy meant taking a certain position, and
that this in turn meant dependence on a certain support. (Fourteen years later, he would verify this fact.
The acclaim of the shopkeepers and the little milliners
would, in its turn, define a policy which charmed
the "crowd" rather than the people.) That night in
New York, he was carried away from a dinner with
Monsignor Spellman and lifted onto a stage in Madi-
son Square Garden while Marian Anderson sang the
"Marseillaise." Half-moved, half-irritated, he snapped
to his aide-de-camp on the way back to his hotel:
"You'll send some flowers to that woman!"

But it was also a trip "that paid." On July 12th, the
American government published a statement in which
it recognized that "the French Committee of National
Liberation is qualified to carry out administrative affairs in France." And at the beginning of the month
of August, De Gaulle, Roosevelt, and Churchill
reached agreement on a text which stated that only
the Provisional Government of the French Republic
should exercise the powers of government—furnishing
assistance to the Allied armies and putting into circulation a legal currency.

Charles de Gaulle was now in a position in which
he could proclaim—immoderately, and resorting for

144

the first time to the use of a "we" in which there was less evidence of the figures of his companions than of an affirmation of a monarchist style: "And now, let the great battle of France go forward. . . . We are bringing back to France her independence, her Empire, and her sword."

He had won the battle against the Allies. And now he was face-to-face with the French people: confronted with those who had fought when he had called on them to fight, and whose enormous hope in him must not be deceived; confronted with those who had come into the struggle for other reasons and who were watching him mistrustfully; confronted with the enormous mass of those who had done nothing but survive, and who scarcely knew his name; and confronted with those who "had followed the marshal," with those who had secretly wished for the victory of the "new European order" when they hadn't actively taken part in it, and for whom he was the enemy. This fanatic on the subject of unity, who had himself taken the risk of secession, was now at the storm center of a conflict in which five years of history had given new stimulus to the class struggle and the confrontation of ideologies.

He felt that there were two possibilities which might still deprive him of the "summit meeting" with the people of Paris, which would be the foundation of his "legitimacy" just as his meeting with the people of Bayeux had been the basis of his new relations with the Allies. The first was a plot of Laval—Pétain's prime minister—to call together in Paris the members of the 1940 National Assembly and set up a new government with Herriot as prime minister; and the second, the proclamation of a new Paris Commune by the Communist party, which now controlled most of the key posts in the Resistance, particularly in the Paris area. In spite of American encouragement, how-

145

ever, the president of the Radical party refused to enter into any of Pierre Laval's schemes; and the communists were less concerned at the moment with seizing the apparatus of the State than with securing an overwhelming option on the later direction and functioning of both government and production.

Did De Gaulle really, at that time, fear the possibility of a *coup d'état* by the party of Maurice Thorez? De Gaulle's chief delegate in France, Alexandre Parodi, sent him cable after cable, attempting to convince him of the fallacy of such an assumption: "Just make an appearance here, and you will see. . . ." But the first security officials he placed in office—Coulet in Normandy, Luizet in Paris—were insistently reminded to be on guard against any infringement of their authority by the various liberation committees, which were deeply infiltrated by communists. His own objective was to break so sharply with the collapsing regime of Pétain that the communists would not be permitted to take exclusive credit, in the eyes of the French people, for the liberation and revolution.

Operation Anvil, in which General de Lattre and the First French Army were playing a major role, had already been under way for five days. The German occupant was caught in an enormous pair of pincers extending from Coutances to Saint-Raphaël, and the uprising in the capital was several hours old, when De Gaulle decided to leave Algiers and "appear" before the people of Paris. On August 20th, he landed at an airport near Saint-Lô and went immediately to see Eisenhower: the American armies were at Mantes and Melun, and while Patton prepared to strike out toward the east, Montgomery was slowly pushing back the troops of Von Kluge.

"And Paris? Why is nothing being done about Paris, where the people are already in arms?"—"It's too soon," the supreme commander answered. De Gaulle extracted Eisenhower's promise that the 2nd Armored Division—Leclerc's division—would be ordered on to Paris "shortly": he let it be understood that if the order were too long delayed, he would assume the responsibility of giving it himself.

In fact, Eisenhower was waging a war of tactics, sound precautionary tactics based on logistics. De Gaulle introduced the psychology of the masses into the debate, waging a total war—in which policy and techniques were inextricably mingled—and reasoning on a level of grand strategy, even though it was on the reduced scale of a single theater of operations. It was a recurrence of his leitmotiv: tactics is the affair of generals, even when they are in command of millions of men, but strategy is the prerogative of governments, even when they are almost without arms. It would be seen again in later years, from Strasbourg to the question of NATO, that whenever he considered something to be on a governmental level De Gaulle felt free *to reassume his freedom of action.* Sovereignty and policy came first. At last, on the night of August 22nd, Eisenhower set the hunting pack of French tanks on the path of their quarry. Paris was within reach: the Constable's triumph would take place the next day.

Not quite. Basing their action on information furnished by the Anglo-Saxons, which led them to think the Allied forces would not be in Paris for weeks, Parodi, his civilian delegate, and Chaban-Delmas, the military delegate, had just accepted a proposal of the Swedish consul, Raoul Nordling, and concluded a truce with the governor of Paris, Dietrich von Choltitz: it was a matter of sparing the capital from a destruction for which the German general had a signed order from Adolf Hitler in his pocket. Did De Gaulle know the full extent of this threat, the real stakes in this desperate game? Since the communists,

147

strengthened by their sacrifices and sensing the enemy trapped, were already preparing to acclaim themselves the victors of a new Stalingrad, he disapproved of this respite.

But the majority of the fighting men of Paris had already disdained the delegates' orders for a ceasefire. Burning their bridges behind them, they had wagered everything that Leclerc would be there in time.

Swept from Nogent-le-Rotrou through Chartres "by a kind of wave of joy," De Gaulle arrived in Rambouillet on the night of the twenty-third. He had told Leclerc he would meet him there ("I expect to be in Rambouillet tonight, and to see you there. I embrace you. C. de Gaulle"). And the man of Koufra was there, the worn kepi accenting the clear, blue eyes of a child, the jaw set and hard, seeming very thin in his dusty battle dress, carrying the cane he had carried in the desert, a young wolf hunting wolves. If ever De Gaulle had looked on anyone with total friendship, it was that night with this young brother-in-arms whom he was sending out to meet the people of Paris. Until tomorrow, at Montparnasse—I envy you! From Athos to d'Artagnan . . .

August 25th: Longjumeau, Bourg-la-Reine, and then Paris, the Porte d'Orléans—so many faces—the Avenue du Maine, the Gare Montparnasse. Here at last, would he give free rein to his exuberance? His son Philippe, an officer in the naval marines, was already there, but left almost immediately to take part in the attack on the Palais Bourbon, which was still occupied by the Germans. And Von Choltitz had just surrendered to Leclerc's men. But because the signature of Colonel Rol-Tanguy, the communist leader of the Parisian insurgents, appeared on the text of the enemy capitulation beside Leclerc's, De Gaulle harshly reprimanded the young general for encouraging the tendency of the Resistance fighters to substitute themselves for the State.

It is for this reason that he did not want to go at once to a meeting with the people of Paris at the Hôtel de Ville. He went instead to the Ministry of War on the rue Saint-Dominique—less from any military reflex than to mark a continuity, to reaffirm a legitimacy. It was from this building that the undersecretary of state in the Reynaud cabinet had departed on June 10, 1940. Inspecting his surroundings with a sovereign eye, he found himself carried back four years, two months, and fifteen days: "Furnishings, hangings, individuals, ceremonial: nothing is missing, except the State. It is up to me to place it here. So it is here that I establish myself first."

But Parodi arrived, breathlessly: "The leaders of the Resistance are waiting for you at the Hôtel de Ville." De Gaulle greeted the unknown man he had made his representative in France—not just because he had stood up bravely to the Nazis, but because, in addition to this, he had been a member of the Council of State (for what reasons had he previously chosen Jean Moulin and Émile Bollaert for the same post, if not that these elected prefects of the Third Republic maintained the continuity of the State within the heart of the Resistance?)—and icily decreed that the leaders of the Parisian insurrection could wait.

It was not until after a visit to the headquarters of the Paris police, who had, in fact, played a decisive role in the liberation of the capital, that he arrived at the Hôtel de Ville. Georges Bidault, chairman of the National Council of the Resistance—who had been waiting for two hours and was indignant that the general should have given preference to "the cops"— welcomed him there, with his communist colleague Marrane at his side; and De Gaulle was lyrical enough to state that "Paris has been liberated by her people."

149

But when Bidault invited him to "solemnly proclaim the Republic" before the people assembled at the Hôtel de Ville, he drew this reply: "The Republic has never ceased to exist. Vichy was always null and void. . . . I myself am president of the government of the Republic. Why should I go out and proclaim it?" The thesis of his permanent legitimacy, which would reappear in 1960 . . .

The personage they saw—many of them for the first time—was possessed of a force, a diversity, a brutality that caused confusion. The man who had just uttered one of the most ardent—and the most "Parisian"—hymns of love to the city that had ever been heard, turned back from the steps of the Hôtel de Ville and was immediately in control of himself again. And in control of every detail of the business at hand —official gestures and tricks of protocol. The control of an artist in politics; quite the reverse of Lamartine in this same setting in 1848. There were many who felt that he might have accorded a more ample tribute to those who had accomplished the liberation of the country under the very guns of the Gestapo. . . . It was not a matter of a comparison of different forms of courage, but in this instance, the cold monster of the State suppressed individual emotions and spirit far too brutally.

The triumphal march would take place the next day, at the beginning of the afternoon. Everyone is familiar with those pictures of Charles de Gaulle striding down the Champs-Élysées on August 26, 1944. There is no point in dwelling on them. What is important here is that the "intractable" De Gaulle was capable of molding himself to the event, of offering himself as "a friend and a brother" to a crowd which might have become a disorderly or a panicky mob. Knowing that he had "neither the physique nor the taste for crowd-pleasing attitudes," he nonetheless

150

knew how to move through this long-imprisoned people—to whom his presence was like a writ of freedom—and maintain a nobility that bore no trace of condescension. Did he say to himself, as Clemenceau had on the night of November 11, 1918: "I would like to die now"? Probably not—less sentimental, less self-centered, less pessimistic, but even more proud, he was thinking of the history of France, of the place of France in the world, of his place in the history of France.

Perhaps he was not even thinking of the terrible risk he shared with this mass of people that surrounded him. He probably did not know that less than fifty miles from Paris a certain General Speidel had received a direct order from Marshal Model (who got it from the Führer) to unleash "a rain of V-1's and V-2's" on Paris. The American General Gerow had wisely tried to prevent De Gaulle's prodigious gamble, but he had been told: "The procession will bring about the political unity of the nation." But one hesitates to imagine what vespers in the churches of Paris might have been like that evening if the inner spring of the Nazi machine had not snapped.

To die? The idea scarcely occurred to De Gaulle even an hour later, when bursts of gunfire that seemed to come from the nearby rooftops scattered the crowds in the Place de la Concorde, then in the great square in front of Notre-Dame, and then within the cathedral itself. While those around him threw themselves to the ground, he leaned against a command car, with a cigarette dangling irritably from his lips. "What is all this commotion?" he demanded of Parodi. Ridiculous smudges across the clean surface of the triumph. It is not hard to picture him adding: "The delegate of General de Gaulle should know how to organize a liberation. . . ."

In his *Memoirs*, he would accuse the communists

(without actually citing them) of having used this means of provoking panic in order to justify the continued "vigilance" of the Resistance organizations, and especially of the Liberation Committee—in short, to maintain their position as guardians of the State. He brought no proof of the charge.

However that might be, on August 28th he notified the members of the National Council of the Resistance and the Paris Liberation Committee that their role in this capacity was finished, and that the irregular organizations would have to be merged into the State, the Government, and the Army—into which the "patriotic militias" would be integrated under control of the new military governor of Paris, General Koenig, who considered the French Forces of the Interior to be "the principal danger." He was to form these diverse groups into the 10th Infantry Division (the division of Paris), which would fight under the orders of Colonel Billotte, then De Gaulle's closest aide. It was just the first skirmish in the war of attrition between De Gaulle and the general staff of the revolution—but he won it.

With help from the "foreigner"? In *Crusade in Europe*, General Eisenhower has stated that the leader of the provisional government asked him for two American divisions at the time, to maintain order in Paris. For his part, De Gaulle says: "Pure invention," and goes on to his own explanation: "Naturally, I greeted the American divisions passing through the capital on their way to combat, but I certainly had not asked for them." As a matter of fact, it seems that General Koenig *did* ask for reinforcements, from an officer on General Gerow's staff. Dominique Lapierre and Larry Collins report this fact in *Is Paris Burning?*, and apparently it comes from a well-qualified source.

An argument between generals? Or a debate on principles? In any case, one thing is clear: being temperamentally averse to calling on foreigners for the protection of the State, and having let it be known that he reserved the right to any final decision regarding the use of Leclerc's troops, he was now planning to dispatch this *Garde Imperiale* on the route to Strasbourg, and was waiting only for the swiftest possible solution to its logistical problems (fuel, munitions, spare tracks for the tanks, etc.).

Now that Paris had invested him in office, the city disturbed him; but the place of France in the world, the prestige of France, and his own weight as a negotiator at the peace, could be affirmed by assuring the liberation of Alsace by French forces. It was a matter of affixing the national seal to the most significant single enterprise in the reunification of the nation. Once again, the mobility of arms was to be put at the service of a policy of symbols and of values.

What remained for him to do? Win the war. Rebuild the Republic. In the face of these tasks, who was he at this time, and what was his place in the nation?

At this stage, the man De Gaulle was, in the most proper sense of the term, insupportable. From this point on, he was to inflict on the entire world the character he had armored and armed against his overpowering allies: a character which was at least partially responsible for the condition of French independence in 1944. His talent had matured and developed, his political experience was already surprising, his "horizons" and his authority were vast. But the instant he took a step in the direction of human kindness—he was wary of it, but occasionally it trapped him—an incident which would form the pretext for marshaling the troops in a defensive square, with bayonets fixed, would occur. It might be a communiqué of Eisenhower's, published without his

153

knowledge; or a statement of one of the liberation committees praising the men of the Resistance and making no reference to the State; or a regiment the Americans had detached from the First French Army to pursue the enemy more closely. Whatever it was, he thundered and drew back into himself.

In the Council of Ministers, he let his people speak and occasionally went so far as to praise a particular summary—then presented his point of view, allowed himself to explain it, and delivered his verdict. His manner, when he preferred to refrain from authoritarianism, was neither negotiation, however brutal, nor conciliation: it was arbitration between two theses and two methods of application, which he would take up, reshape in his own hand, and then slice down the middle. In this manner, he ceded nothing, since the final solution, like the alternative, was his own. All of this was done in the highest style, and generally was imbued with the clearest sense of the long-term interest of the State—which, inevitably, was not always the short-term interest of the greatest number.

He had to discover his place in the opinion of the people at the same time as he discovered France, and he might sometimes have confused the cheers of a crowd with its innermost feelings. But he would define his position primarily in relation to two issues with which the country confronted him: implementation of the program of the National Council of the Resistance, and the matter of purges.

Since the creation of the CNR in the spring of 1943, the *maquis* and the various Resistance networks had theoretically placed themselves under the orders of Charles de Gaulle. But this allegiance did not prevent either the tensions brought about by the efforts of the liberation committees to maintain their positions of power, or the sometimes painful clashes with the leaders of the Resistance. From Lyons to Marseilles, from Toulouse to Bordeaux, De Gaulle was generous with his studied rebuffs to these men. In Toulouse, one of the most widely respected young leaders of the *maquis,* now the military commander of the place, introduced himself: Colonel Ravanel. "No," De Gaulle says icily, "Lieutenant Asher." At Montpellier, at the end of a line of colonels, very obviously newly promoted, he spotted a second lieutenant. His voice carried down the entire line: "What's the matter with you? Don't you know how to sew?"

As things stood, the campaign of the president of the Provisional Government for dissolution of the militias was to develop into a lengthy task: so lengthy and so arduous that the return to France from Russia of Maurice Thorez, secretary-general of the French Communist party, his appointment as vice-president of the Council of Ministers, and even the general's trip to Moscow, would not be superfluous moves. The objective, after all, was an integration of the revolution and the State. But such an operation would not have been possible if the State itself had not taken the initiative of revolution through law.

Although he might be able to survive only by "swimming with the tide" of the revolution as far as the limits he was attempting to fix for it, De Gaulle quickly recognized that the balance of power on which he stood—a fragile balance, in spite of his present prestige—was assured by the precipitous rush to his side of a large group of people that saw in him the preservation of "order" and the protection, not of a regime, but of a society. A bewildered bourgeoisie was awaiting its savior. And felt that it had found it in him: his general's stars, the noble "De" in his name, his taste for authority, and his occasional opportunism, would cause a great many people who had ignored or fought him for the past four years to support him now.

155

Made the leader of a Popular Front by the Resistance in 1942, General de Gaulle was adopted by a much larger group in 1944. Whether he wished it or not, his enemies, until the time of the liberation of Paris, had been the men of the Right. In the future, he would find himself drawn to the Center and to the groups which pretended to take their lead from the Center, conducting a policy which he thought of as one of national unity, but which was often one of compromise—if not of simple tightrope walking.

This was apparent in the choice he made in April, 1945. With the enemy driven at last from the national territory, the greatest national peril was inflation: the disastrous imbalance between the level of production (one third of what it had been in 1938) and the amount of money in circulation after years of systematic inflation by the German occupant. A surgeon was available to probe the wound and stitch it up: Pierre Mendès-France, now commissioner of finance in the Provisional Government.

To blot out this surplus in the means of payment, he proposed to extend to France the system of a change of banknotes, which he had already introduced in Tunisia and Corsica, and which Camille Gutt had carried out in Belgium. Against this method of an authoritarian reduction of inflation, implying as it did a strict austerity and constant intervention on the part of the State, the majority of members of the government cited the inadvisability of inflicting new privations on a population that had already suffered too much, warned that deflation would impede the restoration of industry, and stressed the inevitable unpopularity of a freeze in wages on the one hand and agricultural prices on the other. When the socialist ministers (with one exception) and the communists supported the theses of his "liberal" opponents, Pierre Mendès-France resigned. René Pleven would then be charged with implementing the inflationist policy implicit in the departure of Mendès-France.

General de Gaulle had attempted to arbitrate between the two camps, but he had been unwilling to throw the enormous weight of his authority on the side of Mendès-France, whose policy clearly had his personal approval. Why did he not dare to force acceptance of it? Why did he permit an act which was the origin of the rapid decay of the Republic he had restored? In his *Memoirs,* he states that he was reluctant to "shatter the substance of the sick and wounded nation." It is tempting to color this moving declaration of motive with some political design and to think that he might have been concerned with reassuring moderate opinion by ratifying the choice of a classic and "laissez-faire" policy.

He wanted to channel the course of this revolution, but he found himself being forced to lead it. He was no longer the leader of the Popular Front, but he was the leader of a government in which the Left was dominant because its supporters were in the majority throughout the country. When it is reread today, twenty years later, the program of the National Council of the Resistance is less revolutionary than it appeared at the time, and impregnated with an anti-capitalist theory of economics which is a trifle hazy at best. The role assigned to the State in control of the nation's economic activity and in the stimuli to be given it seemed then to be immense; in the situation of the French economy at the end of the war, this economic planning which so enchanted the Left was not entirely displeasing to the Right, where many people saw it as a splendid means of using public funds to rebuild the nation's capital equipment.

It was not only the nationalization of credit and of the major public services which frightened the French bourgeoisie, but also the question of purges—the punishment of those who had been pro-Nazi and pro-Vichy. In this matter, De Gaulle was not prepared to make any great concessions. In the first place, he felt that only the application of the law (even though the law was of very recent date) could prevent "the basic impulse toward punishment" aroused in the French people by the trials they had undergone—trials which had often been aggravated by other Frenchmen. He also thought that in a time of rebuilding the State it was of particular importance to "display its justice," as both an arm and a symbol. Justice, or State policy? They were often confused, in those days, by a mixture of partisan passions and the opportunism of the prosecutors.

De Gaulle had hoped to employ the severity of the State to prevent vengeance; the solution that resulted would be vengeance on the part of the State—but even so, many who had been guilty of the most terrible of crimes against the nation, the denunciation of patriots, would escape punishment. Revolutionary justice is not noted for weighing its decisions on a chemist's scale. The mistake of the leader of the Provisional Government lay perhaps in the fact that he did not recognize that this was a matter of revolutionary justice and therefore felt himself bound by normal legality. As soon as it seemed to him that it was the State which was dictating its decisions, Charles de Gaulle, the man who brooked no interference from foreigners, became totally submissive. In this sort of thing, he was not the bold man of June 18th.

But this was the General de Gaulle who faced the two great tasks he had assigned himself: resurrection of the national security and independence, and restoration of the State. He was prepared to make use of any means at hand to buttress the position of the French nation against her cumbersome allies and her dangerous neighbors, as well as against the subver-

158

sion which was beginning to crop up here and there in the Empire. His relations with the Anglo-Americans were still heavy with mistrust and wounded sensibilities.

The year 1945 began, in fact, with a new crisis in Allied relations: threatened by a sudden German offensive in the Ardennes, Eisenhower had decided on a reformation of the front lines which involved the evacuation of Strasbourg. De Gaulle reacted immediately, telegraphed De Lattre a thunderous order to hold the capital of Alsace at all costs, and demanded that Eisenhower revoke his order of withdrawal. Churchill hastened to Paris and once again pled on De Gaulle's behalf in favor of the hero's solution: De Lattre would be provided with the means of holding Strasbourg against the Nazis.

But De Gaulle expected more from the Allies than just their help in preserving the integrity of the national territory. He expected to obain their support in a dismemberment of Germany, and to insure French occupation of the whole left bank of the Rhine. Neither London nor Washington was ready to concede such objectives to France; the general, therefore, would look for powerful support in other quarters. In the last days of the month of November, at Stalin's invitation, he left for Moscow. De Gaulle had already taken the measure of the two great men of the West; now he confronted the leader whose savage energy had made Russian patriotism and the great barrier of the Volga into the wall against which Hitler's power had been broken.

No matter how important the objectives he had in mind when he arrived in Moscow on December 2, 1944—the signature of a mutual security pact, the partition of Germany, the hope of obtaining Stalin's agreement to a restriction of the revolutionary impulses in France—it is a reasonably safe guess that

De Gaulle had primarily come because of a desire to meet this fabulous personage. Less as a chief of state himself, perhaps, than as a chronicler of history and a collector of personalities. The personality did not deceive him. And neither did the portrait he drew of this "great Czar . . . with the shadowy charm."

But it may be that what he had sensed most clearly in Stalin was the fact that the leader of the world revolution seemed to confirm so simply, so totally, De Gaulle's own historic theses: even when he is the symbol of an ideology—the most powerful, the most convincing, of ideologies—a man is first of all a national animal, linked to a homeland, product of a collective temperament and a traditional culture. In his writing, he would note that Stalin used the word "Russian" far more often than "Soviet." In short, he found him to be a man of much the same school as his own, if we grant that they were different scholars. . . .

The political result of the journey was relatively slender: Stalin refused absolutely to consider the views of his guest when it came to the matter of Germany. He saw no virtue whatever in a plan for dismemberment of the Reich, and was interested only in denazification, demilitarization, and reparations. For his part, he was attempting to obtain De Gaulle's recognition of the Lublin Committee, the future communist government of Poland; and even went so far as to make this a condition for the signing of a Franco-Soviet pact. The general refused. Only at the moment when he was about to leave for the airfield did he make a concession: he would send a liaison officer to maintain contact with the Polish Revolutionary Committee (this would be Christian Fouchet, later minister of education from 1962 to 1968). De Gaulle had seen Stalin; he had interested the Russian leader, perhaps even impressed him, but in no way convinced him.

This was to become perfectly evident two months later at Yalta.

After so many refusals, rebuffs, and boycotts, this one would be the hardest for the solitary man of June 18th, who was now assured of his legitimacy. There would be only three Great Men sketching out the future of the world in the Crimea. De Gaulle, in a contemporary denunciation of these "secret and tortuous discussions," announced that France would not consider herself bound in any way by decisions she had neither taken part in nor ratified. And he even recalled, in a tone that contained a hint of threat, that France represented an aggregate of one hundred million people on the frontiers of the territory whose future was being decided.

Yalta, however, would turn out to be a French diplomatic success. Faced with Stalin—who gave France no more consideration than that due to a State incapable of mustering more than twenty divisions, and who refused to grant her the slightest priority in the questions of reparations and the occupation of Germany—and with Roosevelt, who was still preoccupied with his project for a world governed by a group of four great powers in which France was not included, Churchill would fight "like a tiger," in the words of Harry Hopkins, to obtain for France a zone of occupation in Germany and a place on the Allied Control Commission. And it was in large part due to the good offices of the British prime minister that Paris was invited to the world conference summoned to set up the organization of the United Nations. Churchill, in fact, had played the part of the Constable's ambassador.

Winston Churchill unquestionably appreciated the irony of the situation. But not De Gaulle. His irritability was at its very height, and it provoked the incident with Franklin Roosevelt which is one of the most unfortunate in a biography rich in demonstrations of clashes of temperament. As soon as the Yalta discussions were concluded, Roosevelt sent De Gaulle word that he would be happy to confer with him in Algiers. In a French city? Did the man think he was going to make him relive "the Casablanca affair"? He refused bluntly to go to meet the ailing President who held in his hands the greater part of the possibilities for a reconstruction of France. The most lucid of today's Gaullists maintain that this refusal was not based on any reasons of protocol or susceptibility, but rather that De Gaulle's primary intent in refusing to go to the meeting with Roosevelt was to avoid giving the impression of having agreed to the Yalta decisions.

The argument is not very good, in the precise measure to which this result was good. The general is one of those men who would rather see a bad play from a front-row seat than a good one from the second balcony.

He would still have opportunity for a few more displays of anger: another denunciation of British maneuverings in the Levant at the beginning of summer, 1945; and the exclusion of France from the Potsdam conference in which the three Great Powers were to decide on the fate of Germany. But from San Francisco, where she took part in the construction of the UN, to the deck of the battleship *Missouri* in Tokyo Bay, where Leclerc sat with MacArthur and countersigned the surrender of Japan, just three months after De Lattre had signed that of the Third Reich, France was beginning to reappear on the scene; not quite so great as he would have wished, but carrying more weight than her current steel production or the size of her armies might have implied. General de Gaulle would have liked to conduct his diplomacy on a grand scale. He wavered between procedure, polemics, and eloquent playacting; but it represented a considerable ascent from the abyss from which he had started.

But there was already a cancer gnawing at this edifice whose facade he was attempting to restore to its original noble proportions: the colonial system on which this fragile power was partially based now threatened its ruin. In Algeria, on the very day of the armistice in Europe, manifestations which had been intended as a participation in this feast of liberty had degenerated into riots. The repressive measures were atrocious, especially in Kabylia: in the region from Bougie to Sétif, there were something like ten thousand dead.

In Indochina, a complete Japanese takeover on March 9th eliminated all trace of French authority. Who could really have believed that the vague statute of autonomy promised to the Annamites by Paris on March 24th would satisfy the nationalist aspirations of a people which had just seen a colonial empire collapse before its eyes? No serious measures were taken to prevent the explosions which took place in Hanoi in August, or in Saigon in September. The Indochinese war was born during the reign of General de Gaulle far more directly than the war in Algeria. Progress in Europe, cracks in the wall in Africa, and a running fever in Asia.

To anyone who taxed him with dictatorial tendencies, General de Gaulle promptly replied that no political leader solicited the approval of his fellow citizens more often than he. Seven public votes in fourteen months, during his first period as chief of state. But was it possible that this electoral debauch contained a hidden motive? Surfeiting starving people with food is dangerous. . . .

De Gaulle was not yet at the point of denouncing

163

the various parties; he was rather attempting to prevent them from becoming the skeleton framework of the new regime. The great battle he was about to launch would be the battle for the constitution. Three theories were in direct conflict. First, that of the communists, who wanted to install the government of the masses by obtaining the election of an assembly which would be both constituent and legislative, and whose mandate would be unlimited. Second, that of the radical party, which wanted to return to the 1875 constitution of the Third Republic. And lastly, that of the general, reluctantly supported by the Mouvement Républicain Populaire, which found itself caught between the old parliamentary regime and a new version of the consular system—rejecting the 1875 constitution, but also refusing a government by assembly. De Gaulle succeeded in having the conflict resolved by a vote of the people.

On October 21, 1945, the French electorate was called on to state its preference: either "yes-yes," as De Gaulle had asked ("yes" for a new constitution, "yes" for a limitation on the mandate of the assembly); "yes-no," as the communists had asked; "no-no," as the radicals had asked. The first "yes" carried 96 percent of the votes cast; the second, 66 percent. In the area in which he had opposed the communists, De Gaulle's majority was slender.

On November 13th, by a unanimous vote of its 555 members, the National Assembly elected General de Gaulle chief of a government which, as of that moment, ceased to be "provisional." The communists had voted along with their colleagues, but it was clear that in the future they would take the path of fundamental opposition. The war in Europe had been over since the eighth of May, and a discipline imposed by the war effort against Germany was no longer *de rigueur.* Obviously, the leaders of the party had re-signed themselves to the dissolution of the patriotic militias and the liberation committees. Obviously, in all of the posts of economic responsibility that they were assuming, they had renounced any thought of a revolutionary seizure of power and chosen the path of legality.

But when it became a matter of forming the government, Maurice Thorez immediately notified General de Gaulle that his party expected to be awarded one of the three most important ministries—Foreign Affairs, National Defense, or the Interior. The general refused. Thorez accused the chief of the government of outraging "the memory of the 75,000 communists who died for France and liberty." In a radio address, De Gaulle replied that he intended to associate the communists freely in the economic and social tasks of the government, but that he would not consider confiding to them "any of the three levers that command foreign policy, the diplomacy that expresses it, the army that supports it, the police that covers it."

The general had found a formula, and one which was Gaullist in the extreme. He was satisfied with this and, having won on the major point, could afford to be generous at a lower level. The communists would be awarded five portfolios, including half of one of those they desired: Charles Tillon, named secretary for armaments, was 50 percent of a minister of National Defense. And Maurice Thorez was vice-president of the Council of Ministers. But this compromise promised nothing for the future but constant bickering and bidding for power—all the more so since the French people, at the end of this year of 1945, were hungry and cold, and since, beyond the frontiers, the great wartime alliance against the Nazis was already falling apart.

The "days of wine and roses" of August, 1944, were far behind. De Gaulle had hoped to create a national unity; he had not been able to create unity among the liberators.

7
Days of Wrath

At noon on January 20, 1946, General de Gaulle, president of the Council of Ministers, wearing his army uniform, entered the Hall of Arms of the Ministry of National Defense. Standing to greet him were the ministers he had peremptorily summoned the evening before. In measured, unemotional tones, he stated: "The exclusive regime of the parties has reappeared. I disapprove of it. But short of establishing by force a dictatorship I do not want and which doubtless would turn out badly, I do not have the means to prevent this experience. It is therefore necessary for me to withdraw. . . ."

Why? We have seen that the guerrilla warfare with the parties had already been going on for some time. The communists had challenged him at the time of the October referendum, and again during the formation of the government. The MRP had only supported his institutional theses with reservations which had annoyed him. The socialists thought him overbearing.

Unable to accustom himself to this contest for power, he had been thinking of withdrawing since the month of October. Jacques Dumaine, chief of protocol in the government, reports in his *Memoirs* that at that time he heard General de Gaulle say to his wife:

167

"We'll retire to Canada. I'll go fishing. And you can cook whatever I catch!" To put an ocean between the parties and himself . . . This temptation, still vague in October, and colored with the melancholy which was a normal echo to great triumphs, would harden in his mind as a result of two incidents which would serve as a pretext for his departure.

On January 1, 1946, from the speaker's rostrum of the Chamber of Deputies, André Philip called for a reduction in military expenditures. The motion was scarcely surprising, coming from a socialist leader. But the general saw in it a sort of personal betrayal by his former comrade in London. Taking issue with the basic reasoning of the speech, he asserted in his own that it was "a fundamental difference in the concept of relations between the government and the Assembly" which separated him from the speaker. And he went on to add: "This will doubtless be the last time that I will speak in this chamber." Words which went curiously unnoticed. Then, on January 4th, he left for the southern coast. The Constable on the Riviera? It calls up a feeling of refuge, of the island of Elba.

On the fourteenth, he returned to Paris. Two days later, he was again present at a meeting of the Chamber, at which the chairman, Édouard Herriot, protested against the award of decorations to soldiers killed in the North African fighting against the Americans, November 8-10, 1942.

To this, the general, at the top of his form, replied that the attitude of soldiers who died bravely, in obedience to orders from leaders who were alone responsible, seemed to him less open to criticism than that of a man who was negotiating with Pierre Laval on the eve of the liberation of Paris. And he added: "With Vichy, ever since 1940, I did not confine myself to an exchange of letters and messages. . . . I proceeded at once to an exchange of artillery."

As usual, it was he whose teeth were sharper. But this time, the verbal victory was more bitter than usual. The Assembly had reacted favorably to Herriot's proposals. And this was a matter of the history of the Resistance, something which, to him, had seemed sacred. Yesterday, a comrade from London had attacked him; today, the elected representatives of the people rejected him in favor of a political leader whose attitude in the past had sometimes been ambiguous. This was no longer a question of a political quarrel, but of a spiritual divorce. Four days later, he was to make his farewell to the rue Saint-Dominique.

Farewell? To all appearances, he seemed to be thinking only of one of those strategic withdrawals to which military men are quite accustomed. When he called them together on January 20th, he had not expected the ministers to hurl themselves at his knees and implore him to remain, but he had almost certainly expected that there would be a public outcry in his favor, that among the intellectual elite and, especially, in the mass of the people, there would be a clearly defined movement that would call for him to reverse his decision.

Three days after his announcement to the ministers, the general wrote to a friend: ". . . as for my departure, it is only an episode. Before coming to any conclusion, wait for the ending." And three of the men who might be considered to express the thinking of Charles de Gaulle from one viewpoint or another— Maurice Schumann in *L'Aube*, Stanislas Fumet in *Témoignage Chrétien*, and Rémy Roure in *Le Monde* —wrote at the time that the general's retirement might very well be of short duration.

There were those who thought they heard the curious sound of marching boots in a now-peaceful Paris —as well as in such distant corners of the Empire as Saigon, where Admiral d'Argenlieu and his staff found it difficult to accept General de Gaulle's departure without some show of reaction. But he gave orders to the most Gaullist of the military leaders to remain calm and to wait until the people recalled the man of June 18th. De Gaulle confided to his closest friends: "Before six months." The people did nothing.

It was not a beaten man who drew aside, but a man embittered by the apparent indifference of the public, and the alacrity with which the political class had accepted his departure (including the president of the MRP, Maurice Schumann, most dedicated Gaullist, who had advocated this party's continuance in power even without De Gaulle in a speech to the national committee). Greeting a visitor in his residence in the Bois de Boulogne, seated on a case filled with archives, he announced in his deepest, most solemn tones: "I am at Longwood (the Saint Helena residence of Napoleon)...."

Taking leave of them, he willed to the staffs of politicians a formula which summed up his fifteen months' experience and assumed the shape of a time bomb: "I don't like the socialists because *they are not* socialists. I don't like the MRP's because *they are* MRP's. I don't like my supporters because they like money...."

Monsieur de Gaulle was in his tower, a tower which he had added to La Boisserie, his pleasant provincial dwelling at Colombey-les-Deux-Églises, to give it a nobler aspect. With his enormous forearms poised on his desk like the legs of the Sphinx, and his head bowed, he was writing. In the large, careless handwriting which seemed to be that of a tired old woman, but in which specialists nonetheless see the man of action—along with the intellectual and the

170

solitary—growing greater with age, he was gravely, patiently, setting down his "Commentaries on the Gallic Wars," which have the air, like their ancestor, of having been thought out in Latin. But which are, this time, written by the Gallic chief . . .

He also wrote a thousand letters—meticulous, refined, ceremonious—in the style of the letter-writers of the *Grand Siècle*. He replied to every shipment of books with an admirable courtesy. He was as attentive to the feelings of the least important essayist on the Left Bank as he had once been to ruffling the feelings of Roosevelt or Churchill. This disruptive statesman was by far the most agreeable of colleagues.

Through the window of his great corner office, he gazed lengthily at the horizon of Champagne, with its stark, denuded hills, at the valley of the Aube, and beyond that at the great forest of the Gauls. A landscape planed and polished by history, fashioned by generations of disunited Frenchmen—builders of cathedrals and plunderers of monks, archers of the king and revolutionists—the people whose Republic he had reestablished. Did he even like this countryside, which he had selected twenty years ago so that he might be "halfway between Paris and the German frontier," between the seat of power and the seat of war? He did not like it. But it was a landscape suited to his mood of gloomy introspection, to the noble phrases of the memorialist.

He saw few people. Paris was a long way off. A few of the faithful came to visit him, however, and were welcomed—Michelet, Vallon, Malraux, Soustelle, Guichard. Let us follow one such visitor: "The house is vast. One passes through a first room, filled with a kind of rustic clutter, and then a second, a large salon furnished in a traditional manner, with no great attempt at elegance. . . . The furnishings, which range from Louis XV, real or false, to Napoleon III and the

English styles, have been accumulated through inheritance, wedding gifts, chance, and the necessities of function and garrison life. Family life is centered on the dining room and the small salon where everyone gathers after meals. The tone of conversation never rises, either in quarrel or in laughter. . . . Before going off to his tower—where neither his children, his wife, nor any guests are admitted—De Gaulle sacrifices a quarter of an hour to social life and talk, his long body set against a background of the Voltaire armchair. . . ." (Emmanuel d'Astier. *Les Grands*, Gallimard, 1961.)

His son, Philippe, married a Montalembert; his eldest daughter, Elizabeth, married Colonel Alain de Boissieu. Anne, the little invalid, died in 1948, at the age of twenty. The general, who had never liked being separated from her, and who alone knew the fables, the songs, that could bring some joy to the endless night of her life, was enormously grieved. At the edge of the grave, as the last shovelfuls of earth were dropped on the coffin, he took his wife's hand in his: "Come. Now, she is like the others. . . ."

But, as Forain said of Degas: "This hermit knew the schedule of all the trains." His constant companion, France, was in danger, in various forms of danger—primarily that of the divisions within herself, and then that brought on by her allies: those of the West, who seemingly would never abandon their efforts to make her into a docile protégée by blending her into a European *fondue*, and those of the East, who were at last revealing their true ambitions and attempting to harvest in France the grapes of wrath.

He attempted to advise or to reprimand from a distance. To a friendly journalist who had campaigned for the constitution he had disapproved of, but which was adopted in October, 1946, he wrote: "If you had been more clear-sighted, we had the opportunity to

crush the Marxists—communists and leftist socialists.
. . ." But such clandestine interventions were no
longer sufficient for him. It was necessary for him to
reappear on the scene: this would mean speeches in
Bayeux (in favor of a strengthened constitution), in
Épinal, in Bruneval. Then, at Strasbourg, on April 7,
1947, he would announce the foundation of the Rassemblement du Peuple Français, just fifteen months
after his withdrawal from public affairs.

So many people had urged him to throw the weight
of his fame into the national debate: the members of
the Gaullist groups, allergic to inaction themselves
and knowing how to exploit the bitterness of a leader
who was not yet ready to be cast into the shadows;
politicians willing to make this symbol into a ladder
for their own ascent; conservatives frightened by
the expansion of communism in France and the pressures of the U.S.S.R. abroad; opponents of the various
plans for European union, who knew how to arouse
the oddly regionalist nationalism of this visionary
man—syndicates of special interests, in short, for
whom it was natural that the lower their aim the
higher they should set their sights in the hope of securing it. The RPF was under way.

In his *Memoirs*, De Gaulle is very discreet on this
subject because he does not know how to portray himself in any kind of defeat except a defeat in the
grand style. And the only style possessed by the RPF
was that of the fear it caused; it was not very grand.
The RPF was essentially a reaction to a panic, and
also a great spectacle.

The great fear of 1947 was that of communism. It
would be impossible to understand anything of the
incredible adventure of the RPF without at least attempting to recall the climate of the times—a climate
of rupture between East and West and the birth of
the cold war; of the creation of the Cominform and

the communist takeover in Prague; of communist leader Jacques Duclos welcoming the prime minister of France, Robert Schuman (born in German-occupied Lorraine), to the chamber of the Assembly, with the cry of "There's the Boche!" while his comrades shouted "Heil Hitler!" at the appearance of Jules Moch, minister of the interior; of such writers as Arthur Koestler and Victor Kravchenko bringing out succulent anecdotes to nourish the already well-nourished anti-communist fever of the public. It was a time when—simultaneously with the appearance of the most sordid accounts of events within the Stalinist state—almost half of the French intelligentsia would dismiss as a "slimy rat" anyone who ventured to doubt the democratic virtues of Joseph Vissarionovich Stalin. It was a time of a war of religion, a climate of apocalypse.

But the RPF was not just a movement which hoped to face the man in the Kremlin with the man of June 18th, to confront Maurice Thorez and his counter-State with a counter-counter-State. The thing that made it unique in the French political landscape was the theatrical atmosphere created for it by André Malraux. The RPF was Charles de Gaulle staged and directed by Malraux. It is tempting to call up an image of Josef von Sternberg, laboring mightily for the greater glory of Marlene Dietrich.

Projectors, platforms, waterworks, backdrops, music: for three years, Charles de Gaulle was a giant Gallic druid confronting the Tartar hordes and the fifth-columnists within the System with an invincible silhouette and a resounding voice—floodlit and recorded in stereophonic sound by the producer of *Man's Hope*.* And even aside from these great spectacles, there has always been something of a theatrical at-

* Malraux produced and directed a film version of his novel of the Spanish Civil War, *L'Espoir*. [Translator's note]

174

mosphere to the relations between the general and the writer. De Gaulle wanted Malraux to run for the Assembly as a deputy from the suburb of Paris where he lived. Malraux refused, and in the course of a conversation one night De Gaulle realized that he was not going to be able to persuade him to change his mind. The following day, Malraux received this note: "Brutus always prevails over Caesar. . . ."

Two souvenirs of the period. At Bordeaux, with his back to the river, standing on a platform built to relatively human scale—the Anglicized Gascons of this city are not taken in by excesses—the general spoke of the French Union to a mildly skeptical public of middle-class businessmen and dazzled shopkeepers. A good speech, not very new, and not antipathetic. In New York, De Gaulle had been acclaimed by the constituents of La Guardia, whom he assumed to be the poorer classes. Here, he was applauded—less— by the constituents of Chaban-Delmas, who had no great worries about the end of the month. As they were leaving the speaker's platform, François Mauriac, who, as a Bordelais, knew what was going on around him, took Malraux's arm and murmured delightedly: "Think of it, Malraux, there I was on *your* left. . . ."

At the Velodrome d'Hiver, two years later in Paris: cavernous gloom, turtleneck sweaters, bicycle caps, the beams of giant spotlights, ladies with opera glasses, banners and trumpets. Embarrassing memories. That plump gentleman who was walking toward the microphone was Jacques Soustelle, who proceeded to recite a list of figures in a voice that was both soft and impassioned. Then someone else stood up, pale and ascetic, and began to speak: "Three centuries ago, a strange form of reed appeared in the lake that forms the center of the garden at Versailles. . . ." The audience of workmen listens to him, open-mouthed. That was Malraux. Then came the general,

175

somewhat ill at ease, to tell the truth, in that atmosphere haunted by ghosts of six-day bicycle racers. But he took advantage of it to announce, as he had before at Rennes: "The Red Army is just two relay stops removed from the cyclists' Tour de France. . . ." It was not De Gaulle at his best. But it should not be forgotten that remarks of this kind were made at a time when the risk of war was great, and Soviet policy was doing nothing to ease it. However, though there may have been nothing objectionable in the desire to face and expose what Stalin represented in the world of 1950, was it necessary to call up the phantoms of ceremonies designed in foreign totalitarian states?

"The RPF—it's the metro," Malraux decreed. The world of subway riders, the middle classes? Yes and no. It was true that the RPF voter was closely related, sociologically, to the voter for the Communist party. In the Paris suburbs, Vallon and Billotte were elected to seats which had been held by communists. But with the exception of the Seine area, the electoral base of the Rassemblement du Peuple Français would differ only slightly from that of any other classic formation of the Right. It was not by chance that typical right-wing politicians like Messieurs Frédéric-Dupont and Barrachin hastened to join his cause and bring him the votes of the concierges and the small businessmen. The public which was sympathetic to the RPF differed, however, from that of the "independent Right": a survey of the subject has noted that it contained more professional people and fewer businessmen, more technicians and fewer executives, and also more women. The military and the church were a trifle mistrustful. Banking circles were tempted, but when Antoine Pinay arrived on the scene in 1952, they gave their allegiance to this perfect bourgeois politician.

The real objective of the general as president of the RPF is something that is still open to question. One of his closest and most intelligent associates has said: "He was not attempting to submerge the regime in a mass of votes, to wash it away in an electoral tide. He was thinking simply of trying to elect enough of his followers to block the functioning of the institutions of government, primarily in the Assembly, and thereby to make inevitable a reorganization of those institutions—a reorganization in which the Rassemblement would have played the role of arbiter, and the ideas expressed in his Bayeux speech would be imposed." A strategy of dissuasion with an objective of substitution.

But what *was* the general in the structure of the RPF? A faraway Symbol, an ikon to be carried about the streets on feast days? This is the thesis held by certain of his lieutenants of the period, but it is a version that is at least questionable. A glance at the articles appearing in the publications of the RPF is sufficient to measure the role played by the general and to recognize that he was truthfully the guiding spirit, the leader of the RPF, and that he not only inspired its strategy but also conducted its tactics of movement. He had, in fact, stated on April 14, 1947, a week after formation of the party: "I am assuming direction of it." His interdicts, his incentives, his sarcasms, were the slogans and the ukases of this "order," which to many was still imbued with the spirit of the Resistance, and in connection with which Malraux frequently invoked the spirit of chivalry.

To many? Only to the best elements in the party. But there were also the inevitable hangers-on of an elite group, the eternal followers of the strong man: the shopkeepers, the giddy young girls, the pious old ladies. There were also the devotees of sensationalism

177

and the professionals of strongarm tactics. And—strange as it may seem in the following of the advocate of the State par excellence—there were the petty, everyday anarchists, the tax-dodgers and scofflaws.

The career of the Rassemblement du Peuple Français was marked with the same brusque, theatrical, demonstrative character as that of its founder. No sooner had he delivered his speech in Strasbourg in April, 1947 ("It is time for the assembly of the French people to form and to organize"), than its membership began to swell: according to its founders, eight hundred thousand people joined it in the first month. Six months later, the municipal elections of October, 1947, gave clear evidence of the triumph of the new movement—it drew almost 40 percent of all the votes cast.

The number of its candidates elected was so large that De Gaulle at one point turned to the secretary-general of the party, Jacques Soustelle, and said: "Have you at least had time to verify the police records?" (A question that arose again after the Ben Barka case, in 1966.)

The RPF reached its apogee during the first months of 1948: at the time of its national convention in Marseille, on April 17th, the hard core of the party workers was estimated to be one million strong. But from that moment on, the Rassemblement declined steadily. Why? In the first place, because the liberal tendencies of some of its most prominent members—Malraux, Vallon, Morandat—caused it to lose the support from the Right, a support that its obsessive anti-communism made it impossible to replace from the Left. Every public opinion poll of the period demonstrated that the people considered De Gaulle the "rampart" against communism. But the parties in power were shrewd enough to avoid a confrontation with the newcomer and to concentrate their own efforts against the Communist party. A considerable portion of the middle class felt that the Third Force of Robert Schuman, René Pleven, and Jules Moch was doing a sufficiently good job of combatting the "reds," and that there was no need to call on a savior whose protection might prove expensive.

As a result, the regional elections of March, 1949, showed a decline in the movement: 31 percent of the vote. In 1950, the ebb continued—until the month of June, when the outbreak of the Korean War restored to the general his prestige as a man for stormy times. If the legislative elections had been held in the fall of that year, the RPF would probably have secured a majority sufficient to control the government. But they were held in June, 1951; and in spite of Korea the Rassemblement emerged as only the second party in the country, with 21.7 percent of the votes, trailing the communists. In other regional elections in 1952: first 13 percent and then only 10 percent of the votes.

"Those who have no will to fight are doomed to lose," the general said. And on May 6, 1953, he recognized "without equivocation . . . that (his) effort . . . has not thus far achieved its goal."

After a final speech in the industrial exhibition grounds at the Porte de Versailles in Paris, in which he reminded his audience that he might yet be called on ". . . when a grave crisis revives concern for the public safety . . ." and reserved the right at such a time "to intervene directly by any means at all, including that of the electoral process . . ." he returned to Colombey.

Monsieur de Gaulle was in his tower. This time he had not come back as a hero too great for the little men around him, but as a prophet who had not been heard and who by now had lost his voice. He worked on the final revisions of his *Memoirs,* of which the first volume was to be published in 1954.

As if in anticipation of the vicissitudes and triumphs yet to come, he took great pains to close the *Memoirs* with a final passage filled with a noble pantheism in which, abruptly, Chateaubriand replaces his habitual models, the classic Latin orators and historians. A lofty romanticism imbues these few pages, which seem intended as a farewell to the earth and to the century—but when it is borne in mind that the final volume of the *Memoirs* did not appear until after he had returned to the hazards of politics and world affairs, it becomes apparent that they are also imbued with ideas and motives for the future.

For General de Gaulle it was a question of making clear that no matter what turn might yet take place in the adventure he had accepted, and even sought— the demon of action, the "divine game of heroes"— the statue of General de Gaulle had been completed at the moment the war ended. He consented to a few ulterior allusions only to dignify the gesture of his withdrawal.

He traveled—from Africa, where the destiny of Free France was assured, to Oceania, whose fidelity to the Gaullist ideal was on a plane with its distance from the ideal's roots. After his return to Paris, he occasionally hurled his thunderbolts at targets such as the European army and the various formulas for economic or political integration. In June of 1955 he held a "last" press conference, in which he used the most chauvinistic arguments to slash at the idea of a "Europe of the Six," and at the same time managed to address a greeting of exemplary nobility to the exiled sultan of Morocco. Then he took leave of the newspaper men "for a long time."

General de Gaulle still came to his office on the rue de Solferino every Wednesday. His staff made his appointments for him with a curiously unequal sense of discrimination: a visitor was likely to see almost anyone, even the führer of shopkeepers, Pierre Poujade.

8
Operation "Resurrection"

During the spring of 1958, a sort of nebulous cloud formed in the skies above Colombey-les-Deux-Églises and swelled rapidly into a storm which was to carry away a republic tormented by two wars, a hundred quarrels, and a pernicious, lingering decline. The Constable, however, told his visitors that his role was finished, and that the destiny of De Gaulle would be to have made an unsuccessful attempt to lift France to the summits. But from time to time, a word which revealed that this netherworld was peopled with projects for the future escaped him. In 1957, Michel Debré came to discuss his misgivings about the Treaty of Rome, which was opening the way for the European Common Market. "What difference does it make?" the general grumbled. "When we are back in power, we'll tear up these treaties."

As they had in 1946, visitors were once again seeking out the way to La Boisserie. Before leaving France after the bloody incident at Sakiet (February 8, 1958), the Tunisian ambassador, Mohammed Masmoudi, came to consult "the conscience of France" and was advised not to "insult the future." A few weeks later, in *Le Monde,* Maurice Duverger published an article entitled "When?". Following a private interview with Pierre Mendès-France and François Mitterrand, he wrote that the problem was not a matter of knowing whether De Gaulle would return to power, but of knowing on what date and under what conditions he would. A few days later, the editors of the left-wing Catholic monthly *Esprit* dismissed the idea of an immediate appeal to the man of June 18th, but did not reject the basic principle.

However, three groups of Gaullists were already preparing the way for the appeal. First, those who believed—or pretended to believe—that only De Gaulle could keep Algeria French: Jacques Soustelle was their leader. Second, the group that had waited through the days of the RPF for the great drama which would force the nation to call on him and now saw in Algeria the powder keg which could propel them into power: Jacques Chaban-Delmas, for example. And lastly, those—far fewer in number—who were counting on the general's prestige to convince the nation that the emancipation of Algeria was inevitable: Edmond Michelet was one of these.

The hermit of Colombey greeted his petitioners with a lofty skepticism. Two visitors, however, brought a spark to his eye and were rewarded with words which sounded very much like acquiescence. First there was Léon Delbecque, who had been regional director of the RPF in the north of France and who now was Chaban-Delmas' personal envoy in Algiers. When this long-time follower asked him what his attitude would be if there were to be an uprising in Algeria in his name, De Gaulle replied succinctly: "I would know how to assume my responsibilities." After this, it was the turn of Lucien Neuwirth, director of the RPF for Saint-Étienne and an officer in the parachute troops, who urged him to act, saying: "And if the

army in Algeria should make a direct appeal to you?"
De Gaulle replied: "I would answer you."

Why should he have put on gloves? The Republic
was about to throw in the towel. On May 5th, an
emissary of President René Coty contacted Jacques
Foccart, one of De Gaulle's most trusted assistants:
on what conditions would he agree to assume the
responsibilities of government? Monsieur Coty's ad-
vances were fruitless; De Gaulle, on his side, sensed
that the fruit was ripening. On April 27th, the various
veterans' organizations in Algiers had staged a mani-
festation which bordered on a revolt, and now the
hypothesis of a change in regime was in everyone's
mind.

The thirteenth of May, 1958. Delbecque had prepared for the seizure of the headquarters building of
the *Gouvernement Général* in Algiers by a commando
unit which would then broadcast a public appeal to
De Gaulle. And the "G.G." building was indeed seized
—but by a group led by Pierre Lagaillarde in the name
of the Committee of Seven, an extremist organization
made up of rabid anti-Gaullists: monarchists, reactionary nationalists, supporters of Pierre Poujade,
fascists of every shape and form. Through skillful
backstairs maneuvering, Delbecque succeeded in obtaining appointment to the Committee of Public
Safety as a member of the staff of General Massu, who
had directed the operation. For a time there was un-
certainty. Who would be the winners and who the
losers: the army, Delbecque, the Committee of
Seven? But toward midnight, dispatches arrived from
Paris, and it became apparent that any sharing out of
the spoils of power would be premature. A new government had been formed, with Pierre Pflimlin as
prime minister. In the corridors of the "G.G." a colonel
murmured: "We've had it now."

On the fourteenth, Algiers and Paris surveyed each

other warily, like two aging boxers clinging to each other for support, but preparing for the knock-out punch. Lagaillarde, the Committee of Seven, and the masses led by the officers had gained a round. But the forms of legality had been reasserted, and anything was possible. On the next day, May 15th, the citizens of Algiers were called together in the vast Forum facing the "G.G." building. General Salan, who was both the then-reluctant leader of the rebels and the cautious appointed delegate of the government, spoke a few phrases which were as ambiguous as his position. He paused and was about to withdraw to the accompaniment of sparse applause when Delbecque appeared behind him, pushed him back to the microphone, and whispered: "Shout *Vive De Gaulle.
. . .*" Salan hesitated momentarily, and then uttered the words the crowd had been waiting for. It was high noon.

Four hours later, on the rue de Solferino in Paris, a message from General de Gaulle was distributed to the press: "The disintegration of the State inevitably entails the estrangement of associated peoples, confusion in the army in the midst of combat, turmoil in the nation itself, the loss of independence. . . . Once before, in the depths of defeat, the nation trusted in me to lead it to safety. Today, in the face of the new trials which confront it, let the nation know that I hold myself in readiness to assume the powers of the Republic." Not a word about Algeria. A solitary allusion to the problems of colonization, referred to in terms of the "association of peoples." De Gaulle neither humbled himself nor made any commitment to anyone. But his intervention had saved the Algerian rebellion against Paris from drowning.

On that day, he contented himself with making an appointment. But from that point on, he would initiate and carry out a typically Gaullist strategy founded on illusion, psychological pressures, and talk. In actual fact, he controlled none of the elements of power, and the "Gaullists" of Algiers were almost as much in the minority as those of 1942 had been. But if Salan was more shrewd than Giraud, and Lagaillarde more decided than Bergeret, De Gaulle himself was stronger than he had been. He planned to play the game on two levels—dangle the powder keg of Algiers over the head of Paris (while keeping the matches carefully out of reach), and hold Algiers itself in check, so that he would not find himself the next day in possession of a capital occupied by rebellious parachute troops.

Dissuasion, persuasion: for the next three weeks it would be a masterpiece of combined strategy and stratagems. He had conducted campaigns which were more praiseworthy, or in any case more pure; but he had led none which demonstrated more clearly the extent to which a "strategy of circumstances" might be applied. Guided by the certainty of acting always in profound accord with the best interests of the nation, there was no act so cynical but what it was justified in his eyes.

Under the urging of various political leaders to reveal his intentions, and especially about the Algerian sedition, he called a press conference on the nineteenth of May: by that date, the affair would have had time to ripen, and he would have had time to polish his weapons. When the time came, he rose to face the press. Since the path of legality still seemed to him the only possible one, and since the socialists held the keys to the Chamber of Deputies, he was lavish with his conciliatory remarks, speaking of his *friend* Lacoste, and paying tribute to Guy Mollet, the two socialist leaders who had assumed, for the past two years, the heavy responsibility of the more and more cruel war in Algeria.

When someone suggested that he should condemn the rebellion, he cried: "The government has not condemned it. I, who am not the government—why should I do it?" (A fallacious argument: a free man, unsaddled by the responsibilities of government, "the conscience of France," invested with an unwritten but potent mandate, he could still demoralize the rebels and cut the ground from beneath the feet of the extremists in the army. He refrained from doing it—in other words, he was keeping his powder dry. . . .)

But when a heckler asked him if all of this was not just leading up to the installation of a dictatorial system, he exploded; he leaned forward across the rostrum, his jaw thrust out angrily, his tone solemn: "I restored the Republic when I could have imposed my personal power. Does anyone think that, at the age of sixty-seven, I am going to embark on a career as a dictator?" But he knew, even as he spoke, that several parachute officers had already arrived in France to lay the foundations of operation "resurrection."

On May 26th, Charles de Gaulle met with Pierre Pflimlin, the prime minister, in the park of Saint-Cloud, still haunted by the shade of Bonaparte. De Gaulle's only grenadiers were on the far shores of the Mediterranean—and even they did not obey him. This did not prevent him from refusing to give the president of the Council of Ministers any assurance that he would dissociate himself from the rebellion; but on the next day he published a communiqué in which he stated his disapproval of "any action, from no matter which side, which disturbs the public order." And all the more so, he went on, since "yesterday, I initiated the regular procedures necessary for establishment of a republican government." The amazement with which the prime minister must have read this text is not difficult to imagine. The regular procedures—this secret interview whose only result was disagreement? But, as Emmanuel d'Astier has written: "Monsieur Pflimlin is not a man of sufficient stature to call the Great Visionary a liar. . . ."

In short, whether regular or not, the procedures would have gone on within the framework of a somewhat bruised and shabby legality if it had not been for the fact that in spite of the resignation of the government, the socialist group in the Chamber voted almost unanimously against any appeal to the general. The path of legality thus appeared to be barred. On the night of May 27th, for the first time in two weeks, De Gaulle had doubts of his eventual success.

Late in the morning of May 28th, at Colombey, he received a delegation of envoys from General Salan, led by General Dulac. He made no attempt to hide his disillusion with the turn events had taken: "They don't want De Gaulle. . . ." Then, addressing himself to his guests: "And you; what are you preparing in Algiers?" He listened silently to Dulac's lengthy "briefing" on operation "resurrection," remarking only that the forces envisaged for the plan seemed a trifle small. As he led his visitors into the dining room, he took Dulac by the arm: "Dulac, we have to find a way to save this ark. . . ." What did he mean by that? Was "this ark" the recognized forms of legality, or was it the nation, rent by the "system" and the parties? General Salan's delegate left Colombey perplexed.

However ambiguous the statement might have seemed, De Gaulle himself was even more so. At the time he made it, he had in his pocket a letter from Vincent Auriol which left him in no doubt that even in the innermost circles of the Socialist party there were still loopholes left open to him. On the next day, again in the park at Saint-Cloud, he met with the presidents of both houses of the Assembly, Gaston Monnerville and André Le Troquer. The former attempted to be accommodating, the latter was peevish. But the responses they obtained from this curious approach resulted in a message to Colombey the next day from the president of the Republic, announcing that he was preparing to send a note to the National Assembly in which he would ask that General de Gaulle be elected president of the Council of Ministers.

On May 29th, shortly before the dinner hour, the general arrived at the Élysée Palace in Paris; a communiqué published earlier in the evening had made it known that a government provided with full powers would undertake a revision of the constitution and that the new text would be submitted to the approval of the people by a referendum. The Fourth Republic was dead.

On the first of June, the general appeared before Parliament for the first time since his bitter departure of January 16, 1946, when he had been followed by the sarcastic remarks of Édouard Herriot. He had consented only to read a ministerial declaration in which he resumed his customary reflections on the misdeeds of the defunct system. But he knew that now that he had conquered, it was still necessary for him to convince. He informed the elected delegates that he would meet with them again the next day to discuss and defend the plenipotentiary law. It was certainly the least he could do. This meeting of June 2, 1958, had to put the final seal to the tortuous, brilliant campaign through the approaches to power—a campaign marked by veiled threats, dramatic innuendos, and abusive communiqués.

Faced with these six hundred judges, whom he had regally consented to receive, but whom he had, in his mind, already deprived of all real power, Charles de Gaulle refrained from mockery. He told them that if they granted him their confidence, he would be conscious of the honor they did him "until the end of my life." Georges Bidault murmured acidly: "Today, chamber music. Tomorrow, a brass band." But he would vote for ratification, unlike his communist fellow-deputy who cried: "Yesterday, operation sedition; today, operation seduction."

That night, General de Gaulle, newly elected president of the Council of Ministers, returned to the Hotel La Pérouse, his Paris residence for many years. The night porter, Albert, was waiting for him and took him up in the elevator, silently respectful. The general gave him a little clap on the shoulder and whispered: "Albert, I've won!"

9
". . . and Legitimate King"

In August, 1944, it had not been necessary to organize a referendum: the Republic was already in evidence, and Charles de Gaulle was a part of it. A walk through the streets of Bayeux, a tidal wave sweeping down the Champs-Élysées, had been enough. But in 1958 . . . Three days before Charles de Gaulle's return to power, 250,000 Parisians—the same people who had made him king fourteen years before—marched from the Place de la Nation to the Place de la République, carrying signs and banners inviting him to return to his pedestal. It was a combination of testimony to the past and alibi for the future which was destined to have no sequel; but it was also a reminder that this time his legitimacy (which he would later claim he had held for twenty years) was in need of a formal foundation.

Eighty percent of the French people were prepared to grant him four fifths of legality: those who were always fascinated by a great man, those who never knew how to say no, the devotees of order frightened by the recent surfeit of disorder, certain of those who were still haunted by the nocturnal voice from London, a majority of the partisans of a French Algeria, and a minority of those who supported its independence. The electoral body of the RPF, plus a commando group of liberals and the mass of the "patriot party." The metro, and the taxis of the Marne.

De Gaulle in power: this ambiguous, frequently unreachable man is a simple and direct Chief of State who might not have explained himself but who had at least announced his position. To assure the independence of the nation, he wanted to rebuild a strong State, and he would not pay too close attention to the means of doing it or to minority interests.

First objective then: to rebuild the State, a State tailored to the measure of this monarchist-minded court chamberlain. For such a purpose, De Gaulle is both an ideologist of imposing continuity of thought and steadiness of vision, and a practitioner of a depressing opportunism and cynicism. He *sees* the French national state with the eyes of a great Jacobin cardinal. To form—or reform—it, he is prepared to employ the ruses and brutalities of any petty official of the Second Empire—measures which the author of *The Edge of the Sword* would have found a trifle too gaudy to be altogether politic.

This dissimilarity between the loftiness of concept and the pettiness of means is noticeable all through the history of the Fifth Republic. But it became more pronounced in its "second age," the period which began in 1962. Before this time, the war in Algeria had practically suspended the norms of legality, and no one took great exception to the fact except the supporters of a French Algeria, who felt they had been duped by the man they had recalled to power in 1958. De Gaulle had been invested with an exceptional mandate, a legality of necessity. He was the surgeon performing an operation, and an anesthetized people waited for him to have done his work. After awakening, they would take stock of things, and the regime would assume its form and its meaning.

Looking back today through the records of the

May, 1958, debates of the Parliament and the Constitutional Committee, it is astonishing to observe the gravity with which the delegates of that period studied the problem of whether or not the government would be responsible to Parliament—if the Republic, in short, would or would not be a parliamentary republic. De Gaulle promised, of course, that the Assembly would control the actions of the government. It remained for him then to free the bases of executive initiative from the tutelage of Parliament, and this he had firmly resolved to do as long ago as the time of the skirmishes at the end of 1945, skirmishes that had certainly hastened his retirement, even though they might not have caused it.

It was this resolution which resulted in the creation of the "privileged domain," a formula whose imprecision left to the president an ideal margin for maneuver and at the same time confirmed De Gaulle's continuing "strategy of circumstances": he intended to leave himself room for movement, to set no limits in advance. It was not a question of demolishing the Parliament, but of being able, when the occasion arose, to bypass it. And the occasion so often creates the thief ...

The Bayeux speech (1946) had provided a readily available synthesis of Charles de Gaulle's constitutional concepts: a republican structure crowned by a leader placed there by a large electoral body—a true chief of the executive branch, invested with real powers of initiative and arbitration, primarily those of naming the ministers and dissolving the Parliament. The general was to make constant reference to this 1946 text until the time, in 1962, when he would accentuate the monarchical aspect of the regime by rooting the legitimacy of its chief in a system of universal suffrage. But its real meaning was quite usefully clarified by a clandestine text distributed in

193

1943 by two Gaullist personalities who have since been identified as Michel Debré and Emmanuel Monick. One of the most notable affirmations of this text is the statement that what the French people desire is a "republican monarch," elected by the nation, of course, but for a term of twelve years. Why twelve years? Because, according to the authors, this is the average length of the reign of a monarch of the *ancien régime. . . .*

More Gaullist than the king? Certainly. But if it was to be founded on such hypotheses, the Republic of Charles de Gaulle would inevitably be somewhat different from that of the bearded bourgeois presidents of the beginning of the century. Charles de Gaulle is not a tyrant, even if one follows the example of Paul Reynaud, the former patron now an opponent, and writes the word in Greek. Authoritarian by temperament, allergic to negotiation, impatient in argument, he nonetheless enjoys himself at council meetings and listens attentively to advice. "Constraint is repugnant to him (Pierre Viansson-Ponté. *Risques et Chances de la Ve République,* Plon, 1960), so he aspires to gain his ends by the scope of his viewpoint and his conscience of what he feels to be the public good.

In this Republic, which seems vaguely ill at ease with the number five—as if it had something in common with the Fourth, which he had also founded, but not in his own image, or with the Third, which had been a constant source of deception to him—it is still possible to contest decisions, to draw up plans for a truly democratic regime, to ridicule, and to publish freely. Since the chief of state is clearly not a disciple of Montesquieu, the separation of powers is the least of the concerns of a government in which edict is casually substituted for law and the magistracy is invited by the presidential palace to judge along the right lines. But the style is not totalitarian: if the monarch reserves to himself the exclusive right to policy decisions, he does not confiscate the elements which constitute that policy. Ninety percent of the French people criticize the regime openly, without fear of reprisal; 80 percent of the press expresses a more or less impatient yearning for a successor; 55 percent of the electorate apparently remains faithful to a despotism lit by flashes of a style that flatters it and the glow of a nationalism that warms it.

Charles de Gaulle could exercise a limitless dictatorial power. He has not yielded to the temptation, primarily because a French intellectual nurtured on classic moralists and liberal philosophers would be incapable of imitating some foreign adventurer. But also because a personage of his stature cannot resist the temptation to invent what no one before him has attempted: a republic based on plebiscite and presided over by an old emperor, returned from the isle of Elba, but deciding against a new campaign that led to Waterloo and anticipating, by a quarter of a century, Monsieur Guizot's famous dictum to the people: "Go out and get rich!"

On occasion, however, he has not hesitated to bring about an open challenge to his own legality. In 1962, when an attempt on his life had recreated an emotional climate similar to the state of alert that had existed during the Algerian war, General de Gaulle, still desirous of having the chief of state elected by universal suffrage, calmly violated the most obvious intentions of the Constitution by resorting to a referendum before any vote had been taken in either house of Parliament. The Council of State, almost unanimously, and the Constitutional Council, with the support of Gaullists as loyal as René Cassin, Léon

Noël, and Pasteur Vallery-Radot, declared this initiative unconstitutional.

Even though he tossed the threat of his resignation into the scales, the general won by only a small margin: 46 percent of the total vote. His legitimacy had dissolved. But his personal ascendancy over the masses remained intact. On November 22nd of the same year, the legislative elections brought him the greatest electoral success obtained by a chief of state since Louis XVIII: with the added votes of a few independent delegates, the UNR (*Union pour la Nouvelle République*, the Gaullist party), disposed of an absolute majority. His political ideal had been realized: a parliament which sits but does not govern. This time, reversing the example of Napoleon III, the authoritarian empire would succeed the liberal empire.

Then, on January 31, 1964, there was the extraordinary press conference in which he handed down the tables of the law, describing the central power as "no longer the plaything of partisan groups, but [a power] of which the chief of state elected by the nation is both the source and the keeper . . ." and the Constitution as "a principle, a set of institutions, a custom." The disputed text of 1958 was thus sandwiched between a principle—which tended naturally toward the arbitrary—and a custom—the custom he had installed, imposed, modeled to his own hand.

Here then was the Legitimate Ruler in all his glory, crowned by History, source and keeper of a power defined by the thinkers of the Grand Siècle and justified by victory, a republican monarch who had brought to pass the old dream of the delegates of 1875: the founders of the Third Republic and the grandson of Charles X, wrapped together in the folds of the tricolor flag, accomplishing the kind of synthesis he had often imagined as he leafed through his history books. To the extent to which a man destroys only what he replaces, he would have destroyed political society if he had substituted for it another set of institutions. In this domain, he has created only precedents.

But this power is perhaps less absolute than it appears. The "privileged domain" is not only the region in which he has regally assembled, under his personal leadership, foreign affairs, national defense, and the French Community. It is also another domain, in which he rarely hunted. This politician who has been unswerving in his efforts to increase the authority of the State is a very timid advocate of the State in matters of economy; we saw that in 1945.

If General le Gaulle surrounds himself with liberal economists and classic financiers, if he—who sees himself as the symbol of national unity and the least bourgeois of men—carries out a policy which, in its overall aspects, is a policy of classes, it is because all of these problems, to his way of thinking, revolve around a single, dominant problem: money. Here again he demonstrates his familiarity with his history books, which teach that political independence is built on the foundation of a stable currency and that it was not any cartel of the leftist parties that had stabilized the franc forty years earlier, but Monsieur Poincaré.

It is also because this man, to whom the concept of the powerful State is almost intuitive, has found a great many inconvenient factors in the economic plans of the State, and primarily this one: a Plan is "complications," additional battles to be fought. The general, who is so attentive to the projection of his image on any terrain where he knows he is at his best—strategy, diplomacy, history—has a tendency in other domains to duck from blows and to ring down the curtain. Confronted with foreign states and rulers, he conducts himself with the boldness of a Richelieu;

197

confronted with groups of interests at home, with the wiliness of a Mazarin. Not too many headlines in the press, nothing too new or startling. To him, the term "stabilization" is the key word in economics. Would he use it in his dealings with Washington or Peking?

Money, first and foremost. To assure himself of this economic groundwork, this base for any *force de frappe*—a striking force which would permit him to issue a challenge to the dollar when the occasion arose—the general surrounded himself with such laissez-faire economists as Messieurs Pinay, Rueff, and Baumgartner, and later with Messieurs Pompidou and Giscard d'Estaing. This Republic whose diplomacy appeared to be to the left of that of the Popular Front; whose programs in matters of the national production would make of it what a member of the socialist opposition termed "the midwife of modernity"; whose discreet support of economic planning succeeded in terrorizing the entrenched hierarchy of industry—in the realm of finances and distribution of revenues, this Republic conducted itself like the old-fashioned Third Republic—with the exception of Michel Debré's "new deal" in 1966.

The Gaullist regime has done away with the deadlock in government, reestablished an equilibrium in the balance of payments, made the franc a solid currency again, provided an energetic impulse for the development of foreign trade, supported industrial expansion, and assured a favorable position for France in the European Common Market. But it has suffered three serious setbacks which, in the long run, will compromise these immediate victories.

Setbacks? In the first place, the troublesome lag in the matter of housing construction. "It is on that that we will be judged," De Gaulle had said. For the moment, the regime must be poorly judged. For fifteen million ill-housed citizens, 370,000 new dwellings per year. In the Paris area, 70,000 per year, although plans already in existence called for 100,000. Another setback is the rise in the cost of living: over a seven-year period it went up almost 30 percent—less than in Italy, but more than in either Belgium or England, and much more than in Germany or the United States. And a setback of primary importance is the increasing discrepancy between the revenue levels of shareholders and salaried workers: in 1964, a 12 percent increase for the former, and a 3 percent increase for the latter. It is no longer, of course, a question of absolute poverty; but in relation to those who are favorably placed on the upward path of industrial expansion, there is a constantly widening gap separating the working classes from a standard of living which a society of abundance has led them to desire and expect.

To a man who sees himself as the promoter and herald of social as well as political "cohesion," it is a deceiving state of affairs. But it would be naïve to believe the legends to the effect that he is sublimely uninterested in it. The anger of the destitute is contrary to his conceptions of a State that is efficient and united, stable and ambitious—contrary to his moral as well as to his esthetic sense.

These, however, are not the only reasons for the partial setback he suffered when he was reelected as President in December, 1965. If 45 percent of the French people whom he claimed to embody refused to back him, it was because of a deep-rooted Vichyism which has been able to survive his victories; because of the bitter aftermath of the struggles for "French Algeria"; because of the sense of frustration within the political establishment, which has not forgiven this "usurper" for depriving it of its cherished activities. Above all, it was because the peasants, a good deal of the working class, and the majority of the intellectuals

199

and youth felt that this regime of "grandeur" is no longer suitable to their present aspirations or to the problems of modern France—democratic planning, the European community, modern housing, the absolute priority of a less stratified educational system.

Fifty-five percent. Perhaps his "successors" will be glad to get such a majority. But for an old-style legitimate monarch, for a man of destiny, what use is a half-sacred rite? And, for such a passionate exponent of national unity, what is the meaning of a vote that shows a loyal North and a contemptuous South, an angry countryside balancing the more favorable cities, a majority among those over forty years of age and a minority among those under thirty, and a greater following among women than among men? It is a bitter victory, not the victory of a man who considers himself the symbol of France. The Fifth Republic was born of chaos transcended and ennobled by a Machiavellian hero; the Fifth-and-a-half Republic derives from a legality which is clouded by the sunset of a great destiny.

But of what importance are ordinary days or the problems of daily living, of what importance are even the forms of power, by comparison with the major objective which Charles de Gaulle had assigned himself: assuring the *independence* of France on a *level* worthy of this *nation* which he sees as the instrument of the Maker's designs.

10
The Nation
Above All

The "petit Robert" is the best practical dictionary in the French language. Since its latest edition was published under the Fifth Republic, one might think that its editors had General de Gaulle in mind when the following definition was prepared: "Nationalism: a) a passionate attachment to the nation to which one belongs, sometimes accompanied by xenophobia and a will toward isolation; b) a doctrine founded on this sentiment, subordinating everything to internal policy or to the development of national power" (cf. Maurras, Barrès).

Such, clearly, is the philosophy that inspires the words and deeds of Charles de Gaulle: all human activity revolves around the nation, the supreme collectivity molded by history, armed by the State, rooted in a territory, united by interest, led by the hero. Against this bloc, ideologies—illusions whose origins either are in the East or in shoddy rags borrowed from German philosophy—are useless.

Nothing prevails against this force, at once dreamlike and carnal, stemming from the depths of time. Only racial factors could emerge to cloud the spirit and threaten cohesion. No matter what his judicial status may be, can an Arab, a Maltese from Algeria, a Madagascan, have the same "idea" of France as Charles de Gaulle, an idea that can only have been formed by visiting the Invalides at an age when other children were rolling hoops; by reading, at twelve, the tales of a drummer boy of the Revolution; at fifteen, the *Memorial de Ste. Hélène;* and at thirty, Péguy's *Jeanne d'Arc?*

We cannot measure the strength of this nationalism and the vigor of its expression without citing some of the general's remarks, at various periods of his career. Consider for example, his *Memoirs* of the war:

"To Notre Dame la France, we have only one thing to say, and that is that nothing is of any importance to us except serving her . . . on the day of liberty, let her open her arms to us in a maternal embrace so that we may weep with joy and so that on the day when death comes to take us away she may wrap us gently in her good and sacred earth . . ."

And his speech to the crowd in Algiers, with the now famous declaration: "Never more than here and never more than tonight have I understood how fine, how great, how generous is France" (June 4, 1958).

And again, adopting an altogether different tone, familiar, almost comradely, in a speech delivered on the night when Algiers rose in insurrection against his power, January 29, 1960: "I address myself to France. Well, my old and beloved country, so here we are together, once more confronted with a heavy task."

And there is yet another style, this one borrowed from the language of the sportsman but expressing just as forcefully the old man's nationalist passion: "I seem to hear a murmur that resembles a worldwide sentiment, a general feeling—go France! go France! go!" The tone is all the more curious for having been employed in front of the cathedral of Chartres, the high altar of French spirituality, and on the occasion of the twenty-fifth anniversary of his call to arms of June 18, 1940. But with De Gaulle, one must always expect anything.

France would assuredly be finer and even more beautiful if she were not a nation of changeable people who betrayed Vercingetorix, detested Richelieu, guillotined Danton, forgot Clemenceau, tried and condemned Pétain. But the less worthy the French are of France, the more ardent—because the more stark—must be devotion to this sublime entity, constantly menaced by stateless interests and greed poorly camouflaged as internationalist doctrines and coalitions.

His own words notwithstanding, one need not overemphasize the religious aspect of the general's "faith." The components of Gaullist nationalism are at least partially mystical, and it is not by chance that one of Péguy's most fiery poems has been cited in reference to them. One need read only the three or four essential texts of Charles de Gaulle, from *The Edge of the Sword* to the speech "on the Republic" of September 4, 1958, to measure the extent to which Gaullist nationalism is positivistic.

Charles Maurras? Of course. But here again we must beware of going too far. "Maurras is a man who is right to the point of madness," De Gaulle once said. Maurras, if not a strategist, is at least an excellent professor of military history. And the memory of lost battles has inspired in him a certain sense of realities, though leaving him free to return, with the help of the Maurrasian demon, to the myth of "France alone."

Another source is the geopolitical estheticism of Barrès: A fascination with places and horizons; a nostalgia for the return; an attachment to the rhythms and words of the tribe; a will toward incarnation of the group; a passion for speech; the cult of energy expressed as attitude; an overwhelming contempt for any form of collectivity which is not the nation; an appeal to the past; the vision and conscience of a certain form of biological unity of the fatherland. De Gaulle emerges from Barrès as Churchill did from Kipling.

However severely one may judge nationalism in either a man or a people who, for many years, have been in a position to measure its real possibilities and its profound risks, it is still proper to weigh it against the test of fact. It has not always been summary and provocative. Let us recall a few dates.

When, in 1934, Major de Gaulle led his campaign for armored divisions, with the help of Paul Reynaud, it was not to assure the supremacy of France on the continent; it was to permit her to honor her signature and hold to the commitments of "collective security." How could Czechoslovakia or Romania be saved if the means did not exist to strike out from the ghetto of the Maginot line? The arguments of that day are closer to those of De Gaulle the statesman than those which fed the campaign for the nuclear striking force, twenty years later.

When, in June, 1940, in the depths of disaster, Churchill put forward his stunning and grandiose idea for a total union between France and England— surely the most anti-Gaullist idea of which anyone might dream—General de Gaulle hastened to Bordeaux in an attempt to see it carried through. Here again, the interest of the greatest number, which is not necessarily defined by the line of a frontier on a map, is considered of more importance than national egotism. Things can be restored to their proper order, later.

When, in November, 1942, the Allies—behaving toward De Gaulle in the most offhand, not to say contemptuous, manner—launched the invasion of Algeria without even notifying him in advance, his initial reaction was one of thin-skinned nationalism. "I hope the Vichy people throw them into the sea!" he cried. But he very quickly changed his mind and launched yet another of his great appeals to the French people; the cause of liberty had taken precedence over the pride of the leader.

When, in 1948, the chairman of the RPF attempted to gather all of the French people around the man who had been the leader of June 18, 1940, his most pressing argument was not strictly nationalist: it was a matter of joining with the anti-communist West to checkmate the "Cossacks" and the "totalitarians." So, the Atlantic Community was brought to the fore, the American alliance extolled, the council of the "free world" convoked. This was not the time for "France alone." But, at the same time, the EDC* was denounced as an absolute evil; De Gaulle certainly wanted allies, but, no matter how varied the force itself might be, he also wanted to be certain that the kepis and the insignia of rank of the French would be recognized.

When, in 1958, Charles de Gaulle returned to public affairs, his first gesture was not to withdraw France from the coalitions in which the leaders of the Fourth Republic had made her a partner; it was to call for the organization of a tripartite directory of the Western alliance. Was this simply a step on the road toward isolation? In spite of the bitter commentaries with which he surrounded the rejection of his proposal by Washington and by London, this objective may, for a time at least, have been his true objective —leaving him free to make life more difficult for his

* EDC: The European Defense Community; an American-sponsored project for a multinational European army, which was rejected by the French Assembly.

two partners than for the adversary, in accordance with a tradition he had perfected.

And if Charles de Gaulle's policy with regard to overseas nationalism remains strictly in keeping with his line of thought, it is not the policy of a common nationalist. To transfer to others a faith of this nature, to acknowledge that a passion for his homeland may burn in the heart of an Algerian as well as in that of a Frenchman, requires, in spite of appearances, a certain fineness of spirit and a certain openness of heart.

The nationalism that had not ceased to inspire, support and impel him, was controlled intelligently enough so that, once reestablished in "legitimacy," De Gaulle knew how to form a diplomatic strategy animated by other motives and weighted with a better lead. But no matter how attentive he might have been to the prolongation of peace and the defense of liberty, progress and international solidarity, one can see in the elderly leader the demanding passions that carry us back to the themes of the young cadet at Saint-Cyr.

From 1958 to 1963, occupied with the disengagement from Algeria, and thus concerned not to alienate too abruptly the official allies of France, he demonstrated his ability for maneuver, his aptness for cooperation. However, once "liberated" by the Evian agreements, he apparently decided to exact repayment from the world for this exorbitant concession of French nationalism. Thus, he set out in battle against the Anglo-Saxon world: January 1963, July 1965, February 1966, December 1967, March 1968; no blow was too hard if it was delivered against those whose shadow for too long had clouded the landscape of France.

Xenophobia? For the "petit Robert," the word could not be entirely dissociated from the concept of nationalism. Nor can it be separated from an attentive description of the general's diplomatic behavior. However noble may be the will to resist the American hegemony; however occasionally diverting the fencing match Charles de Gaulle invented for the purpose; however penetrating his analysis and refreshing his blows—from Pnom-Penh to Santiago—the Gaullist game stems too clearly from a strategy of temperament to be truly healthy.

General de Gaulle has certainly always been aware of Nietzsche's comment that the twentieth century would be the century of national confrontation. We must admire him for this awareness; but we must reproach him with having done nothing to belie this pessimistic prognosis. It is one thing to be conscious of the permanent virulence of nationalism and another to maintain it with apparent delight. The general likes to say that: "A state worthy of the name has no friends." Are the friendships resulting from a perspicacious diplomacy with regard to the "third world" no more than blameworthy weaknesses?

We have already cited Roosevelt's judgment of him: "He is highly sensitive to anything concerning the honor of France. But I think that he is essentially an egoist." And we have mentioned De Gaulle's comment on the matter in his *Memoirs:* "I will never know if Franklin Roosevelt thought that, in anything concerning France, Charles de Gaulle was an egoist for France, or simply for himself."

It is a question which others, better informed now than Roosevelt was, continue to ask.

11
To Liberate France
from Her Colonies . . .

            At the beginning of this century, the French army was made up of two types of officers: the "colonials" and the "mainlanders." The former considered Joffre and Gallieni to be their leaders. The latter, Foch and Pétain. As we have seen, Charles de Gaulle chose the second path immediately on graduation from Saint-Cyr. He served in Arras, under Colonel Pétain. For him, the military profession was not to be a matter of "pacification" or —in Lyautey's phrase, of "spreading oil on the waters." Nor would it be the "improvement" of the subsoil of Tonkin or the government of the Bambara tribes of French West Africa. It would be firepower, modern techniques and the strategy of movement.

It would not have required much stimulus for this nationalist intellectual to arrive at the conclusion that the French army, in pursuing the trails of Samory and El-Hiba, was wasting its time and burying itself in the past. He might even have agreed with Lord Salisbury's statement (and Clemenceau's thought) that "in scratching its claws in the sand of the Sahara" the French nation was employing its energies to no purpose and dispersing its forces, forgetting the Rhine frontier, "revenge," Europe, and the world of the twentieth century. In De Gaulle's particular case, there was also the concern of a young officer with a passion for research, to whom the problems of the present were not on the Niger or the Mekong rivers, but in the coal mines, the factories and the laboratories.

"Sacred egoism," a sense of history, or a prophetic feeling for the future of technics? Lieutenant, then Captain, then Major de Gaulle, saw the problems of his work and life only in "European" terms and in the perspective of the industrial universe of which he was a part. No Frenchman was less concerned with what is now called the "third world" than this Parisian native of Lille.

And yet, in 1930, the De Gaulle who dreamed, spoke and wrote only in terms of fortifications, major units of armies, offensives and techniques of firepower, found himself in a place where his ideas and his fund of knowledge played a minor role—Lebanon. France governed there at the time, under a mandate from the League of Nations and with no excess of violence. It was through the influence of this rather pleasant semi-colonization that Major de Gaulle first approached the colonial question. He was not fascinated by it. The letters we have cited to his friend Lucien Nachin demonstrate that De Gaulle did not believe in the necessity for a "French presence"— except as a means of changing man.

But he did judge it possible and useful to change or create structures, as is evidenced by the only public statements he made in the course of his stay in the Levant. Here is a fragment of one such text, one of the rare "unpublished" statements of Charles de Gaulle: "Devotion to the common good, that is what is needed . . . for you, the youth of Lebanon, this great duty takes on an immediate and imperious meaning; for it is a nation that you have to build. On this marvelous soil, steeped in history, sheltered by the rampart of your mountains, linked by the sea to the activities of the West, aided by the wisdom and strength of France, it is up to you to construct a State. Not simply as a means of sharing in its functions, of exercising its prerogatives, but of bringing to it this proper life, this internal strength, without which there are only empty institutions. It will be necessary for you to create and nourish a public spirit, a voluntary subordination of the individual to the general interest, a condition without which there can be no true authority of leaders, no true justice in the courts, order in the streets, or a consciousness of duty in civil servants . . ."

Already so like De Gaulle . . .

Less than a year later, after his return to France, he took up again his work on the "army of the future" with the help of Paul Reynaud (who, coincidentally, had just left the Ministry of Colonies). The armored divisions failed to materialize, but De Gaulle was interested in nothing but them. The Levant was far away.

Then came the war, and De Gaulle's assignment on the Rhine. Then, the command of the 4th Armored Division, and then his appointment as Undersecretary of State for War. In the midst of the debacle of 1940, there was his famous conversation with Weygand, who sighed, "All is finished!" "And what about the Empire?" was De Gaulle's furious reply. Suddenly, he was aware of an overseas world which, as strategist, he had forgotten and was rediscovering in the hour of disaster. Throughout the "days of agony" of June 1940, Charles de Gaulle talked about the "Breton stronghold," but was thinking primarily of Africa.

On June 18th, the thesis he developed in his appeal

to the French was one of war in world dimensions, France beyond the seas. From this time on, Africa became a part of himself, almost an obsession, first as a litany of disasters: Mers-el-Kebir, Dakar; and then of hopes: Douala, Fort-Lamy, Brazzaville . . .

It was in the heart of the dark continent, as much as in front of the microphones of the BBC, that Free France was born. Gratitude is the least of Charles de Gaulle's faults, but memory is his most exceptional gift. He would not forget his first meetings with Eboué, the Negro governor of Chad. It was from this that the most truly French part of his fortune was to emerge; the African peoples were a part of it. After the disaster of Dakar he appealed directly to them and to their attachment to France. A link between them would remain.

June, 1941. One year after the first call from London, De Gaulle and Catroux, on the eve of confrontation with the Vichy forces, officially recognized the independence of that same Levant in which Major de Gaulle had not wanted to see France too deeply or lengthily engaged.

Clearly, the policy of Free France in the Levant was not always to be inspired by Catroux's evolutionist spirit, even before the bombing of Damascus by Gaullist forces in June 1945 ruined for a long time a moral credit already undermined by London policy. But, in many of the most conservative reactions of General de Gaulle in the years 1941-43, there is clear evidence of the exasperation provoked in the man of June 18th by the actions of General Spears and other British agents.

Be that as it may, the Levant emerged from the war independent. De Gaulle, through a thousand intrigues and ambushes—willingly or not—had carried out the policy defined as early as 1936, under the ministry of Léon Blum, by the man who was now his ambassador in London and one of his closest advisers, Pierre Viénot.

But, for some time now, the axis of Gaullist strategy had inclined toward the West and those Algerian sands on which the fortunes of Charles de Gaulle would be repeatedly decided. The Allied invasion of November 8, 1942, brought him back to Africa.

From this point on, decolonization was a problem he could not avoid. It was in January 1944, at the Brazzaville conference, that the Gaullist theses on the colonial question were formulated. What De Gaulle said on the speaker's platform and what his minister, René Pleven, put into the final text, does not go very far and may be summed up thus: the liberation of men, but not of nations. Political and social emancipation within the framework of a unit in which France would retain ultimate power. It was specified that, in no case, would matters be carried as far as self-government.

Brazzaville was far more a preface to integration than an announcement of self-determination. De Gaulle, in this instance, is the heir of radical humanists of the type of Jules Ferry rather than the precursor of the President of the Fifth Republic.

He had given evidence of this and was to confirm it in the course of two crises which put the question of French overseas power to a brutal test. In the first days of 1944, the newly created Moroccan Istiqlal party laid claim to independence and began manifestations in the streets of Rabat and Fez. The Second Armored Division, which was then encamped near the Moroccan capital, was charged with "restoration of order" and set about it with all the means at its command. At the same time, René Massigli, General de Gaulle's personal emissary in Rabat, was instructed to inform Sultan Mohammed Ben Youssef (a man

212

for whom De Gaulle had a vague feeling of fellowship, later expressed by an invitation to France in June 1945 and recorded in one of the happier pages of his *Memoirs*) that France would tolerate no agitation for so long as the war continued.

The very day on which the war ended, May 8, 1945, 'he Algerian masses descended into the streets to demand that this struggle be fulfilled by liberty for colonial peoples. Violence erupted and several dozen Europeans were killed. Repression was terrible, bringing bloodshed to most of Kabylia. More than ten thousand people were killed. Decidedly, the De Gaulle government, which was responsible for the action, was not taking the path of decolonization.

The general, however, now found himself constrained to revise his relations with the territories and peoples overseas. If the French presence remained solidly anchored in Africa—despite crises—it was already confronted with developments of a different order in Asia. On March 9, 1945, the Japanese garrisons entrenched in Indochina since July 1940, seized complete control of the country, massacring or interning French military and civilian officials. The colonial administration was utterly destroyed. Clearly, the Japanese power was already enfeebled after continued attacks by MacArthur and Mountbatten; the situation in Indochina constituted temporary conquest. But who could have foreseen that, five months later, the atomic bomb would seal the fate of Japan?

In the meantime, the loss of Indochina was seriously disquieting. The French no longer possessed a fleet. The United States—the only power which could provide the key to a possible return—was declaredly hostile to the French cause in Indochina. So, in the hope of once again finding the path to Saigon open, on March 24, 1945 (two weeks after the Japanese takeover) the French government published a declaration of intentions of distressing timidity. There was in it no question of autonomy, except within a federal framework.

Progress toward emancipation? Cambodians and Laotians might think so; but the Vietnamese, to whom the Japanese, in fact, had just granted an independent government, greeted this text with no enthusiasm whatever. For one thing, it separated the three *kys* (Tonkin, Annam and Cochin China), thus setting itself in opposition to the unitary inclination of a people very conscious of their common civilization and history.

Not content with thus indicating to the Vietnamese that the hour for independence had not arrived, the De Gaulle government began preparing an expeditionary corps destined for the Far East. It could certainly have been said that the objective assigned to Leclerc was the defeat of Japan, rather than the reconquest of Indochina. But even after Tokyo had capitulated, on August 15th, no thought was given to disbanding the armada gathered together in Marseille. A great many people who considered themselves engaged in a struggle against the Japanese, were instead to find themselves implicated in an enterprise of colonial reconquest.

But Charles de Gaulle was soon to retire from power, anticipating, precisely over Indochina, a confrontation between the two halves of the wartime Gaullist movement: a conservative spirit on the one hand, and a theme of innovation on the other. These were symbolized in the Far East by Admiral d'Argenlieu and General Leclerc. D'Argenlieu (or those around him) advocated an intransigence which made no distinction between a Nazi occupation and the will toward freedom of colonial peoples. Leclerc (or those around him) thought in terms of adaptation to new situations, refused to apply the "I shall maintain" theories of 1940 to these overseas rebels, saw in them the nationalism and spirit of the Resistance.

In this phase of decolonization, De Gaulle would truly have failed. What is remarkable is that he recognized this fact. In 1946, he had declared himself in favor of his conservative friends, the Argenlieu team, and opposed to his innovating friends, Leclerc and Sainteny. But, in 1953, when Jean Sainteny's *Histoire d'une paix manquée* was published and France's former representative in Hanoi told the story of the failure of his attempts at a peaceful settlement with Ho Chi Minh in 1946, and of the cost of this failure to France—a long and devastating war—the hermit of Colombey summoned the ex-High Commissioner of the Republic and said to him: "Well, Sainteny, so it was you who was right."

In the intervening period, of course, De Gaulle had lived through the unfortunate adventure of the RPF, which, on the pretext of gathering together an assembly of all Frenchmen, had brought him to the brink of leadership of a neo-fascist movement uniquely intransigent on the subject of the Empire, hostile to any new status for Algeria, and to any concessions on Indochina. An authentic liberal such as Catroux had been intelligent enough to dissociate himself from the RPF at a very early stage. This feeling of having almost become the hostage of the most obtuse proponents of colonial conservatism contributed to the awakening of the man of June 18th.

It was, therefore, about 1953 when his "epoch" (in the sense that his teacher Charles Péguy gave to this word) of decolonization began. He was returning from a trip through Africa. During a stopover in Tunis, the local leaders of the RPF asked him to make a speech against the "terrorism" of Bourguiba's Neo-Destour party. De Gaulle refused; he had finally realized that a national sentiment might traverse the frontiers of the hexagon of metropolitan France and that a courageous Tunisian need not be a "fine young Tunisian" in the sense intended by his local partisans.

It was at this time, as we have seen, that his Indochinese reconversion came about and he made his remark to Sainteny. To these private gestures, he was shortly to add a public statement of position that would arouse the hopes of the colonial peoples. In June 1955, he convoked his "last" press conference, and before several hundred journalists he replied to a question on the Moroccan situation by paying tribute to Sultan Sidi Mohammed, "my companion." And this at a time when the Sultan was still living in exile in Madagascar.

The conference caused something of a sensation. The words themselves may certainly be interpreted in a sense other than that of liberalism. One can see in them, within a typically Gaullist perspective, an intention to associate allegiance to his person with any form of relationship to the France of "proper order." This Sultan whom you others have exiled forms a part of the Gaullist legend; it is that which is important. We are here at the heart of the mechanism of Charles de Gaulle's thought. That disciple of Mithridates would say, "Rome is no longer in Rome, but wherever I may be."

The blow was fully effective. Colombey, once the sanctuary of Empire, became the Court of Appeals of the colonial peoples and of the advocates of decolonization. Jean Amrouche, François Mauriac, Mohammed Masmoudi joined together to create the legend of a De Gaulle who was the patron of liberties. It was clear that he no longer believed in the Empire. He was seeking new formulas. He said as much. But only in private.

When he had departed from the scene in 1946, France was recognized—with a condescension which doubtless irritated him—as one of the "great powers." When he returned, he found her (or professed to find her) limited in her independence by pressures from both above and below. Above was the American protectorate exercised through the North Atlantic Treaty Organization and the various European alignments; below was a colonial system which bore out the old revolutionary principle that "a State which oppresses another is not free."

In 1946, he had said that only a great crisis would bring him back to power; in 1952, he had added that the French would think of him when they became fearful of losing Algeria. But did he know what path he would choose? Had he formulated a doctrine during the years of retreat at Colombey? Had he decided to support, and even to speed up, the political emancipation of Algeria? He had, in fact, decided on only one thing: to assure the independence of France with relation to Algeria. He does not seem to have measured quickly what this proposition implied in return.

Actually, there were few questions to which he had given more careful thought over so prolonged a period of time. In April, 1944, in Algiers, three weeks after the announcement by the Provisional Government of the relatively liberal statute granting French citizenship to an important sector of the Moslem population, André Philip, the minister charged with application of the law, told De Gaulle that the measures thus far taken had not been enthusiastically received and that it would probably be necessary to grant complete autonomy. "Autonomy, Philip? You know very well that all this will end with total independence!"

This lightning flash of insight did not, however, prevent General de Gaulle from dealing harshly with autonomists of the type of Ferhat Abbas, or from as-

217

suming responsibility for one of the most terrible repressions ever unleashed in Algeria—that of May, 1945. Nor did his lucidity as a historian prevent him, as chief of the RPF, from taking a stand in a speech delivered in Algiers in August, 1947, against the evolutionary statute proposed by the socialist minister Édouard Depreux. Because the risk of war at that time was such that France could no more have envisaged depriving herself of such a strategic base than she could have in 1942? Or because, on the eve of the municipal elections, the RPF had to be made to appear to the voters of Algiers as the party of imperial stability? In the case of De Gaulle, who always has "two irons in the fire," there are also always two plans of decision: one for history and one for the varying winds of fortune.

In 1955, the Algerian writer Jean Amrouche came to visit him at Colombey. "Algeria will be emancipated," the general told him. . . . "It will be hard; there will be damage done, a great deal of damage. . . ." But that same year, at the press conference in which he saluted—in the person of Sultan Sidi Mohammed—the idea of independence for Morocco, he spoke of Algeria only in terms of integration.

Two years later, just before leaving for a meeting of the United Nations General Assembly at which he would have to defend French policies, the minister of foreign affairs, Christian Pineau (his former minister of supply in 1945), also made the pilgrimage to La Boisserie. "There is only one solution for Algeria, independence . . ." De Gaulle announced. Pineau was astonished. "But, general, you must say so—it would change everything!"—"No, Pineau, this is not the time. . . ."

And four months after that, on February 8, 1958, Maurice Schumann, who questioned him on the future of Algeria, was answered with a complete summary of the plan for self-determination which De Gaulle would make public in September, 1959—a year and a half later. Long before that, he had also told Maurice Clavel: "I am not Bonaparte, but I will say, as he did about the revolt in the Vendée: no more fighting. . . . It is time now for talk."

And so? And so, when the events of May 13th took place he contented himself at first with going to see Algiers for himself: force of things . . . On June 4th, he made a speech in the Forum and informed the people of Algiers that they have been *understood*— by which he meant the past has been understood. The popular climate of Algiers impressed him, but not to the point of preventing him from paying tribute—in the face of this single-minded crowd—to "all the fighters." And that same night, he said to one of his closest collaborators: "Now, everything depends on what the *Fellaghas* are going to do. Do you think they'll come down?" And when Soustelle displayed astonishment at the remark, which seemed to presage negotiations with the rebels, the general said: "You should reread Lyautey, Soustelle; do you think that the Moslem Arabs really want to be Frenchmen?" But none of this prevented him, two days later in Mostaganem, from launching a cry of "Long live French Algeria!" It might always be useful. . . .

In the time-period necessary to resolution of an Algerian policy, he set out to create the "structure" for an eventual welcome to an emancipated Algeria. In a tour of all of Africa, he offered independence to the island of Madagascar and to twelve French territories on the dark continent itself. The one of the twelve who took him at his word, Sékou Touré of Guinea, was so promptly dismissed into the outer darkness that one wonders whether the general had not hoped that there would be one "no" to ratify so many "yeses," a "no" which would raise the curtain for a settlement with Algeria. "If all goes well, we will have a Houphouet-Boigny (the "yes" of the Ivory Coast); if not, it will be a Sékou Touré (the "no" of Guinea)...."

Algeria would see herself promised a *choice position* in a Community which more and more closely resembled some form of nebula. Raymond Aron ironically saluted "the style of abandonment." The fact remains that he accomplished this necessary African operation, which the Fourth Republic had approached with hesitation and squabbling, with an audacity and a nobility which created a concrete bridge between France and the people of Africa.

But there was a difference between Algeria and the rest of Africa—a war. The first thing required was for the fighting to cease. On October 23, 1958, he offered the Algerian *maquisards* a "peace of the brave," which made no reference to the white flag that would have given the affair the appearance of surrender. But it was necessary to go even further than this. On September 16, 1959, Charles de Gaulle announced his three-paneled plan for self-determination: *francisation* (a term whose deliberate ugliness made it clear that this political esthete wanted none of it); independence, which was termed *secession* and described as a catastrophe; and *association*, which was obviously what he wanted. The FLN (Front de Libération Nationale)* reacted reasonably to the basic meaning of the plan if not to its details. But Algiers burst into flame, and barricades were thrown up in the streets by the organization of "French Algeria."

At eight o'clock on the evening of January 29, 1960, Frenchmen gathered around their television screens saw a picture of an old brigadier general with a wax-white countenance, dark-circled eyes, and an irritable

* The FLN—the party of Algerian nationalists fighting for independence. [Translator's note]

air. In his most arrogant tones, he barked a few orders and there was nothing for the barricade chief, Pierre Lagaillarde, to do but to send his friends in search of a colonel who was waiting in the back room of a café, and hand in his sword.

The peremptory Jacobin leader Frenchmen admired and followed that night would still take some strange detours before he arrived at his goal, and he would even go to Algeria and talk to the officers in their clubs about a total victory over the rebellion. But he already knew that negotiation was the way to peace. "It will be an ugly business . . ." he confided to his ministers, and advised them to "hang on to the mast, because the ship is going to rock."

On the fourteenth of June, he made a direct offer to talk with the leaders of the GPRA (Gouvernement Provisoire de la République Algérienne). But five days earlier, two of the leaders of the Algerian *maquis,* Si Salah and Si Mohammed, had come to see him at the Élysée Palace. Si Salah had promised him to win popular acceptance for the "peace of the brave" and to form a "party of reconciliation." Less than two weeks after this, however, he had permitted the participants in these secret talks to fall into the hands of worried rivals, and was conducting a lack-luster series of meetings with other Algerian delegates in Melun. And at the same time he was using his left hand to carry on still other conversations with the prisoners (Ben Bella and three others) on the island of Aix, even though he knew that their relations with the GPRA were clouded. It was no longer two irons he had in the fire, but an entire set—as if he were afraid of seeming less oriental than his opponents, but primarily as if he were afraid of concluding the business too quickly and thereby becoming the victim of a bad bargain.

In the end, he was to meet with the formal delegates of the GPRA in Évian when the army in Algeria again attempted to veto his program. At dawn of April 22, 1961, four generals took control of Algiers. Nineteen stars, and not a single head. They were not up to the task they had assumed. De Gaulle sent his minister of state for Algerian affairs, Louis Joxe, and General Olié, his chief of staff, to make up the minds of those military leaders who were still undecided; had Prime Minister Michel Debré issue an appeal to the people which was so naïve and absurd that his brilliant second-in-command won a degree of sympathy he had never before enjoyed; and himself took to the radio with a combination of sarcasm and orders which exploded through every transistor in Algeria—where every draftee listened to and followed him.

The Évian agreements were signed, and a few courageous men, French and Algerian, clinging to each other in the tempest that raged around them, set to work to apply them in the face of the incendiaries and assassins of the OAS and the less intelligent of the leaders of the FLN. The agreements were not a great achievement? The art of conducting a successful retreat is the most difficult in all of military science. The general wanted to give proof of this.

Could it have been done better—or not quite so badly? For the immediate future, France might have obtained better terms at Évian if the general had allowed Louis Joxe to negotiate. Negotiate? Charles de Gaulle does not understand the meaning of this word very well; he knows better how to defy President Roosevelt and to back down slowly before Ben Youssef Ben Khedda. But no matter how the texts signed in Évian might have read, they would have made little difference in 1966, when Paris was forced to admit a fact no one could have blocked—Algeria's move to socialism.

Anyone seeking the areas in which General de
222

Gaulle's policy in Algeria was partially a failure will find them in the refusal of Algeria's French population to accept any solution but their own. Taking their earlier behavior into consideration, was it possible to associate this million people with a solution of which they felt themselves to be the victims? Charles de Gaulle never seriously attempted it. In his relations with the people he was compelled to carry with him into a new period of history, he spoke only the language of constraint. The safety of the State demanded extreme measures; it did not, however, demand the contemptuous brevity in which he indulged when he was confronted with a people no lucid historian could condemn, a people whose only immorality was the situation in which they had been placed, since 1830, by the French nation. Making peace was the task the French people had assigned to the general. But why not try to make peace with everyone?

He did, however, succeed in ending this war the country no longer wanted, and in maintaining the necessary relations between the two states—and even between the two peoples. It is easy enough to say what might have been done; he was the one who did it, taking his risks and considering those he ran personally as the least of them. That fact should not be forgotten.

In 1960, in the course of a discussion with some other political personalities on the chances of making peace in Algeria, former prime minister Edgar Faure stated: "The Algerian problem is insoluble so long as it is encased in a three-dimensional area. To arrive at a solution, it will be necessary to move into the fourth dimension. I know of no one but De Gaulle who is capable of it. . . ."

Thus, Algeria was independent—and so was France. For this had been the essential objective of the general-president. He knew that one people which oppressed another was not truly free itself. He knew that the American protectorate would weigh more heavily on France for so long as she ruined herself in colonial enterprises and linked her diplomacy to situations inherited from the past. Algeria's independence would bring with it the political freedom of France, a restored prestige abroad, an army brought home to assume more modern tasks; a return to the dreams of 1930, dreams of a military force cast in the mold of a phalanx of cadets.

Twice the old sovereign had found it necessary to go before the nation on television, his features twisted in the righteous wrath of the leader, hurling orders that were not to be disputed. Then, France was decolonized and freed of extremists. The third world was open to her. For De Gaulle, the United Nations ceased to be a court of petty sessions, disdained as nothing more than a theater for the performance of one's best speeches. And in spite of a few spots on her robe, of a few profitable arrangements with Pretoria and Salisbury, a few bursts of gunfire in the Gabon and in Djibouti, France has willingly taken the stage and assumed the role of the wise virgin.

De Gaulle became a decolonizer only because decolonization was inevitable and served both the independence and interest of France and his own freedom of action. But many others, who might have taken note of these same realities and projected their consequences, neglected them.

12

A Guerrillero
in the Élysée

General de Gaulle's foreign policy is constructed on a foundation of three major ideas. France must occupy a place in the front rank of nations. Relations between states—whether allied or not—are based only on power and guile. Ideologies are of relatively little importance, and the only real forces confronting each other in the international arena are individual nations.

The first idea is a part of his intrinsic character. He expressed the second in its crudest form at a meeting of the Council of Ministers. When Couve de Murville spoke of the "states which are friends of France," the general interrupted: "The minister of foreign affairs [should know] that a State worthy of the name has no friends." The most surprising example of the third idea occurred in an observation he made to one of his collaborators who suggested in November, 1944, that Mr. Churchill's wish to take part in the forthcoming Franco-Soviet meetings be granted, and that the pact expected to be signed be made into a tripartite affair. "Inadmissible," the general said. "There is no means of equating the relations of France and Russia, who have no differences, with relations between France and England, who are still separated by serious divergences of interest. . . ."

The general had no sooner taken up the reins of power again, laid the foundations for the French Community, and completed the draft of the new constitution, then he laid his cards on the table with France's allies. In a message addressed to Washington and London on September 24, 1958, he set forth perfectly clearly the problem which he considered fundamental —equality of treatment with the Anglo-Saxon nations in the conduct of the affairs of the West. What Charles-the-Alone could not obtain from his powerful protectors during the war, General de Gaulle, invested by the French people with an almost limitless power, would now demand from his partners. The era of Teheran and Yalta was past. The only replies he received were evasive, and he therefore decided to force the gates of this somewhat too exclusive club.

There are several paths he might have chosen to arrive at his goal. Avoiding the temptation to rely exclusively on the energy and potential of the nation— nationalist dreamer though he may be, General de Gaulle knows how to add—he could have attempted to dissociate London from Washington, conclude a new Entente Cordiale, and open the way for a "greater Europe" which would provide a counterbalance to American power. He could also have accelerated the union of the Europe of the Six and attempted to make of it an instrument for continental independence. Or he could have made another trip to Moscow and indulged in the most classic form of international blackmail: equality or neutrality. And finally, with peace concluded in Algeria, he could have aroused the sensitivities of the recently emancipated nations against the dominance of the dollar and made himself the spokesman for peoples aspiring to freedom and economic development—a strategy which might have caused concern in Washington. But he took, at first, another path.

He chose to see in Germany, not a powerful, prosperous, and disciplined fragment of the Europe of the Six, but an ancient adversary of the Gallic peoples whose redemption could now be assured by the magnanimity of a great man. In Aix-la-Chapelle, speaking in the name of the war-torn continent, he gave a solemn and dramatic character to the historic reconciliation between the two *nations* and reconstituted the Holy Roman Empire. Chancellor Konrad Adenauer, a native of the Rhineland who was easily susceptible to the eloquence of the Gauls, came to Colombey in September of 1958 and allowed himself to be seduced. But on July 30, 1960, at Rambouillet, the charm was suddenly broken by the two words which to the general's mind gave meaning to the whole effort of seduction: fatherland and independence.

On that day, General de Gaulle attempted to secure his guest's adherence to a plan for reconversion of the postwar Europe of the Schuman Plan and the Common Market into a league of individual nations, and to make of this classic coalition an instrument of war against American hegemony. The chancellor, even if he had wanted to, could never have taken such a path: the portion of Europe he governed was actually an American fragment of the Old World, more closely integrated with the production systems and the strategic arsenal of the United States than any other nation on the continent—and all the more closely linked with Washington by the fact that reunification of the German fatherland depended almost entirely on relations between the White House and the Kremlin.

Since that time, the general has tried again to associate Bonn with his enterprises: a spectacular trip to Germany, and the signing of a solemn treaty have maintained a form of illusion. But since the old gentleman from Cologne turned over the chancellery to a Bavarian who is less responsive to the prestige of French eloquence than to that of American prosperity, the attempt has lost whatever credibility it once possessed. It is no longer possible to achieve the desired goal through a miraculous union that would alter the course of history for Frenchmen and Germans; the only path now left open is that of a slow fusion in the European crucible—where the French element may remain at the top, permitting Paris to inspire, and even to influence ideas and policies, but not to dominate (in the Gaullist manner) a continental diplomacy.

England? The general is apparently still haunted by the words Winston Churchill had spoken to him on June 5, 1944. "Every time we must choose between Europe and the open sea we will choose the sea. . . ." He does not seem to have as clear a memory for the prime minister's efforts at Yalta to force the Americans and Russians to recognize France's right to both a zone of occupation in Germany and the power of veto in the Security Council of the United Nations. As a result, he has never devoted any great thought to the idea of an association with London against Washington. Once, however, he did: at Rambouillet, with Mr. Harold Macmillan, in December, 1962.

The British prime minister was preparing to leave for the Bahamas, where he was to meet with President John F. Kennedy. American cancellation of production of the Skybolt missiles, which had been planned as standard equipment of the Royal Air Force, had placed him in a difficult position for discussions that involved a reevaluation of relationships within the North Atlantic Alliance. And Macmillan did not want to align himself too exclusively with Washington without first having assured himself that he would not be cut off from Europe.

Since the explosion of the first French atomic bomb in the Sahara five months earlier, General de Gaulle had considered himself reinforced by a considerable power of persuasion, and was particularly on guard against Washington. Paradoxically, instead of reassuring him with respect to France's position as a privileged ally, the great firmness displayed by President Kennedy in the Cuban affair had seemed to him to confirm his favorite thesis: the Americans might risk the worst when their immediate security and the national territory were threatened, but they would have no desire to engage themselves totally in defense of the European continent.

Did it occur to Mr. Macmillan at this time to propose to the general an association between their two countries for the production of atomic reactors, which would permit them to depend less on the Americans? De Gaulle expected an offer of this nature, but the only thing that was forthcoming was a request for French support of Britain's entry into the Common Market. Did De Gaulle, for his part, make it clear that he considered as Europeans only those who did not depend on the Americans? Whether he did or not, the conference progressed from silence to veiled or direct threats, and ended on a note of almost total disagreement. It was said that Mr. Macmillan wept. He would have done better to explain his position clearly: the two former companions of Algiers, in 1943, missed the opportunity to establish a broad policy of Franco-British association which could have provided a fair counter-balance to the United States and opened the gates of Europe to Great Britain.

It was a result that was made even more distressing by the fact that the intentions of the British prime minister were highly favorable to such a policy. The proof of this is evident in the text of the Nassau agreements concluded a month later by Macmillan and Kennedy. While everyone—and De Gaulle first of all—had thought that the prime minister was going to the Bahamas only to agree to President Kennedy's conditions, the visitor actually brought back an extraordinary diplomatic success, obtaining direct deliveries to England of the Polaris missiles (far superior to the abandoned Skybolt) without passing through NATO, and also the right to utilize them if "the vital national interests of the country were at stake."

And even more than this: Mr. Macmillan had obtained from President Kennedy an agreement that France should benefit from the advantages he had just secured for Great Britain. André Fontaine reported this in *Le Monde* on November 18, 1964, and on very good authority; it was President Kennedy himself who had told him of it.

The general does not like gifts. He rejected this one from the Bahamas just as he had pretended to ignore the fruits of Yalta. Any other statesman would have grasped at the positive factors in Mr. Macmillan's offer and then attempted to enlarge this first opening in the gates and minimize the price of admission. De Gaulle recognizes only victories he himself has secured. So he neglected this one. And as payment for his good offices in the Bahamas, he slammed the door to Europe in the face of Mr. Macmillan, who had to resign as prime minister.

In summing up his attitude from 1940 to 1944, a question was asked: War with whom? Now the question is: Peace with whom? De Gaulle fenced brilliantly, but his thrusts rarely reached anyone but the neighboring companions and allies of his own country.

Was it because he hoped to obtain advantages from the East? The abortion of the summit conference which was to have been held in Paris in 1960 shattered (until his visit to Moscow in 1966) General de

Gaulle's idea of making himself the leader of a policy of arbitration between East and West. Of Mr. Khrushchev's visit to Paris, he especially retained a vivid impression of an incident which served as an admirable illustration to his own historic theses. In the course of a boat trip on the Seine, the Soviet leader had suddenly grasped both of his hands and said: "You and us, we are white. . . ."

In refusing to sign the Moscow agreement on the banning of nuclear tests, and in advocating a policy of unyielding firmness on Berlin, the general has limited his margin for maneuver with the Soviet Union—but not with the peoples' republics of East Europe. With them, he has conducted an intelligent long-term policy ranging from French recognition of the Oder-Neisse line as the western frontier of Poland to a vast increase in economic exchanges with Warsaw and Bucharest—a policy extended in 1966 to the U.S.S.R.

However "white" he may be, and however attached to a technical civilization which is the product of European culture, General de Gaulle has established relations with the "emergent forces"—from Algiers to Peking and Santiago de Chile—relations which constitute the most original and the most attractive aspect of his diplomatic strategy. Whether or nor he overestimated the harvest he might reap from recognition of Red China, it would not be possible simply to put it down as a gesture of defiance to Washington—where, as a matter of fact, a good many people judged that the lesson received was also a service rendered.

Until his challenge to NATO, in 1966, Gaullist diplomacy—that mixture of effervescent swagger, icy realism, and generosity—was in a tradition which no Frenchmen could disown without being unduly cynical. Too much pomp and ceremony for the results obtained? Perhaps. But the results that are obtained

231

are not contrary either to the essential genius of France—which is of "communication"—or to the maintenance of peace, or to the hopes of impoverished multitudes.

The assault on NATO began in February, 1966. Nothing could have been more foreseeable. In many respects it was a gesture that gave expression to all the deepest impulses and prejudices on which his diplomacy is based: cynicism and ruthlessness in the relations between states (even between the so-called friendly states); supremacy of national sovereignty over any ideological concept or alliance; France's standing among the nations. But however typical it was of Gaullist diplomacy, the gesture—being so tough, so abrupt, so challenging—succeeded in taking everyone by surprise.

Why does a man who is so polite in private life behave so rudely and with such contempt for the spirit of classical diplomacy and the letter of historic treaties? Why does he now behave the way he once reproached Bourguiba and Sékou Touré for behaving? Why is Charles de Gaulle so keen to play the role of Gamal Abdel Nasser, if not of Lumumba? It is not only because of his old prejudice against the United States—the old memories of Yalta and Casablanca— nor is it only because Mr. Rusk's State Department was too worried about Vietnam to be interested in the cables from Europe, or because the president of the Fifth Republic is too old to lose any time. It is because Charles de Gaulle is not confident in the Gaullist faith of his "heirs"—if such a term can be applied to his lieutenants. It is because he felt he had to go to the point of no return to prevent the men who surround him (with the exception of Michel Debré and Couve de Murville) from giving in, as he fears they will give in, to Washington policy after his death.

French public opinion has generally been favorable so far: one never appeals to the nationalism or the self-satisfaction of a people without a certain amount of success. And the machinery of NATO is, or was, so outdated that even reasonable men could approve a large part of De Gaulle's initiative. But in condemning the bloc strategy as old and unsuitable to present relationships between the West and European Communism, in condemning this strategy as a hindrance to any solution of the German problem, De Gaulle is going back to an older diplomacy. He denounces the *"diplomatie de papa."* But why should he revert to the *"diplomatie de grandpapa"*—the diplomacy of national alliances, bargaining threats, and parochial armaments? It is possible to see the positive aspects of such a move—the opportunity for the Eastern states to recover their autonomy and for the Western states to reorganize their relations outside the old framework of *de facto* United States hegemony. A Western alliance thus reorganized could have the advantage of questioning and limiting what Senator Fulbright has called Washington's "arrogance of power."

However, the negative and most dangerous aspects of the initiative taken by Charles de Gaulle in 1966 would seem to outweigh the positive aspects. The most dangerous negative aspects are: the revival in West Germany of the old anxiety about encirclement (and the Germans have never been a people in whom anxiety led to wisdom); the temptation for Washington to build its whole European strategy on Bonn; and, above all, the development of what can be called De Gaulle's nuclear nationalism. One H-bomb for everyone? What kind of world are we preparing? He told a friend, in 1965: "Dissemination is not a threat. Nobody will use the bomb. It's only a diplomatic argument. . . ." In the old world, the world of Gladstone or Wilson, this could be true. But has

233

Charles de Gaulle forgotten the state of world affairs when he stepped into history, when he had to replace, by what would seem to be either complete folly or greatness of imagination, the narrow vision of men swept along by the tide of events? Before the bomb, to be a Hitler it was necessary to have the following of a great nation and to be endowed with a patient perversity. But now . . .

General de Gaulle is a man who says wise things in a foolish manner. When he denounces the system of ideological "blocs" or the system of the "gold exchange standard," when he judges the entrance of Great Britain into the Common Market premature in 1963, or when he criticizes American involvement in Vietnam, it is possible to remain in agreement with his basic reasoning. But the provocative brutality of his speech, the arrogant aggressivity of his tone remove any curative power from his proposals. He resembles a doctor who announces to his patient: "You have galloping consumption . . ." and sends the patient to take a cure in the slums. He knows how to discern the illness, but seems to have no objective other than that of seeing his pessimistic diagnosis confirmed. "*So you are dead? Now you will see that De Gaulle was right. . .*"

De Gaulle, like T. E. Lawrence, often gives the impression of conducting a guerrilla warfare for a cause whose true significance only he understands. Among the many skirmishes he has launched between 1963 and 1968, three have been crucial to the career of this rebel in power: his harassment of American policy in Vietnam, his assumption of a favorable position toward the Arabs in the Israeli crisis and his assault on the "gold exchange standard."

In all of these cases, Charles de Gaulle begins from

rational positions. However, in pursuing their consequences to the bitter end, he occasionally conducts himself like a character subject to an hallucinatory xenophobia. To understand this behavior, it is not enough to remember that De Gaulle is a man better suited to the struggle with great events than to "ordinary days"—and therefore is tempted to invent storms so that he may better display his mastery of them. It is necessary to dismantle the intellectual mechanisms in which the weight of the past, the bitterness, the ghosts of Roosevelt, Churchill and Stalin, and the sequels to Yalta and Potsdam play an important part.

In fact, De Gaulle is a man who has too much memory. This faculty, which is of enormous service to him in his public appearances, particularly on television, brings an incurable weight of bitterness to bear on his diplomatic strategy.

Let us take the matter of Vietnam as an example. It is impossible to understand anything of this if one does not bear carefully in mind the circumstances of 1944-45, when the OSS, in obedience to the strict instructions of President Roosevelt, tried to prevent the reestablishment of French colonial rule over the whole of Indochina—in any event, over that portion of it located north of the 16th parallel which had been promised to Chiang Kai-shek since 1943. American policy in the matter seemed all the more unfriendly to De Gaulle because the British authorities, led by Lord Louis Mountbatten, were doing their best to facilitate the return of the French to the southern region of Indochina—which had been provisionally allocated to them at the Potsdam Conference.

In an Asia that was obviously prepared to take every possible measure to prevent a rebirth of the colonial regimes, Charles de Gaulle's concern with reinstalling France in Indochina might be considered absurd. But, as noted before, it should not be seen simply as a reflex of a nationalist conservative. There was also the will to efface the humiliation of 1940 through demonstrations of power, to reply to the accusations by the men of Vichy that De Gaulle was the "liquidator of the Empire," and the determination not to give in to the injunctions of the American superpower. From the moment that Roosevelt willed him out, it was of vital importance to him to be in . . .

In short, the spirit of revenge has played a large part in Gaullist strategy in Vietnam since 1963. From Machiavellian considerations, which the general normally prefers, it is in De Gaulle's "egoist" interest for the Americans to dig their own graves in Vietnam, as he looks on in ironic pity. Viewed objectively, from the nationalist point of view, American involvement in Vietnam is the best guarantee of French independence. It is because the strategists of Washington have allowed themselves to become trapped in the rice paddies of Vietnam that French diplomacy has been able to play so audacious a game in the rest of the world.

An America free of Vietnam would have been in a far better position to call the French back to order and reassemble the European world under its guidance, primarily by hindering the Franco-German *rapprochement* of 1967-68. Since 1963, French diplomacy has thrived on the American adventure in Vietnam, just as French engagement in Africa after 1871 gave free rein to the growing power of Bismarck's Germany, and as the dispersion of Great Britain's global responsibilities at the beginning of the 20th century almost permitted William II to impose his law on the sea as well as on the continent of Europe.

From the "governmental declaration" of August 29, 1963, to the Pnom Penh speech of September 1, 1966, and constantly since that time, the theories expounded by General de Gaulle on Vietnam have been well calculated to exasperate the Americans rather than to calm them. Is the French president knowingly poisoning an abscess which serves his policy? We cannot be certain. The tone he adopts in these circumstances is not the result of a deliberate calculation, but of a sensibility in which is mingled bitterness, the certainty of being right, and an ironic view of a particularly awkward and unpopular policy.

It must, however, also be recognized that the Third World was waiting for a voice to be raised against the American enterprise. That this voice should be his and should come from France, embarrassed (or so it would seem) only the Americans, and quite a few Frenchmen, but certainly did not embarrass the principal interested parties, the Vietnamese. With relation to the masses of Afro-Asiatic peoples, the campaign conducted against American intervention by Charles de Gaulle since August 29, 1963 is one of the most popular of his long and curious career.

On September 1, 1966, the orator of Pnom Penh, facing a gigantic image of himself created from the waving of ten thousand flags, spoke for hundreds of millions of men. The challenge to the greatest power in the world by an arrogant and solitary old man, near the combat zone, on the soil of a fragile, threatened nation, will remain one of the high points of this bizarre career of sporadic decolonization.

De Gaulle here expresses himself in the most Gaullist manner: preaching a lesson to America, egocentrically citing the Algerian precedent and his own glory in it as an example. De Gaulle the strategist points out the advantages of withdrawal; De Gaulle the intellectual makes a well chosen reference to the American philosophy of history; and De Gaulle the lucid paternalist briefly pleads the cause of little peoples.

In his relations with the Arabs, as well as with the

Socialist camp, De Gaulle is essentially a strategist who employs everything granted him by history. His conduct of Arab affairs cannot be considered in terms of any other motive, except occasionally one of common cause against the United States.

Three non-psychological motivations for De Gaulle's Arab policy are Algeria, oil and the struggle against American hegemony. But to these must be added another element of some importance: the character of Franco-Israeli relations under the Fourth Republic— a character which, in his view, was improperly close. It was partially as a reaction to the effervescent and too little "national" style of the relations between the leaders of the two capitals that De Gaulle took a "dislike" to Israeli diplomats and visitors. Able as they may have been, the Israelis did not always know how to redefine in the light of new circumstances a presence and procedures which were considered normal in the time of Mollet and Bourgès-Maunoury, when "every Israeli had two countries, his own and France."

Immediately on his investiture as chief of state, De Gaulle put an end to certain forms of cooperation between Paris and Tel Aviv, notably in matters of military intelligence. However, after an interview with De Gaulle in Paris in August 1958, Mme. Golda Meir stated: "The bonds which unite our two countries are not the fruit of passing conditions, but the reflection of a community of thought . . ." Israeli leaders felt reassured.

A new alarm occurred at the end of 1959, when the nationalized Renault company and Air France decided to break their contracts with Israel rather than suffer the boycott of the Arab League. Was this a signal for a reversal of alliances? Not at all. Six months later, it was Mr. Ben-Gurion's turn to talk with General de Gaulle and declare that the friendship which united Israel and France was based on "essential and common" values.

But if the Israeli prime minister received a friendly and reassuring welcome, he committed a blunder in suggesting to the general a settlement of the Algerian affair based on partition. At the time, De Gaulle may have had nothing against such a formula; but this intrusion by the Israeli leader into "his" affairs, with a solution *à l'Israelienne*, annoyed him.

Because, over a period of four years, it was in Algeria that the fate of his regime was to be decided, De Gaulle was constrained to emphasize his relations with the Arab world. He did not believe, as his predecessors had, that the Algerian revolution was nothing more than a product of Nasser's strategy. However, he had summarily gauged Arab solidarity and understood that, if the war was to be won or lost in the streets of Algiers, peace could ripen elsewhere.

In ameliorating his relations with Tunis and Rabat, in avoiding any systematic affront to Cairo or Baghdad, De Gaulle was placing the Algerian war in its true context. He knew that, in many ways, Algeria was the test by which the Arab world wanted to see the best of itself confirmed.

Thus there developed—between De Gaulle and the FLN and its allies—a kind of objective complicity, due primarily to their common hatred of the partisans of "French Algeria." From the moment he decided to end the war at whatever price—in order to insure at last France's independence of the other Great Powers—De Gaulle discovered in defeat a hope for France and for his own strategy. Could not this Algeria, born during his reign and, in the last phase, with his blessing, become a privileged partner, a prestigious ally of France and a guarantee of his policy toward the Third World?

This was the starting point of a strategy—not without audacity or imagination—which took shape notably during the interviews between General de Gaulle and Ahmed Ben Bella in the Chateau de Champs, in 1963. The doors were opened to a general reconciliation between Paris and the Arab world.

But, in one sense, a liberated Algeria was still no more than a matter of "sentiment"—the poorest form of raw material for a strategy of the type practiced by De Gaulle. It is even more for motives which can be summed up in the single word oil that the general resolved his differences with the Arab world and assumed certain risks with relation to Israel. For oil and gas are the means to what might be termed independence of energy. No objective is more important to Charles de Gaulle than his independence.

At the time of his return to power in 1958, the French depended on Iraq for their oil supply, although France controlled less than 10% of the Iraq Petroleum Company. She was counting, of course, on the future of Algerian oil, which the war threatened. The Suez operation of 1956 had brought about a crisis of gas and oil in France.

From this time on, much of Gaullist diplomacy was devoted to: 1) "liberating" Algerian oil by establishing cordial relations between the two countries, relations also made necessary (until 1965) by the nuclear experiments in the Sahara; 2) obtaining access to the reserves of the Near East, either by encouraging the revolutionaries then occupied with a revision of the oil status quo of the region (Sheik Tariki and the Syrians), or by improving his relations with producers such as the Saudi Arabians and the Iraqis; 3) making himself the promoter of a new type of relationship between owners and exploiters of oil properties, no longer founded on divisions of property (which seemed an intrusion on the sovereignty of the nation concerned) but on the principle of "the operator."

De Gaulle's strategy was developed in three phases. In March 1962, in Évian, the Algerian representatives won their points in every other field, but France extracted from them conditions which, to all intents and purposes, safeguarded the status quo in matters of drilling for oil. Algeria was independent on the surface; below she was still a protectorate. It was in July 1965 that she freed her underground wealth through an agreement which modified the relation between the country supplying the raw material and the country acting as a distributor. It placed both parties henceforth on an equalitarian basis of association, caused the Anglo-Saxon interests to tremble, and gave a great many new ideas to those—from Tripoli to Teheran—who had long dreamed of freeing their own reserves of oil. Finally, in September 1967, the general gained access to the oil of the Near East by signing an agreement with Iraq which made France— and eventually the Soviet Union—the beneficiary of the economic emancipation of Baghdad.

It was not only a profitable operation for French consumers and directors of the economy; it was also a hard blow to London and, especially, to Washington (Kuwait and Ryadh are not populated only by the deaf and the blind). Nothing intrigues General de Gaulle more than chipping away at the American positions, wherever they may be; this, in fact, is the third key to his policies with respect to the Arabs. For him, it is a matter of proposing to any of their possible partners, everywhere and always, solutions more attractive than those put forward by the Americans. That is not very difficult.

It is thus in the light of these three signs—Algerian friendship, the will toward independence in matters of oil, and the anti-American guerrilla war—that the latest phases of this diplomacy must be considered. They include the establishment of amicable links between the general and King Hussein (scorning ideologies as he does, De Gaulle concerns himself little with the particular ones symbolized by any individual, and has even given a cordial welcome to Tshombe himself); the reception in Paris of Marshal Amer and the denunciation of the assassins of Ben Barka (he knows the value the Arab world attributes to the word of honor and to the rights a guest may expect from his host); and, finally, the position taken by the French government during the Arab-Israeli war of June 1967.

Here, as we have observed before, it is once again necessary to take due note of personal factors. De Gaulle's denunciation of the Israeli offensive stems largely from the fact that the general considered intolerable Tel Aviv's apparent disregard of the advice he gave to Abba Eban on the 24th of May: "In any event, do not attack!" These people who do not listen to De Gaulle are not worth a great deal. More importantly, the Israeli operation altered the balance of forces in the Near East in a sense favorable to the American camp and prevented France, in the May crisis, from playing the role of arbiter that her dual friendships had caused De Gaulle to hope for.

We know now that the choice of Paris was not—in the actual event—as clear-cut as General de Gaulle's statements seemed to imply. Despite the fact that he called the Israelis a "domineering people"—which, for the General-President, is not entirely abusive—military relations between the two capitals were not affected by this until after the 7th or 8th of June. Information on this subject was made public on January 7, 1968, by the deputy to parliament Pierre Clostermann, a hero of the air war of 1940-45 and an expert on the three subjects of Gaullism, aviation and Arab-

242

Israeli relations. He made it clear that General Rabin's army had continued to receive French equipment for the duration of the hostilities.

In fact, De Gaulle's personal choice is probably more clear-cut than this rather banal double game (words for the Arabs, planes for the Israelis). The French chief of state is still the man who, in Beirut in 1942, was urged to base the French positions in the Near East on the Zionist bastion. "Look at the map and listen to the crowds of Damascus," was De Gaulle's reply.

This general considers geographical areas and occasionally even popular trends, if they affirm themselves strongly enough, as they did in Algiers in December 1960. He certainly does not neglect technical values, and on this level he is impressed by the Israeli organizational staffs and the ardor in combat of Rabin's army. The letter he addressed to David Ben-Gurion on January 9, 1968, bears witness to that. But his analysis of the future of the Near East is based essentially on the long-term possibilities of Arab development. Charles de Gaulle is a man who knows how to be patient, at least when it is a question of the patience of others.

De Gaulle today makes use of the independence of the Arabs, which France was so long in recognizing, as an instrument in the game of French diplomacy, which is primarily a guerrilla war against American hegemony.

But it is perhaps in the matter of gold that the gap between the solid foundation of Gaullist theses, the absurdity of their presentation and the excessive manner of their manipulation is most striking.

Charles de Gaulle is a man whose character in public life has been formed in two periods: between the two wars, when he recognized that the constant depreciation of the franc with relation to the pound and the dollar was one of the causes of French dependence on allies in London and Washington; then, during World War II, in which he was reduced to begging in order to survive.

This is why one of his first acts after his return to power in 1958 was to restore to the franc first an appearance and then a reality—in spite of his placid ignorance in matters of both finance and economy. The "heavy franc" operation launched at the end of 1958 might have seemed ridiculous: it succeeded, as a result of the confidence of the French proprietary class in Charles de Gaulle—the strong man—and Antoine Pinay—the quiet man.

Reassured by this restoration (in the manner of Poincaré) and advised by Jacques Rueff, an economist noted for his crusade in favor of a return to an international gold standard, De Gaulle decided to call into question a worldwide monetary system founded on the privilege accorded to the dollar and the pound in Genoa in 1922.

The "Gaullist doctrine," which is in fact a synthesis of three policies—those of Rueff, Valéry Giscard d'Estaing and Michel Debré—may be summed up in three propositions: (a) all equivalence with gold determined in terms of the currency of a given nation, expresses the hegemony of this nation; (b) this situation was perhaps true for Great Britain from 1922 to 1940, and for the United States until 1965; but the financial situation of Great Britain as a result of the second world war, and of the United States as a result of the Vietnam war and a general prodigality, no longer forms a basis for the privileges of earlier years; (c) in the period intervening before the creation of a more equitable system, only gold represents a truly international means of exchange.

A mixture of good sense and mediocre conservatism,

this doctrine was resolved as early as 1962, in a form less decisive than it has since assumed. At that time, barely liberated from the Algerian war, De Gaulle was launching his first thrusts against American hegemony. The first blow to the Genoa system, which Washington had attempted to consolidate or to save in 1961 through the creation of the "gold pool" and the reabsorption of the American deficit, was the proposition made to the International Monetary Fund by Valéry Giscard d'Estaing: it came in the form of a proposal to create a new currency, the "united collective reserve," independent of the dollar and based on gold. The offensive was still discreet, since De Gaulle had made the proposal only through the voice of a subordinate. But Washington was not entirely taken in and, in spite of the appeasement preached to his collaborators by President Kennedy, American financial circles realized that the gold reserves of Fort Knox were decreasing and that the French leader might profit from this situation. They began to grow anxious.

On February 5, 1965, in one of his most surprising press conferences, Charles de Gaulle declared open war on the international monetary system: "The convention which attributes to the dollar a transcendent value as an international currency no longer rests on its initial base—possession by the United States of the largest part of the gold of the world . . . The United States is running into debt gratuitously . . . The dollar, far from being an impartial and international symbol of exchange, is no more than a means of credit appropriate to one State."

American humorists dubbed the general "Gaullefinger." But it required more than that to stop him. Even though others might be less outspoken than he, they nonetheless played their own game against a god whose sacred character had just been questioned.

As the child in the old story said, "The emperor is naked," De Gaulle had said, "The dollar is fragile." The pound was the first victim of the operation. But the dollar was to follow: throughout the year 1966, and to an even greater extent in 1967, the American currency grew weaker, drained by the hemorrhage of Vietnam and eaten away by worldwide speculation and the adventurous policies of Washington.

In the same period, Michel Debré, the most faithful Gaullist of them all, appointed Minister of Finance by a general eager to push his advantages to the limit, was striving to make Paris a great financial center by restoring freedom of movement in gold, then by withdrawing France from the "gold pool," and then by refusing to supply the London market in order to maintain the price of gold at $35.00 an ounce. Both Americans and Englishmen murmured about treason, and some English newspapers asserted "undeclared war" between Paris and London. But this was still no more than a prelude to the battle of March 1968.

On Wednesday, March 13th, at the height of the crisis, when competent observers were evoking the dramatic precedent of 1929, Jacques Brunet, governor of the Bank of France, had decided to follow the example of his American and British colleagues and close the gold market of the Paris stock exchange on Friday: it seemed to him that he would simply be obeying an exigency of collective safety. As soon as he learned of this decision, General de Gaulle summoned Michel Debré, the Minister of Finance. "Does the governor of the Bank of France occupy his position in order to play the game of the Americans?" he demanded. The market was to remain open, making it possible to bring to light the present-day absurdity of the "gold exchange standard" and to impose the necessity for a reevaluation, perhaps even to make Paris the prime world market of free gold. But none of this prevented De Gaulle from announcing through his representatives: "France has nothing to do with what is happening. She has not exchanged dollars for gold in almost two years. Who else can say as much?"

French "moderation" was, however, extremely strange: since the summer of 1967 Paris had been inciting her allies in Western Europe, and particularly those of the European Economic Community, to act in accordance with the same principles and to participate in the stag hunt against the dollar. On March 24, 1968, Charles de Gaulle stated in a speech at Lyon that France might even reconsider her adherence to the Common Market if her partners did not follow French monetary policy. This was perhaps going rather far . . .

In acting thus, was De Gaulle generally supported by French public opinion, or, in any case by his own collaborators? It is not certain. We know, for instance, that during the meeting of the Council of Ministers on March 20, 1968, the text of the communiqué he had prepared with Michel Debré was contested and overruled—at the instigation of Maurice Couve de Murville, the man who, for ten years, had been the faithful interpreter of the general's thought. Although De Murville had the active support of the most independent of the ministers, Edgar Faure, this "revolt" had no sequel.

It did, however, demonstrate that the general's methods, even more than his ideas, were meeting with increasing resistance, after ten years in power. Many of those who, in this particular matter, had adopted positions similar to his own condemned the excesses with which he abused his provisional victory. Paraphrasing his famous statement of 1940, *Le Nouvel Observateur* wrote at the time: "De Gaulle has won a battle, the battle of gold. He has not won the war of the dollar."

247

13
A Realist of the Imaginary

"By what signs are we to recognize the
man . . . who leaves his mark on the
events which destiny places in his path?
Is it not that he encompasses a more or
less long succession in an instantaneous
vision? The greater the portion of the
past he holds in his present, the heav-
ier the mass he propels into the future,
to press against eventualities still un-
formed. . . ."

Henri Bergson

Let us study him for a moment
as he appears on the television screen—which he has
made into an arm of government—reaching out to the
international observers who, in the opinion of his
skeptical people, are the proofs of his universal glory.
The De Gaulle of television is an eye, a mask, forearms, and hands. The eye of an elephant, of ruse and
rancor, glittering with enormous wisdom or with cold
rage; the mask, in which age has ceased to carve its
lines and begun to smooth over the planes, hardens
abruptly when he is angry, relaxes again for the pa-
ternal or the bantering words. And then there are the
forearms, which he hurls out in front of him like
tanks on the slopes of Abbeville or a sword at the
feet of Caesar. He uses them in the same way when
he is speaking directly to the crowds, like a semaphore

whose action is independent of its base, signaling the De Gaulle who is in love with the nation—with the "common people," the "honest folk . . ."—while the other De Gaulle soberly contemplates the future of the State, faced with "foreigners" and "intermediaries."

In front of these cameras, these witnesses, this dazzled and sometimes worried people, *Le Grand Charles* indulges in his favorite alchemy: he replaces facts with a representation of facts, and objects with ideas he wants to propose for them; he forages in history for the basic matter of "his" history; he snatches at that portion of the real which coincides with his dream, and employs his talent, his will, and his arrogance to make of it another form of reality. He knows the past well enough to remold it to conform with his passion; and he controls his passion well enough to remold it to conform with what he has decided is the public interest. The interest of a France "assembled" as a State and guided by the man who expresses the nation.

Here, in fact, is where the transmutation begins. The France young Charles de Gaulle saw as a princess of legend, the France whose history Captain de Gaulle recounted to the cadets of Saint-Cyr—General de Gaulle has seen this same France divided, inert, forgetful of her past, reluctant to consider the future. An absolute has crumbled before his eyes, a totality has fragmented in his hands—but he knows no way of acting except in the name of an absolute and a totality.

For this man who has so profoundly doubted the French people—and judged it with such cruel lucidity —but who refuses to accept the sleight-of-hand of a Maurras which would oppose the "real nation" to the legal nation, it is constantly necessary to recreate an ideal France. He might like to employ the methods of Richelieu and depict the ending of his work as a recreation of the France of Saint Louis; it will not be that, but neither will it be a recreation of the Fourth Republic. A constant reconversion of the real makes of Charles de Gaulle the singular statesman he is: a realist of the imaginary.

When the dream ends, will France fall back into the hands of the ordinary presidents of "la belle époque"? He predicts it. Perhaps, sarcastically, he desires it. He has influenced history, but he does not claim to have channeled it into an eternally beneficent course. To him, history is not the objective and infallible divinity the Marxists have substituted for the Greek concept of destiny. History is a force of gravity that can be eluded, thwarted, suspended. It is the rock of Sisyphus, which he holds at arm's length from him, strengthened by his knowledge of the past and drawing from it the skills and ruses he needs, but well aware of their vanity. The machine is opening paths which he himself had taken as a young man in armor, but of which he is apprehensive in his later years. He talks of the atom, but he dreams of a return to gold. And what role does he assign to youth in this State he means to build?

It is not because the De Gaulle of thirty years ago had taken a stand in advance of his times when he advocated a mechanized army which might have changed the course of events that the De Gaulle of today invests his atomic *force de frappe* with the same virtues he once ascribed to the armored corps. At that time, France was a necessary rampart to the liberty of the world; due to the Nazis, war was unavoidable, and it was tanks or Hitler. The situation today is quite different; France is on another level, and the nuclear weapon is far more an instrument in a diplomatic game between allies than a bulwark against an imperialistic or a totalitarian enemy.

Dialectic has no place in the unequivocal system of this nationalist Catholic for whom the world turns and is organized around an ideal France. But the thing that is truly original in this "possessed" man is the clarity of his vision. The more intense his sentiment of nationality and the more obvious the roots of his faith, the broader the scope of his lucidity; it is so authentic and fundamental a thing that he has an easy grasp of what is authentic and fundamental in others.

This deep-rooted man is the most flexible of gamblers. Above everything else, he is a strategist of movement and space: a player who knows the value of distance, who wins because he knows and uses the trick shots, the rebounds, the ricochets. In twenty-five years of adventurous diplomacy, his primary victories have been won by other warriors in other places. Chance has played some part, but basically his good fortune has been the success which crowned operations based on persuasion or dissuasion, in which he was careful to remain always one move ahead of his opponent. De Gaulle has done many clumsy things— in so many extravagant enterprises!—but the odd fact is that his adversaries' mistakes always seem to have been planned by him.

Among the thousand or more challenges that this baroque figure has hurled at the laws of modern social history, none is perhaps more curious than his strange dialogue with the army—from June, 1940, to the Évian agreements for Algeria; from the insurrectionist trials of 1962 to the drastic reductions in troop strength in 1963 and 1964. "When I entered into it, the French army was one of the greatest things in the world," he wrote. When he departs from history, it will be one of the smallest bodies of the State. Could it be that in his mind the army should follow in the path of the Vatican—an institution he admires to a somewhat un-Gallic extent—on the theory that the narrower its area of temporal action the greater its influence will be?

But if history is no more than a succession of accepted challenges, if death puts an end to his solitary endeavor, if his death is the end of *the* history? "Reassure yourselves, I shall not fail to die. . . ." He speaks in the jokingly ceremonious tone one uses to describe something that is thoroughly familiar. And there are even times when a word or a gesture seems to reveal a kind of obsession. On the morning after one of the attempts on his life, a friend received this message: "Would my exit have made the best ending?" The attitude of an esthete of history rather than of an intimate friend of death. The general does not, like Malraux, maintain an almost mystical commerce with death; he is more inclined to treat it as an irritating interruption of the irrational into a plan of life founded on the conscious will.

Valéry spoke of "man leaning against his death like a speaker with his back to the fireplace." For De Gaulle, it is not the fire that is important, but the attitude, the style, the frame, and also the sense of limits. This baroque man has no difficulty fitting himself into the classical mold, and he goes so far as to claim that he enjoys only the formal gardens of the French school. He denounces nothing more ardently than excess of any kind, and the description he gives in *France and Her Army* of the career of Bonaparte and the ruins it bequeathed to France is the work of a disciple of the masters of classic *mesure*. He likes to repeat Talleyrand's phrase: "What is excessive does not count," and he says of Bismarck: "All the same, he was a great man because he knew when to stop." But himself?

"A generous intelligence at the service of a temperament which is not," is the summation given by Philippe Serre, one of the political figures who fought at his side in the battles for the armored divisions. An intuitive, instinctive intelligence; a disciple of Bergson armed by Péguy. Emotional reactions that are curiously restrained, repressed—the reserve resulting from a family life in which this giant is quite the opposite of a singular man. A friendless life? But Leclerc, at the time of rejoining him in Paris, received a hastily scribbled note which ended with the "I embrace you" of Napoleon to Lannes, his favorite lieutenant. Emmanuel d'Astier, at the conclusion of a bitter telephone conversation in London, was astonished to hear from the other end of the wire a murmured "I'm very fond of you, Bernard" (the war name of the future minister). And the general feels for Malraux the affection of a fellow artisan, an accomplice in both adventure and altitude.

When a man is "Christian by race," as Péguy wrote, is he concerned with adding charity to his inherent virtues? The life of this personage who wills himself capable of anything the needs of the State may require is overshadowed by the idea of sin; at the very height of a political debate, he used the word to Edmond Michelet. Born in the Jansenist quarter of Lille, he was a pupil of the Jesuits, who do not trifle with this matter; but the greatest ordeal of his life—that inflicted on him by the infirmity of his daughter—provided fuel for an obsession which could have led him to the idea of predestination.

What makes De Gaulle run? The thought of installing France in the front rank, like a duchess in Versailles at the bedside of the Queen? Making it possible for Frenchmen to pay in South African gold for a national reconstruction that would have been poisoned by a statement drawn up in dollars? What is this great man, whose wartime goals have always been more clear than his peacetime objectives, offering to his beloved France? An increased assurance in the initiatives and efforts of her diplomats, a greater confidence on the part of her distant friends, irritation on the part of her closest friends, a striking force which is a force only in relation to the weak and would be incapable of striking, an increase in the specific weight of France in the world, in the noise she makes, in the reserves in her treasuries?

To some, he is only the flamboyant alibi for French political underdevelopment, and to others, the necessary agent of an abrupt transition into the industrial era: an operation they will willingly qualify as Caesarean. So long as he lives, Frenchmen will feel they know the weight of this abusive man, this hypnotist who watches over their political sleep; but his greatness, true or false, will be measured more accurately when he is gone.

Then the ruses of personal power may seem incidental to the constant struggle for liberty; the rebel may win out over the monarch.

Epilogue:
The Barricades
of Spring

Charles de Gaulle has called himself a "somewhat fabulous personage." From June 1940 to the Operation Resurrection of May 1958, and from the Algiers "putsch" to the follies of Québec, the exceptional, the inordinate, the unexpected have marked a destiny worthy of a fabulist from the South of France. But before the spring of 1968, some fragments of classic reason and measure still clung to his career, relating it to the tradition of the *Grand Siècle*, which he claims to embody.

From the first of May to the thirtieth of June, 1968, the biography of General de Gaulle moves from the fabulous to the incredible. It is characterized by misfortune, absurdity, imposture, concealment; by ill-considered attempts and dramatic returns, comings and goings between zero and infinity, by flights from beatitude to the abyss and from humiliation to triumph. Such phenomena have only a dubious bearing on politics, and even less on history. They're more in keeping with a literature of the improbable, which, until now, has been more often the style of Germanic poets and the prophets of the desert than of French essayists.

France in the past twenty-five years has not been the best model of equilibrium or of rationalism. Collapses and restorations have not always been clearly motivated. In this troubled period, De Gaulle often seemed the one man of, if not wisdom, at least clarity of vision and firmness of plan.

But in the storm that swept France in May and June of 1968, he succeeded in adding to the confusion, in blackening the dark storm clouds. His final triumph was not that of Prospero, but of Lear: He did not conquer the tempest, but was swept along by it, by the weakness of his opponents and by the general fear.

A man ordinarily so firm in the midst of the extraordinary, so much at ease in peril, was now wavering and hesitant; passing from brutality to calculation, from the temptation of withdrawal to the dizziness of the harshest forms of repression. He risked too much and then talked of removing himself altogether. He was evasive, always on the move and yet never really in movement: old, too old—dull, disoriented, uncertain—finding his former self-assurance again only for a few minutes in a radio speech which was splendidly opportune from a strategic point of view.

After ten years of undivided power, which he employed with an inimitable mixture of contempt, simplicity, severity and tactical skill, Charles de Gaulle had triumphed over all of his adversaries: politicians, colonels, terrorists and "Eurocrats." It seemed that he might now drowse in a grandiose twilight, free to choose between the retreat of Charles V and the last days of George Washington, and thus become the first French sovereign to fulfill his mandate since the Revolution. Then came the month of May, 1968.

"Great events," Nietzsche said, "arrive on the footsteps of doves." To all outward appearances, what could have been more serene than this spring of 1968 in Paris, in spite of the imminent last phase of realization of the Common Market on the first of July? The general was preparing to leave for Romania, there to reap the fruits of his strategy of two-sided nationalism; M. Pompidou was going to Iran, where France was consolidating its oil policies against the Anglo-American interests. Who could have foreseen that it would be in Paris, for once, that the destiny of the Fifth Republic would crystallize?

On the first of May, attention was centered on the entrance of Governor Rockefeller into the American presidential race, on Hanoi's refusal to meet Washington's representatives aboard an Indonesian warship, and on a statement of Mr. Dubcek's in Prague concerning the necessity for making socialism "attractive." Few were concerned with the fact that a certain Daniel Cohn-Bendit, the instigator of the "rebels" of the University of Nanterre, had been summoned before a faculty disciplinary council and threatened with expulsion for having instigated the occupation of the buildings by the students. Those interested in radical movements were busy following developments at Columbia University in New York or at the University of Rome.

The next day, however, the Parisian students began claiming attention: following on a new demonstration by the "rebels," the University of Nanterre was closed. And on the following day, the combat was transferred to the Sorbonne, in the very heart of Paris: the rector, M. Jean Roche, called on the police who, for the first time in centuries, invaded the symbolic institution and forced the students out—arresting several hundreds of them. The Sorbonne was closed.

The third of May, 1968, marked the date of a scandal, of a new abuse of power, and the beginning of a crisis which almost overthrew that power. Three days later, a formation of students clashed with police in the neighborhood of Saint-Germain des Prés, and set up barricades in the street. There were several dozen wounded, but, on May sixth, the intellectual youth of Paris had reinvented the city's revolutionary strategy and defied the regime. Paris was preparing to receive the American and Vietnamese delegates, De Gaulle—welcoming Walter Lippmann at the Élysée Palace—was flaunting himself as peacemaker, and a revolutionary situation was emerging in the "capital of peace."

From the seventh to the tenth of May, the fever mounted steadily. The Gaullist government denounced the actions of "minute groups" of agitators—but it was by the tens of thousands that young people threaded through the streets of Paris, forming regular columns and demanding the reopening of the Sorbonne, the withdrawal of the police and the liberation of their comrades. On May eighth, De Gaulle stated to a group of parliamentary delegates: "It is not possible to tolerate violence in the streets, which has never been the means of setting up a dialogue. . . ." The next day, however, Alain Peyrefitte, minister of education, an "unconditional" Gaullist, promised that the facilities of the university would shortly be reopened. But when the students of Nanterre took the initiative and reoccupied their university, Peyrefitte refused to evacuate and reopen the Sorbonne.

This was the detonator: On May tenth, everything exploded. The students occupied the Latin Quarter in accordance with a strategic plan, and constructed barricades in the streets. The majority had decided to do battle here to obtain application of their "three points." That evening, the dean of the university attempted to negotiate but refused to free the imprisoned students, whose leaders broke off the discussions. They decided instead to hold the fifty barricades which now stretched across the Latin Quarter.

At about two o'clock on the morning of the eleventh,

the Prefect of Police, Maurice Grimaud, announced that he had received orders to reduce the barricades. But who had issued them? The CRS (Compagnies Républicaines de Sécurité) launched the attack. Two hours later there were 367 wounded; more than 500 persons had been arrested and more than 100 automobiles set on fire. The police forces bludgeoned fugitives, pursuing them into private apartments. They struck out at those already wounded, and were greeted with the cry: "CRS—SS!"

That night, the regime had dishonored itself. As for De Gaulle, no one, it was reported, had dared wake him after ten o'clock on the tenth or before six o'clock on the eleventh—in other words, throughout the drama. What is there to say of a power which lashes out blindly when a leader sleeps? The prime minister was in Afghanistan; the minister of the interior and the minister of education had acquired the habit of waiting for orders. And the general was asleep. On Saturday, the eleventh, Georges Pompidou returned from Kabul, disavowed the police brutalities, freed 24 of the 28 imprisoned students, and announced the reopening of the Sorbonne for the following Monday. The student leaders, meanwhile, were at work persuading the major union organizations (the pro-communist CGT, the socialist FO, and the Christian progressivist-inclined CFDT) to declare a general strike for Monday the thirteenth.

The thirteenth of May was the tenth anniversary of the Algiers uprising which had brought about the Gaullist "restoration." But it was not a holiday for the regime. More than half a million people, led by the student leaders, liberal professors, union leaders, and leftwing political leaders, marched through Paris. "Ten years, that's enough!" they shouted. "Happy anniversary, general; we are a minute group!" The government dared not confront this human tidal wave.

Since the police had prudently evacuated the Latin Quarter, the students occupied the Sorbonne—now transformed into a "Critical University." The cultural revolution had conquered its fortress, and won the first battle.

De Gaulle attempted to ignore this crushing defeat. Refusing to postpone his trip to Romania, he left for Bucharest on the fourteenth. On that day, however, the situation became even more serious when the workers took up the student rebellion. Near Nantes, the Sud-Aviation factory (manufacturers of the Franco-British supersonic plane, the Concorde) was occupied by its workers. On the fifteenth, it was the turn of one of the Renault factories. By May sixteenth, work stoppages and factory occupations had infected the whole of French industry.

The government became all the more alarmed because the movement was obviously not controlled by the CGT and the Communist party, forces which it understood and could restrain, but by the working class "base" which the students had apparently won over to their cause. It was for this reason that the prime minister, after showing moderation, gave a threatening speech on the night of the sixteenth. But, the next day, the reporters of the RTF (Radio-Télévision-Française), the state-controlled radio-television network, decided to disobey governmental directives. Following the student rebellion and the workers' strike, their action constituted the third phase of the "May revolution."

Acclaimed by the students of Bucharest on the 17th, De Gaulle nonetheless decided to cut short his trip to Romania; he landed at Orly on the morning of the 18th. After the general had conferred with several of his ministers, Premier Pompidou summed up De Gaulle's position: "Reform, yes; *la chienlit*, no!" (*Chienlit* is an old word signifying both disorder and carnival, but its generally accepted tone is extremely contemptuous.) The intellectual youth groups were insulted; the tension was aggravated. On May 22nd, the general strike continued to paralyze the French economy. In the ensuing parliamentary debate, two important Gaullist deputies, René Capitant and Edgard Pisani, dissociated themselves from the government, while the minister of the interior forbade the return to French territory of Daniel Cohn-Bendit who, as a German citizen, had gone home.

This was yet another detonator. On the twenty-fourth, as the general agitation seemed to be reaching into the farm areas, violent demonstrations took place in front of the Gare de Lyon in Paris and in the major cities of Nantes, Bordeaux and Lyon—where a police superintendent was killed. During that evening, General de Gaulle gave a television speech which had been announced a week earlier and was eagerly awaited. In a moment of national peril, could he once again find the words and the ideas which would save him?

But his appeal, mediocre and hesitating, was little more than the announcement of a referendum in June. It betrayed the confusion of the governmental forces and encouraged the rebels. Denouncing the referendum, Pierre Mendès-France exclaimed: "A plebiscite does not confront the problem; it combats it." Was this to be civil war?

Georges Pompidou attempted to dissociate the union organizations from the totality of the movement by opening negotiations with their leaders. On May 26th there was a projected agreement calling for a considerable increase in base wages (from 10 to 30 percent) and a reduction in the hours of work, but not for payment of days on strike. On the morning of May 27th, when he presented these terms to a meeting of workers at the Renault factory in Billancourt,

Georges Seguy, secretary-general of the CGT found himself spat upon. There would be no agreement with the labor leaders, who seemed as confused as the government itself.

On that May morning, France appeared to be in a state of anarchy. De Gaulle's offer of a referendum had become a laughing matter, Pompidou's proposals had been scornfully rejected by the workers, and the police had disappeared from the scene. Factories and universities were occupied, and even the largest organizations of the left—including the Communist party —did not seem to have any control over the masses of the people. This regime—sworn to insure order and stability—was passing away; lamentably, irrevocably, under the pressure of "minute groups" of students and non-violent workers.

Anything seemed possible. That day or in the days that followed, a Lenin or a Castro could have seized power. All of the security forces were concentrated on Paris and three or four of the major provincial cities. From the 26th to the 30th of May, 65 prefectures out of 90 were entirely stripped of police forces. Commando groups could have occupied them without striking a blow. And on the 28th—ironically, symbolically—Daniel Cohn-Bendit, who had been forbidden to return to France, held a press conference at the Sorbonne. De Gaulle said nothing.

On the 29th, everyone assumed that the seat of power had been vacated. At the Ministry of the Interior, people came and went without knocking; the official ushers had disappeared, the switchboard operators no longer answered. A rumor ran through Paris that the prime minister had advised the general to withdraw. At eleven o'clock outside the Élysée Palace, government members who had been summoned to a meeting of the Council of Ministers found the gate closed. De Gaulle had left for Colombey, where he was "reflecting." Left for Colombey? With his suitcases? In secret? Was this the flight of Louis XVI to Varennes? Of Napoleon III to London?

By noon on Wednesday, virtually everyone believed that the old sovereign had preferred retreat to defeat, and that he had "retired to his village and his sorrow"—as he had often threatened to do. During the afternoon, M. Mendès-France stated that he was ready to assume the direction of a "provisional government" if he should be called to it "by a reunited left." (Earlier, on the 28th, François Mitterrand had declared that he was still a "candidate for the succession.") But the communists announced their mistrust of this proposal, and organized an imposing march through Paris to demonstrate that, on the left, they were the dominant force.

On Thursday morning, May 30th, who governed France? De Gaulle had made his major objective the restoration of a strong state. That morning, a gendarme would not have dared collar a student who had struck a minister of state. Before the morning had ended, however, Robert Poujade, a Gaullist leader, stated on the radio that great events were in the offing.

Early in the afternoon, General de Gaulle returned to Paris. On the preceding day, following a mysterious itinerary, he had disappeared for several hours en route from Paris to Colombey. It developed that, in the course of this strange journey, he had conferred in Baden-Baden with the commander of the French armed forces in Germany, and that he would speak on the radio at 4:30 p.m. Was it to announce his withdrawal, or his revenge?

His first words were: "I have decided to remain at my post." His tone was sharp, threatening: In terms of form, the Charles de Gaulle of June 18, 1940, had replaced the flaccid De Gaulle of May 24, 1968. He declared combat "against totalitarian communism" (which had just saved the regime by damming up the revolt at its base). The prime minister was retained in office and congratulated. "Committees for civic action" were created. Our impression was that the general-president was assuming the risk of civil war. Denounced and defied in such a manner, the Communists would surely proclaim a general strike. De Gaulle, who had assured himself the day before of the support of the armed forces, would attempt to force the workers back to their jobs; the shock of conflict was inevitable.

But the Communists made no move. Their spokesmen contented themselves with stating that "the struggle for revisions of wages continues." And the announcement of the dissolution of the Chamber of Deputies, opening the way to new general elections, seemed to give them cause for rejoicing. Their passivity, coupled with the threats of General de Gaulle, seemed to strike the whole of the opposition dumb, while the partisans of the entrenched power emerged suddenly from their lethargy and gathered on the Champs-Élysées. Gaullism, like Lazarus, had been resurrected from the tomb, triumphant and noisy. The prophet had spoken; it was time to live again. And this party of frightened deaf mutes found itself abruptly masters of the streets once more.

On May 30th, in the space of the six minutes of the general's speech, the nature of France and the nature of its master were altered. Before 4:30, France was almost Cuba; after 4:36, she was already Portugal.

From that moment on, everything hung in the balance. Frozen on the brink of action by the constant talk of their leaders, the firm decision of the Communists to take no major risks, and the sudden revival of General de Gaulle's authority, the revolutionary forces saw their gains and their alliances

264

turned back at every point. They had created fear without assuring themselves of the power to transform this fear into obedience. They had aroused illusions without satisfying them. They had created a void without filling it. They had allowed their chance to escape. And at the very moment when the nation, seized with vertigo, was prepared to deliver itself to anyone who would command it, it was the old general who had spoken and acted.

Power is a profession, and its primary component is a sense of the favorable moment and the realization of the horror of nothingness. On the 30th of May, De Gaulle had understood this very popular fear and exploited it. On the 29th, the forces of the left had been denied the favorable moment by the Communists.

The strategic genius of the general had enabled him to reverse the situation. But his partisans became all the more numerous as the gas stations began to flow again. Dismayed by the immobility of their automobiles and the deprivation of their weekends in the country, Frenchmen were enchanted by the fact that they could drive again. Was the consumer's society, denounced by their children, really so pernicious? This revolt of the young, which had been regarded almost affectionately, was it not really leading the country into an abyss? Those red flags of socialism, those black flags of anarchy—what did they conceal? For many Frenchmen, there was a long distance to cover before the elections of the 23rd and 30th of June. In the event, they gave Gaullism a majority without precedent in the history of French Republics—less than a month after it had been thought ruined. The New Left frightened people; the Old Left commanded only pity. So the Right won.

Thus we see the Fifth Republic entering its third phase, after that of the settlement of the war in

Algeria (1958-1962) and that of the triumph of the franc (1962-1967). The Spring crisis of 1968: the six weeks of strikes, the increases in base wages, the weakening of the myth of stability, have brought a rude shock to the economy and opened another phase —one of austerity, embodied by that phlegmatic technician, Maurice Couve de Murville.

Important to us, now, however, is not the value of the franc in the world market, or even the determination which these incredible reversals of situation may inspire in De Gaulle. He was unable to foresee and therefore to design a grand policy for the future; only his talent and his audacity enabled the regime to survive. Whether he feels the urgency to withdraw or the necessity to remain, what is of importance now is the extent to which his most recent test will have corrected and completed De Gaulle the personage.

From the 3rd to the 30th of May, one seemed to be seeing and hearing his double, his caricature. De Gaulle, considered aware of his time, self-admittedly preoccupied with the problems of youth (as he told Mohammed Masmoudi, the ambassador from Tunisia), was conducting himself in May like an old dictator, preoccupied only with the maintenance of order in the streets.

During the bloody night of May 10th, it was clear that his responsibilities were great. No one dared wake him; but if Christian Fouchet, the minister of the interior, ordered the prefect of police to launch an assault against the barricades—risking the worst— it was because he *knew* that De Gaulle did not want to awaken to the red flag floating over the rebellious areas of the city. Paris was not Saigon; De Gaulle was not General Thieu! In this affair, it was from him —and not from his ministers—that repression stemmed.

It was also from him that the insult stemmed. All things considered, this revolt on the part of youth: excessive, disorderly, inconvenient, was an honor to the nation. It was greeted as such by intellectuals who are not revolutionaries. Instead of being proud of the proud youth of his nation, De Gaulle spoke of *"chienlit."* Confronted by pride, he refused to understand it. Worse than contempt, this was stupidity—a new element in the complex armor of this general.

The incredible effectiveness of his speech on May 30th—which will remain one of the classics of Gaullist literature—is undeniable. But how could a person of his stature lie so deliberately and carry imposture so far? One must despise a people very strongly before asking it to withstand an attempted overthrow by a "totalitarian communism" of which one was, at the time, an objective ally. It has been said, but it must be repeated: Since the 27th of May, governmental power had been demolished, authority dissolved. The members of the Gaullist hierarchy had said nothing; the police and a large part of the army stood waiting to learn where and how the authority of government would show itself, so that they might follow.

The Communists knew this better than anyone else. Faced with a situation of which a Trotsky or a Mao would have dreamed, they paraded, talked about wage adjustments and even about a "popular government." But with what form of action, with what gesture did they carry forward these proposals? They forbade the students to seize the headquarters building of the Radio-Télévision-Française—the only project of direct action. They criticized so harshly a transitional government under Mendès-France or Mitterrand, that their commentary amounted to a veto—and thus denied themselves the only legal path.

The French Communist Party leaders judged the

267

situation not "ripe" from the social point of view. They were unwilling to inherit an economic situation depressed by strikes, were disturbed at the thought of invasion by their leftist and student allies, and thought it repugnant to serve as a leading force to men like Mitterrand and Mendès-France. Perhaps advised by Moscow, which had been content with the Gaullist regime for many years, the Communist leaders did everything in their power to channel—if not to colonize—the movement and to maintain it within the framework of economic reformism.

De Gaulle's May 30th denunciation was thus an imposture. It served as a *leitmotif* for the entire electoral campaign, which permitted the installation of a National Assembly that no doubt expresses the real deception of the nation before the incapacity and senility of the left. It also expresses an artificial fear, appealed to and utilized by Charles de Gaulle, who behaved like those "politicians" he claims to scorn. Politics works no better without the use of a lie than medicine works without poison. But after a certain dosage, poison kills.

One week later, at the start of the electoral campaign, the general-president attempted to explain himself. For an entire hour, answering the questions of a respected journalist, he gave his version of the events of May, and confessed that he had come close to withdrawal (as he had in 1946). He compared himself to the protecting angel of a medieval fresco, denounced once again the communist "plot" and claimed ability to resolve the conflict between capitalism and socialism, both of which he condemned, while proposing a "third path:" *participation.*

This is an old formula, which would have seemed timid in other times, which already seemed timid when it was one of the key words in the program of the RPF. In the revolutionary light of this particular month of May, it took on an even more laughable meaning, since the general had presented himself as a "revolutionary."

How old he was that night—beyond time, beyond reality. He thought himself audacious; he believed in what he said, and what he said was empty. The inspired strategist had won the battle of the 30th of May. But the old man was more and more walled up within his historic solitude. He thought himself a revolutionary who had retained his power. But it was no more than a counter-revolutionary power.

Observe the manner in which the Gaullist regime brings sharply to light the contrasts of French society, where profoundly insidious constraints are concealed beneath formal liberties.

A short time ago, Michel Crozier, a visiting professor at Harvard University, entitled an article "France, Land of Discipline." This profound authoritarianism of French society is at the origin of the explosion in May. It aggravates the inherent frustrations of a consumer's society, and especially frustrates those groups, like the young intellectuals, that are dedicated to confrontation and eager for social and political advancement. Unless reforms which are unforeseeable at the present time take place, there remains the basic flaw which will mark the end of the regime of a man who has concentrated so strongly on the acclamation of the students of Rio de Janeiro and Bucharest that he has forgotten that the young people of his own country find themselves strangers at home. Young Frenchmen are alienated within the heart of a system idiotically hierarchical and partitioned, in which the patron of the divine right of kings echoes the voice of the professor-prophet.

In ten years of Gaullism, the industrial—or rather, the technical—structures of France have changed, but not the mental and administrative structures. She remains a "blocked" country. She is attempting, in vain, to become a governing democracy, but remains a "governed democracy," in the words of Georges Burdeau, a professor in the faculty of law at the University of Paris.

Charles de Gaulle is largely responsible for this situation. And even the more so since, from the electrifying speech of May 30th to the triumphant vote of June 30th, he has refounded his regime on a lie, and pretended to defend his republic against those who, in fact, permitted it to survive its technical collapse. The fabulous career of Charles de Gaulle is founded on a call to resistance against mortal peril, in the face of a diabolical enemy. It is for this reason that his career deserves respect. On May 30, 1968, Gaullism found new life on the foundation of a call to resistance against an imaginary enemy. Marx wrote that historic events repeat themselves, but on the pattern of delusion, of caricature. The resurrection of the Fifth Republic is an example of this.

In an issue devoted entirely to the crisis of May-June 1968, Jean-Marie Domenach, the editor of the Catholic Liberal review *Esprit,* wrote:

"What will be the condition of our policy when the great man leaves? The difficult operation involving the amputation of French Algeria was not of the same order as the problem that presents itself today. At that time, it was a matter of ending something; now, it is a matter of beginning something. In effect, what we have lived through is the first shock of a revolutionary process. A new society has arisen, like an upheaval in the depths of the ocean, heralded by a tidal wave. And what this society is demanding is what Gaullism cannot give it: a voice, participation, the reorientation toward human ends of the economy, of technics, and of the social sciences.

"Gaullism has 'hyper-activated' the insurrection of

youth in two ways: first, by its authoritarian and contemptuous behavior; second, by grasping the political destiny of the nation—which the nation, it must be admitted, handed over to it in good faith—it left citizens to their own habits or their own fantasies. It was in this climate of disdainful liberalism that the movement took form, outside of politics, because politics was monopolized by the authority that resided in the Élysée Palace. Since De Gaulle made policy, other people could concern themselves with other things. A shock of this nature would be impossible in a dictatorship; it would also be impossible in a democracy in which active citizens and young people felt themselves concerned by the exercise of power. In France, everyone had become irresponsible —an old French temptation, aggravated by the style of a governmental power which itself was the product of the impotence of the politicians and the indiscipline of citizens. We had all the forms of liberty; it was exactly that which provoked outrage. They could be used only for profit, not for decision. . . . The revolt has not shattered the system: to the extent to which it thought itself capable of that, it was mistaken. The system is flabby, even though its bludgeons are still hard. But, from this time on, it is attacked from within; it is from within that it will be transformed, unless other shocks occur."

The Gaullist government surmounted and employed to its profit the springtime crisis of civilization. But General de Gaulle, as a figure of myth, as an incarnation of a system, as an heroic projection of a certain order, is no longer anything more than a survivor. The man whose life has been only his own choice and his own will has submitted. The man who represents nothing but action has contented himself with reaction.

Some day, perhaps, a patient sociologist will devote himself to the most instructive of inquiries into Gaullism: a comparison between the social origin and the ideological beliefs of the crowd which greeted De Gaulle, the liberator, along the Champs-Élysées on August 26, 1944, and the crowd which again assembled along the same Champs-Élysées on May 30, 1968.

Chronology

1890	Birth, in Lille, of Charles André Marie Joseph de Gaulle.
1894	*The Dreyfus Case.*
1898	*Fashoda.*
1905	*Wilhelm II at Tangiers.*
1910	De Gaulle enters Saint-Cyr.
1912	De Gaulle serves under Pétain, at Arras.
1914	Baptism of fire.
1916	Taken prisoner at Verdun.
1917	Tanks, first British, then French, employed for the first time.
1918	Armistice.
1919	Instructor, then active combatant, in Poland.
1921	Marriage to Yvonne Vendroux. Professor of history at Saint-Cyr.
1922	De Gaulle at the War College.
1923	*French reoccupation of the Ruhr.*
1924	Publication of his first book: *Discord Among the Enemy.*
1925	On Marshal Pétain's staff.
1927	Three lectures at the War College.
1928	Commanding officer, 19th Light Infantry Battalion, at Trier. Birth of Anne de Gaulle, a handicapped child.
1929	Trip to the Levant.

1930		On the general secretariat of the Ministry of National Defense.
1932		Publication of *The Edge of the Sword*.
1933		*Hitler comes to power in Germany.*
1934		Publication of *The Army of the Future*.
1935		Campaign for an armored corps: Paul Reynaud intervenes.
1936		*The Popular Front.*
1937		De Gaulle commands the 507th tank regiment at Metz.
1938		Publication of *France and Her Army*. *Munich.*
1939		*War.* De Gaulle in command of tanks of the Fifth Army.
1940	January	Distribution of De Gaulle's leaflet, "The Advent of Mechanized Power."
	May	German offensive. De Gaulle named to command of the 4th Armored Division. The front line is broken. De Gaulle given temporary rank of general.
	June 5th	Charles de Gaulle named undersecretary of state for national defense.
	June 9th	Mission to London.
	June 15th	*Resignation of the Reynaud cabinet.*
	June 18th	First radio speech from London.
	July	Mers-el-Kebir.
	August	Churchill–De Gaulle agreements on the status of Free France.
	September	Dakar.
	October	Creation of the Council for Defense of the Empire, in Brazzaville.
1941	June	Anglo-Gaullist military operation in the Levant. *The Wehrmacht invades the U.S.S.R.*
	December	*Pearl Harbor: Japan attacks the United States, bringing that country into the war.*

1941	December	Gaullist operation in Saint Pierre and Miquelon.
1942	November	Allied landings in Algiers.
	December	*Assassination of Admiral Darlan.*
1943	January	Jean Moulin parachuted into France. *Stalingrad.* Casablanca conference.
	May	De Gaulle in Algiers.
	June	Giraud and De Gaulle co-presidents of the French Committee for National Liberation.
	August	The Committee is recognized by the Allies: De Gaulle now its sole chief.
1944	January	Brazzaville conference.
	June	Allied invasion of Normandy.
	July	De Gaulle is Roosevelt's guest in the United States.
	August	Liberation of Paris.
	November	Maurice Thorez returns from Russia.
	December	De Gaulle in Moscow.
1945	February	Yalta conference.
	April	Resignation of Mendès-France.
	May	German surrender.
	August	*Hiroshima. Japanese surrender.*
	October	Referendum: "yes" on the vote for a new constitution.
1946	January	De Gaulle resigns.
	June	Bayeux speech.
	October	The constitution is adopted by referendum, in spite of De Gaulle.
1947		Foundation of the Rassemblement du Peuple Français (RPF).
1948		Death of Anne de Gaulle.
1950		*The European Coal and Steel Authority is founded.*
1951		Legislative elections: partial success of the RPF.
1953		De Gaulle recognizes the failure of the RPF.
1954		Publication of Volume One of the *Memoirs.*

275

1954		*Mendès-France government.*
		Geneva agreements on Indochina.
		Insurrection in Algeria.
1955		The general's "last" press conference.
1956		*The Algerian rebellion becomes a full-scale war.*
1958	May	Algiers extremists attempt to force the government into a showdown.
		De Gaulle offers himself as mediator . . .
	June	. . . becomes president of the Council of Ministers and goes to visit Algiers.
		First trip to Algeria.
	July	Meeting of the Constitutional Convention.
	August	Trip through French Africa, to which he offers independence.
	September	Memorandum to the "Anglo-Saxon" governments, calling for equality of treatment for France.
	October	Proposal for a "peace of the brave" to the Algerian rebels.
1959	January	De Gaulle is president of the Republic.
	September	Algeria is offered self-determination.
1960	January	Barricades (of European extremists) in Algiers.
	June	Meetings with Algerian (FLN) representatives at Melun.
1961	April	"Putsch" of the generals in Algiers.
	May	First conferences with Algerian representatives at Évian.
	July	The Bizerte crisis with Tunisia.
1962	March	The Évian agreements on Algeria.
	July	Explosion of a French atomic bomb.
	September	Referendum on the election of the chief of state by universal suffrage.
	November	Legislative elections: the Union pour la Nouvelle République (the UNR-Gaullist) controls the National Assembly.

1963	August	Declaration on nonintervention in Vietnam.
	November	*Assassination of President Kennedy.*
1964		Journey to Latin America.
	October	*Eviction of Nikita Khrushchev from the Soviet government.*
1965	January	*Death of Winston Churchill.*
	February	De Gaulle comes out in favor of a return to the gold standard.
	December	De Gaulle reelected head of state with a narrow margin.
1966	February	He announces that France quits NATO.
	June	De Gaulle goes to Moscow.
1967	March	Legislative elections: defeat of the UNR (Gaullist).
	June	De Gaulle's assumption of a position against Israel in the Six Day War.
	July	Journey to Québec.
	September	Journey to Poland.
1968	May 3-30	Student and worker rebellion, known as "The Barricades."
	May 14	Journey to Romania.
	June 23, June 30	Legislative elections which assure an absolute majority to the Gaullists.
	July 10	Replacement of Georges Pompidou by Maurice Couve de Murville as chief of the government.

Index

282

284

285

287